BANDS DO BK

BANDS DO BK
A GUIDE TO BROOKLYN
BY BANDS
FOR EVERYONE

SAM SUMPTER

LIT RIOT PRESS
BROOKLYN, NY

Published by Lit Riot Press, LLC
Brooklyn, NY
www.litriotpress.com

Copyright © 2022 by Sam Sumpter

Lit Riot Press and the logo are registered trademarks of Lit Riot Press, LLC

All rights reserved. No part of this publication may be reproduced, distributed, or transmitted in any form or by any means, including photocopying, recording, or other electronic or mechanical methods, without the prior written permission of the publisher, except in the case of brief quotations embodied in critical reviews and certain other noncommercial uses permitted by copyright law. For permission requests, please contact Lit Riot Press through www.litriotpress.com.

Cover creative concept by Sam Sumpter
Book and cover design by Lit Riot Press, LLC

Library of Congress Control Number: 2022932919

Publisher's Cataloging-in-Publication Data

Names: Sumpter, Sam.
Title: Bands do BK: A Guide to Brooklyn, by Bands, for Everyone / Sam Sumpter.
Identifiers: LCCN 2022932919 | ISBN 978-1-7351458-4-6 (pbk.) | ISBN 978-1-7351458-5-3 (hardcover) | ISBN 978-1-7351458-6-0 (Kindle ebook).
Subjects: LCSH: Music. | Music--Performance. | Popular music. | Music fans. | Popular music fans. BISAC: MUSIC / General. | MUSIC / Essays. | MUSIC / Genres & Styles / Rock. | MUSIC / Genres & Styles / Punk. | MUSIC / Genres & Styles / Pop Vocal. | BIOGRAPHY & AUTOBIOGRAPHY / General. | BIOGRAPHY & AUTOBIOGRAPHY / Music. | BIOGRAPHY & AUTOBIOGRAPHY / Personal Memoirs.
Classification: LCC M3469.S16 2022 (print) | LCC M3469 (ebook) | DDC 780--dc23.
LC record available at https://lccn.loc.gov/2022932919.

For the bands (and bartenders) that make life in Brooklyn so beautiful.

"Every place that is dear to me in Brooklyn is dear because of how I choose to live my life."
—Lizzie No

TABLE OF CONTENTS

AUTHOR'S NOTE	1
INTRODUCTION	7
DRINK ABOUT IT	17
SEE AND BE SCENE	19
The Anchored Inn	23
Bar LunÀtico	26
The Brooklyn Inn	26
Carmelo's	27
The Commodore	28
Duck Duck	29
Easy Lover	30
Freddy's Bar and Backroom	30
Hartley's	31
The Levee	31
Lucky Dog	32
Night of Joy	33
The Palace	34
Rocka Rolla	34
Temkin's	36
Troost	36
Tradesman	37
BEHIND THE BAR	39
Golden Years	42

One Stop Beer Shop	43
Pokito	44
Reclamation Bar	45

RAISING THE BAR — 47

The Adirondack	51
Barcade	51
Beer Street	52
Branded Saloon	52
Call Box Lounge	53
Captain Dan's Good Time Tavern	53
FourFiveSix	54
Fourth Avenue Pub	55
Fresh Kills	55
Left Hand Path	56
Maracuja	56
Skinny Dennis	57

DIVE IN — 59

Boobie Trap	61
Brooklyn Ice House	61
Bushwick Country Club	62
Capri Social Club	63
The Charleston	63
Do or Dive	64
George & Jack's	65
The Graham	66
Honore Club	67
Pinkerton Wine Bar	68
Sunny's	69

EDIBLES — 73

JUST BREW IT — 75

Cafe Madeline	79

Crema BK	79
CUP	80
Cup of Brooklyn	80
Daytime	80
Der Pioneer	81
Dweebs	81
Fiction	81
Jessi's Coffee Shop & Stella Di Sicilia Bakery	82
Marcy & Myrtle	83
Parlay	83
Partners Coffee	84
Sunrise/Sunset	84
SOUNDBITES	**85**
Champs Diner	87
Joe's Pizza	88
La Isla Cuchifrito	88
Loving Hut	88
Luigi's Pizza & Giuseppina's	89
Nam Nam	90
Newtown	90
Peaches Shrimp and Crab	91
Pies 'n' Thighs	91
Taco Bell	92
Taco Rapido	92
Tacos, Twins and Trains Taco Cart	93
Vamos Al Tequila	93
GOOD TASTE	**95**
A&A Bake and Doubles & Ali's Trinidad Roti	97
Brooklyn Crab	99
Cafe Erzulie	99
Cheryl's Global Soul	100

Chinar	100
The Empanada Lady	101
La Loba Cantina	101
Le Paris Dakar	102
Momo Sushi Shack	102
Ponyboy	103
Red Hook Lobster Pound	103
Risbo	103
Sushi Noodle	104
Sweetwater	104
Together	104
Wei's	105
Yolanda	105
OLD-SCHOOL EATS	**107**
Bamonte's	109
Di Fara Pizza	110
L&B Spumoni Gardens	111
Little Purity	112
Paulie Gee's & Paulie Gee's Slice Shop	113
Roll N Roaster	114
Sunset Diner	115
Tina's Place	116
Tom's Diner	117
HANGOVER HELPERS	**119**
He Cherokee	121
Mable's Smokehouse & Banquet Hall	121
La Mesita	122
Tortilleria Mexicana Los Hermanos	122
Williamsburg Pizza	123
MARKET RESEARCH	**125**
Best Deli	126

The Brooklyn G	127
Brooklyn's Natural	127
Four Seasons Grill Deli	128
Mr. Kiwi's	128

LIVE FROM NEW YORK — 131

STAGE RIGHT — 135

Alphaville	140
Baby's All Right	144
The Broadway	146
Brooklyn Steel	149
C'mon Everybody	150
The Gutter	151
Hart Bar	154
Littlefield	154
Muchmore's	155
Music Hall of Williamsburg	157
The Nest	158
Our Wicked Lady	159
Pete's Candy Store	164
Prospect Park Bandshell	166
Rough Trade	166
Saint Vitus	168
The Sultan Room	169
Union Pool	171

DIY, TOGETHER — 175

Bohemian Grove	180
Dodge 112	180
East Williamsburg Econo Lodge (EWEL)	183
Hartstop	187
Market Hotel	190
Pet Rescue	191

Rubulad	192
ThL2	193
Zoos Studio	195
POP-UPS AND PLATFORMS	**199**
61 Local	201
Barclays Center	201
Feng Sway	202
The Greenpoint Loft	203
Green-Wood Cemetery	204
The Metropolitan G Stop	205
Two Boots	206
BEHIND THE SCENE	**209**
OFF THE RECORD	**211**
Brooklyn SolarWorks	216
Complete Music Studios	216
Danbro Studios	217
Our Wicked Lady	218
Pirate Studios	219
Savaria Studios	220
A Shipping Container in Bushwick	222
The Sweatshop	223
STUDIO CITY	**225**
Black Lodge Recording	231
The Bunker Studio	233
Brooklyn Recording	235
The Creamery Studio	235
Degraw Sound	236
Figure 8 Recording	237
Mousetown	238
Spaceman Sound	239
Studio G Brooklyn	240

Trout Recording	241
Wonderpark Studios	242
OFF THE CLOCK	**243**
PARKS AND REC	**247**
Brooklyn Botanic Garden	250
Brooklyn Bridge Park	250
Coney Island	251
DUMBO	252
The Edges of Brooklyn	252
The Gowanus Canal	254
Maria Hernandez Park	254
McCarren Park	255
McGolrick Park	255
Most Holy Trinity Cemetery	257
Prospect Park	257
Sunset Park & Green-Wood Cemetery	259
SHOP TALK	**263**
The Cowrie Shell Center	266
Earwax Records	266
Green Village Used Furniture & Clothing	266
The Guitar Shop	267
Human Head Records	269
Koch Comics Warehouse	270
Main Drag Music	271
Molasses Books	271
Stranger Wines	271
The Thing	272
Unnameable Books	272
Vinyl Fantasy	273
JUST FOR FUN	**275**
Alamo Drafthouse	278

Bossa Nova Civic Club	278
The Brick Theater	279
Brooklyn Skates Club & Sugar Hill Supper Club	279
Class One MMA	280
Cobble Hill Cinemas	281
Friends and Lovers	281
The Lot Radio	281
Russian Bath on Neck Road	282
Sunshine Laundromat	283
Syndicated Bar Theater Kitchen	283
Whisperlodge	284
A SNAPSHOT OF A SCENE: BROOKLYN TODAY, TOMORROW, AND BEYOND	**285**
ACKNOWLEDGMENTS	**289**
SAM SUMPTER	**291**
BANDS DO BK ONLINE	**292**
NAMES TO KNOW	**293**
INDEX	**303**

AUTHOR'S NOTE

Hello! Thanks for being here. I'm so, so happy to have you.

First off, an explanation feels necessary, lest you stumble upon this book at The Strand (I'm manifesting), or atop your friend's toilet (also cool!), and you notice some obvious, inevitable holes based on your quite understandable expectations. So, before you dive into these pages, eighteen chapters of recommendations and stories and snapshots, I'd like to offer a few notes on my process in advance and provide some answers to your potential questions.

I'll start from the beginning. When I began this project, a book based on the Bands do BK blog, I had no shortage of pre-existing material to work with. At that point, in the summer of 2020, I had two-and-a-half years' worth of transcripts from in-person interviews that took place at bars, restaurants, and venues across the borough, as well as in the closet-sized booth of Radio Free Brooklyn, where I was meeting with bands for on-air interviews once a week to discuss the music they were making and the places where they were hanging out. In addition, I had recommendations that musicians had already submitted in writing, which I had previously posted on my website and social media platforms to offer my audience exposure to new local music with a side of artist-approved destinations in Brooklyn.

So, let's talk about the bands included in this book. When I officially signed a publishing deal, the opportunities it presented, the importance of this project, and the permanence of print hit me

1

like a stranger's sweaty shoulder in a mosh pit. To ensure this book would best represent the audience, participants, and overall community of Bands do BK, I began seeking out and soliciting more NYC musicians for contributions over email and Instagram message, via publicist and in person, and even through an internet open call. My goal was to make sure my favorite local artists, responsible for my favorite music and memories, all had an opportunity to contribute. My greatest fear was forgetting or omitting someone.

That was silly though, because exclusion was, and is, inevitable.

There are countless communities in Brooklyn that are constantly expanding and changing shape, and I truly believe that every musician is unique and important and plays an integral role in the music scene and the overall fabric of this beautiful borough. But including *every* artist in *every* genre would be impossible. I knew that. I *know* that. And like any individual, I have opinions. I prefer punk to polka, rock to hip hop or doom metal, pop to electronic or country or jazz. As a platform, Bands do BK is not objective, it's subjective. I'm not just reporting, I'm curating. I'm also not that willing to explore the ska scene.

This is all to say that while there is some variety, as a blogger and a one-woman show, coverage naturally swings more in the direction of my own music taste and far away from anything, say, Juggalo-adjacent. In addition, while throughout these pages there's mention of Brooklyn's music "scene," it's one that's made up of a million sub-scenes, each built around venues, friend groups, genres, and geographies. And naturally, the more I lean into and learn more about one, the more my work in that sector snowballs through relationships, referrals, word of mouth, and the almighty algorithm. Bands who share bills and beers with artists I've previously featured reach out to me for coverage and collaboration, and as I discover, meet, and befriend more people, these connections result in my diving deeper into certain worlds rather than skimming the surface of every single one in existence.

Preferences aside though, in the end my goal is truly this. For Bands do BK to be a resource and a community that's free and inviting to all, and that musicians, no matter their size, style, or number of Spotify streams, all feel welcome. Ultimately, my main hope when sourcing material for this book was that both the artists I sought out, and those who found me, had the opportunity to heed the call. I wanted to ensure that the individuals who have been kind enough to enter, exist in, and contribute to the Bands do BK ecosystem could opt to share their thoughts. And, to my immense delight, dozens took me up on the offer.

Since I sent out initial interview inquiries in 2018, for a blog that had yet to launch, I've been blown away by artists' generosity and honored by their willingness and even eagerness to participate. The reaction to this book has been no different, and I'm humbled by the amount of people who responded and reached out, who were willing to correspond, converse, and share recommendations and recollections.

It's worth noting that I created a good portion of the writing in this book deep in the middle of the COVID pandemic. This was admittedly a strange time to discuss the places that at that point we were not allowed to enter, businesses that were scrambling to survive and may or may not have ever opened their doors again. Many still haven't. Others, like Rough Trade, have since relocated. However, while it was unpredictably bizarre, more than anything, this period drove home the importance of our favorite spots. After all, you don't know what you've got until it might be gone. And as musicians desperate to save their cherished spaces were donating to bars' GoFundMe campaigns to support out-of-work staff and raising money for struggling venues via live-stream shows, they were extra intent on declaring their love and paying homage to the haunts and holes-in-the-wall that have served as the setting for their personal NYC experiences.

This increased outreach offered me even more material, acquired through occasionally awkward and often hilarious interviews over Zoom and FaceTime. Some artists approached it almost like a job interview, while others broke out beers or packed bowls right in the middle of our conversation. It also resulted in far more written contributions, created and sent over to me specifically to include in this book.

Some bands submitted written pieces on behalf of the entire band. Other times, band members spoke or wrote as individuals. And some people preferred to remain semi-anonymous.

You'll find there are musicians who appear frequently throughout the book and those who just make a brief cameo in the form of a short sentence or shout-out. No matter the length or type of contribution, you'll find corresponding names and projects listed in the "Names to Know" section at the end of the book. One note about that list. While many musicians play in multiple projects, throughout the body of the book, I typically used one project to identify individuals for simplicity's sake, usually the one that's most well-known or through which I've primarily encountered or covered them.

Because of the different types of participation and styles of submission involved, the entries in this book differ in tone and length. Some stories are long. Some recommendations and descriptions are short. Many are poetic. While a handful are a little bit profane. And while there are detailed and well-researched listings that read almost like magazine articles, others just sound like a group of friends hanging around and shooting the shit, often because that's exactly what was happening.

One prime example of an exceptional entry can be found in the prose submitted by Mike Borchardt. If the Brooklyn music scene had an official hype man, it would be Mike. In addition to playing in multiple bands, he seems to be in the crowd of every show I attend, posting dozens of photos and videos and constantly supporting the artists, outlets, and venues that make up our community, both on the internet and in real life. Given this enthusiasm, it was no surprise that he went above and beyond, showing off the power of his pen with lengthy, romantic write-ups of the places that rank among his favorite Brooklyn spots.

And then, on the opposite end of the content style spectrum, you have listings for places like Our Wicked Lady and The Anchored Inn, which each feature the voices of at least a dozen artists, who over the last few years have submitted their thoughts to me in writing or shared them aloud. These spots were repeatedly mentioned and praised for their role within certain scenes, and their significance is clear in the number of artists who, unprompted, took this opportunity to call these places out.

This brings me to another point. When asking artists about their favorite places in Brooklyn, I usually left it open-ended. Rather than interview subjects about a specific spot, I asked them to tell me about the places that meant the most to them, whether they were bars, breweries, bodegas, boutiques, barber shops, or anything else. This means that some chapters and sections are naturally far bigger than others. It also means that if there's a killer cocktail bar, well-known venue, or prominent recording studio that feels like it should be listed but isn't, it wasn't intentionally excluded. It certainly doesn't speak to a lack of relevance, and it doesn't mean it's not worth checking out. It simply means that it wasn't mentioned often, extensively, or notably enough for inclusion by the selection of artists with whom I've spoken.

The only exceptions to this interview style are a few DIY spots run by artists. I did reach out to some musicians for background on the venues they created and operate themselves.

One last note. While this variance of voices is in a way symbolic of the eclectic personalities you'll find among artists and my experiences in working with them, it did make it difficult to decide exactly how to organize it all. So, within the obvious sections like food, drink, and live music, given the overlap I broke up chapters thematically as best as I could, based both on the primary meanings assigned to these places by the individuals interviewed and the memories they hold. A few places appear in multiple sections because they've played different roles to different artists, and occasionally two separate spots are paired together because they were recommended in relation to each other. And in a few instances, it's less about a specific destination and more about a journey, an *experience*.

In this book you'll find long professions of love, as well as entries woven together with opinions and experiences so aligned it feels like the artists weren't speaking or submitting in a silo, but all sitting in a booth having this conversation together. These are the tales and truths you likely won't find on the business's "about" page or social-media bio, details that wouldn't be incorporated into most reviews, and characteristics that likely don't factor into any Zagat rating. The stories that, if these walls could talk, they'd definitely be telling.

Since the book is arranged this way, I invite you to approach all the entries with this in mind. Beyond being stoked on a show or a sandwich, put yourself in the Docs or Vans of the artist behind each recommendation. Consider the role that the place is playing in the Brooklyn music community, and best of all, the fact that both your beloved and soon-to-be-favorite bands are likely hanging out within those very walls right now.

INTRODUCTION

Somewhere in Brooklyn, all over Brooklyn, bands are recording and rehearsing, stage-diving and crowd-surfing, taking walks and taking shots, slurping noodles and shooting pool, biking and beaching, shopping and plotting. And apparently hanging out in cemeteries.

But where is all of this happening? Where are the local musicians we love, whose art and style we admire, spending their time? Where are they working and playing, on stage and off, around the clock and across the borough?

I decided to find out.

Before we get started, I want to offer some background on who I am and how this project came to be. As your tour guide on this journey, I want you to know where I'm coming from, and most importantly, why this work means so much to me.

First off, let's get the answer to the obvious question out of the way. I moved to New York City in September 2016. However, like many, I've dreamed of living here for far, far longer.

Growing up in Texas, I was one of the few people I knew who wanted to get out. Despite years of traditions and routines bordering on brainwashing, like rodeo-themed songs and assemblies, pledging allegiance to the state flag, and being reminded twice a day to remember the Alamo, the BBQ-flavored Kool-Aid didn't take full effect. And the summer trip my family made each year to visit my grandparents in California, tantamount to an annual

Rumspringa, was a recurring reminder that there was indeed life outside the Lone Star State, even if you had to drive like a thousand hours to reach it.

To clarify, I wasn't unhappy. On the contrary, I had a perfectly pleasant childhood among the strip malls, neighborhood pools, and one hundred percent humidity that characterized the Houston suburbs. And those ridiculous rituals? Honestly, a pretty good time! After all, an assembly celebrating "Go Texan Day" was still more fun than whatever else would've happened in fourth grade that afternoon, and if we're talking about high school, I will gladly vouch for the enchantment of those famous Friday-night lights.

In the end, it wasn't so much about the place I wanted to leave. It was more about where I desperately wanted to go.

While I'm now reminded how much I love NYC every time I step outside to be smacked in the senses by the signature shouts, sirens, and sometimes disconcerting combination of sights and smells, I can't put my finger on the original reason I wanted to move here. It might have been an early addiction to fashion magazines, or a love of bright lights and big crowds, or maybe just a lot of television. All I know is that it's been my dream destination for as long as I can remember, a fantasy that morphed into a mission when I visited with my parents one Spring Break in high school and finally saw the city of beloved sitcom settings in full-blown 3D form.

Now I wish I could say that the day I turned eighteen, I kissed my friends' faces goodbye, turned my back on cowboy boots and bluebonnets, and never looked back. But that wasn't quite the case. While I genuinely envy the boldness of every individual whose Big Apple origin story involves the fabled one suitcase, one-way ticket, and one week's worth of cash in the pocket of their only pair of jeans, I lacked the courage to break out of my comfort zone. I wasn't brave enough to take the leap, make the move, and sleep on acquaintances' couches, fingers crossed that a friend's cousin's cousin could get me an unpaid internship at *Highlights* magazine. Also, had I gone to NYU, my hypothetical great-grandkids would probably still be paying off student-loan debts long after I died.

So instead of heading northeast after crossing the stage in

2007, I stayed in Texas to attend college and study journalism in Austin, which was far enough away to feel like I had legitimately left home, even if it was still seventeen hundred miles from where I most wanted to be. However, as luck, fate, or whatever some higher power might have decreed, it turned out that Austin was the ideal first stop for semi-adulthood. Not for the football, swimming holes, or breakfast tacos, but because that's exactly where, a decade after many of my peers, I finally fell in love with live music.

Now before college I had probably only attended a handful of shows, one of which was a Britney Spears concert with a friend and her parents in fifth grade. And I can't blame location for my general lack of interest. The smallest of towns often birth the biggest of fans, and across the country mind-blowing music is always blossoming in the garages and basements of the 'burbs. Plus, Houston is a huge city home to some impressive venues, and I'm pretty sure there was even a local hang down the street called Java Jazz where local bands with names like Breath of the Dying would play. However, music just wasn't *my thing*, and while seemingly edgier sophomores and seniors were skateboarding, applying elaborate eyeliner, and burning CDs that weren't just the first eighteen tracks of the Top 40, I was probably playing soccer, hanging out at Barnes & Noble, or being suffocated by second-hand Fierce while digging through the clearance pile at Abercrombie & Fitch. And to be honest, my curiosity and concert-attendance record didn't improve much during my four years of college in Austin, when I was either in class, studying, or pre-gaming with *Jersey Shore* before spending too much time in too little clothing with the rest of the "twenty-one"-year-olds on Sixth Street.

But like many things, that completely changed after graduation.

Home to South by Southwest, Austin City Limits, and a relentless nightlife, it's no secret that Austin is the Live Music Capital of the World, and after trading the college bubble for civilian life, I started dipping my toes in social scenes that didn't revolve around tailgating and sketchy bars with names like Treasure Island. Free of the world of frats and no longer living in an apartment complex called University Estates, I finally began to explore not just the city but who I was, what I was interested in, and what I really loved and cared about. And I soon learned that what it was, what it still *is*, is music.

When I started really going to shows at the ripe age of twenty-two, I discovered what most music fans do as teenagers, the feeling of adrenaline, elation, catharsis, and comfort that comes with being in a crowd at a concert. The sensation of being seen and understood, of experiencing your own emotions reflected in song and familiar feelings expressed in an album. In other words, I finally understood the true magic of the medium, and I was, like any human being with two ears, an average amount of angst, and the frequent desire to dance, immediately and totally hooked.

Almost overnight, music became my life. Invigorated, inspired, and hell-bent on making up for lost time and lost tunes, I was suddenly spending all my evenings and most of my money on shows and vodka sodas at venues across the city. On weekends and weeknights, with friends or all by myself, I headed out to see the Austin acts I loved and to catch the touring bands whose hits I'd heard on SiriusXM and added to my ever-growing favorites playlist on Spotify. I also started using my local writing gigs to score press passes, honing my interview skills in the media tent and meeting my new music heroes while enjoying sweet perks like free concert tickets, cocktails, and kale chips.

However, while my personal revelation and revolution, a long overdue coming of cultural age, was finally happening in Austin in the early 2010s, it in no way stifled my urge or diminished my desire to move to New York City. It just changed what that fantasy looked like. While I had previously envisioned a glamorous *Sex and the City*-like lifestyle spent strutting down the streets of Manhattan in shoes I could neither walk in nor afford, now I dreamed of sweaty shows and cheap beers in dark bars in Brooklyn, of a scene where many of the bands I had recently fallen in love with had lived and played and first started creating the music I was now consuming like candy. And as I was enjoying my quarter-life anti-crisis, I was simultaneously applying for writing jobs at magazines and websites in NYC, throwing applications and carefully customized cover letters into the ether with no response, and to no avail, for years.

Until finally, in September 2016, I made it there. Made it *here*!

Despite all the hours I had spent scouring job sites, in the end, it had nothing to do with persistence or a good LinkedIn game. Instead, it was an unexpected phone call I took from my boss's boss in a CVS parking lot, followed by a lot of screaming in my Hyundai Elantra, that granted me the greenlight to go to NYC with a copywriting nine-to-five job and the steady paycheck that my total lack of savings account required. Later that summer, when my lease was up and my goodbye tour was nearly done, I spilled a few farewell tears onto the carpet of the now-empty studio apartment where my adult life had really begun. Come Labor Day weekend, I stuffed my car with everything it would hold and officially traded Austin, Texas for Brooklyn, New York, where I rolled up to my new Craigslist-sourced home in Crown Heights beaming like Will Smith in the introduction to *The Fresh Prince of Bel-Air*.

And I immediately hit the ground running.

Although I frequently made amateur NYC mistakes like paying eight bucks for peanut butter and taking the train approximately twelve stops in the wrong direction, I was thrilled to report to friends, family, and fellow Uber Pool passengers that I was *home*. Despite some self-doubt and what a select few individuals might describe as commitment issues, in at least one way I'd always known what I wanted, what I *needed*. Each day and each night, every encounter, and every experience, solidified for me that this is exactly where I'm supposed to be. The city didn't just meet my expectations, it exceeded them. And of course, that was mostly because of the music.

As Patrick Phillips of Brooklyn punk band Namesake (formerly known as Honduras), who had left Missouri for NYC in 2006, would tell me years later during an interview, "New York's a place you can make your home." And while I lacked the network of friends that I'd left behind in Austin, music immediately enveloped me in its embrace, offering me an instant itinerary, emotional fulfillment, and a new family in audience form every evening as

I flew solo to shows at Sunnyvale and Silent Barn, Music Hall of Williamsburg, and Baby's All Right. Besides going out on my own, I also started volunteering for the NYC branch of Sofar Sounds, a global organization that produces intimate shows in secret locations, through which I had the opportunity to meet and support local artists across the genre spectrum. My first two years in Brooklyn were a well sound-tracked whirlwind. It was borough exploration by show, self-discovery through song and sweat. I was by myself, and I'd never felt more like myself.

Once again, music had delivered. And I knew I had to give back.

Confident I had found my forever home and no longer constantly plotting an exit strategy, it was time for me to take on a bigger role in the music community beyond being an occasional volunteer or a faceless fan in the audience. I wanted to find more consistent and significant ways to help the artists I'd fallen head over heels for. I didn't just want to consume. I wanted to connect. I wanted to collaborate. I wanted to *contribute*.

As you've probably guessed by now, I'm not exactly a musician myself. The acoustic guitar I spontaneously put on my Christmas list after Avril dropped "Sk8er Boi" gathered dust for a decade in my childhood bedroom, while the electronic drum kit I purchased to chase my rock-star dreams in my thirties has primarily served as a drying rack for my delicates. If you could learn music by osmosis, I'd be Beethoven. Or maybe the least-famous member of Fall Out Boy. But long ago I picked up a pen instead of a pick, and I'm far more adept at finding rhythm in words and on paper than on stage and in song. So rather than participate by creating music, I knew I would once again contribute through covering it, this time by harnessing my journalism degree, writing experience, and passion for promotion to create something of my own. A new platform with which to amplify art, spotlight local talent, and shout from the digital rooftops about the projects I'm most passionate about.

However, while I had officially decided that I wanted to start a music site, I didn't want to build a knock-off or simply follow in the steps of existing blogs-turned-behemoths like *BrooklynVegan*,

Pitchfork, or *Stereogum*, established publications staffed with experts adept at capturing sound in sentences, offering educated insights, and either bestowing prized praise or throwing brutal barbs in the form of 2.4-out-of-10 ratings and snarky reviews. While I had a photographer friend I could pay in beer, a spreadsheet of interview candidates I was certain could be convinced to participate, and the seventeen dollars necessary to purchase a domain name on GoDaddy, I knew I needed a unique approach, an *angle*.

And one night, or more accurately one early morning, I found it.

It was the crack of dawn in summer 2018, when after emerging bleary-eyed from an after-hours party in the basement of a bar I didn't even know had a basement in Bushwick, I had a very sudden, very sobering realization. *Shit. The sun is about to come up.*

Now every nightlife lover knows there's no bigger buzzkill than the sound of chirping birds signaling the start of a new day when you're just ending your night. The real walk of shame is the one in which you're dodging dogs and strollers while avoiding eye contact with stand-up citizens grabbing coffee or, God forbid, *jogging* at six a.m. So with a fear of daybreak only degenerates and actual vampires could ever understand, I darted across the street to avoid a suspiciously chipper-looking stranger and yanked my phone out of my purse to call a car before the remaining half of the sun slid up.

Mercifully, even at seven percent battery, Uber greeted me with speed and without judgement in the form of a one-click invitation to hail a ride home. But just as I raised my thumb to confirm, I noticed that the address the app listed for "home" wasn't that of my actual residence. Instead, the app had helpfully, at around 7 a.m., presented me with the coordinates of The Crown Inn, the neighborhood bar located a way-too-convenient three-minute walk away from my apartment.

After a moment of confusion, it was then that I had a startling realization. *The Crown Inn is literally where Uber thinks I live.*

Along with being an amusing, albeit slightly alarming, anecdote that I filed away for future bar banter and maybe a free drink, the app's algorithmic conclusion was undeniably accurate. Crown

Inn was typically where I started my evenings. It was often where I ended my nights. And after two years of frequenting my favorite bars, coffee shops, and venues in Brooklyn, I suddenly became completely conscious of my reality. Beyond a very necessary ride, the early-morning Uber experience served as a major lightbulb moment as I realized that here the concept of home isn't confined to the world inside our apartment walls. Instead, home is defined by the places *out there*, where we actually spend our time and live our lives.

After all, no one exists in Brooklyn the exact same way, and there's no identical experience. Unlike the suburbs that served as the setting for most of my childhood, this borough isn't characterized by clusters of standard-issue shopping centers with slightly varying combinations of Starbucks and Barnes & Noble, never-ending breadsticks at Olive Garden, and Bloomin' Onions at Outback Steakhouse. There are no Stepford-style compounds composed of similar streets lined with identical houses. No list of guidelines for where to go or who to be.

Instead, you have a universe completely unique to you, a life in a one-of-a-kind world you've constructed for yourself. There are *your* bars where you go to toast your triumphs and drown your sorrows, *your* coffee shop that fuels your commute, and *your* deli that, God willing, cures your hangover. There's *your* club where you dance until 4 a.m., *your* diner where you talk until 7 a.m., and *your* parks, benches, and bridges where you hang out and make out and break up and make up.

That's *your* Brooklyn. And Bands do BK? It's the Brooklyn of artists.

Three years after its launch, Bands do BK is a blog, a radio show, a weekly newsletter, live shows and streams, and now, as you're well aware, a book. One you can use as a guide or a gift or entertainment on the L-train, that you can read at a bar, flip through at the park, and reference while planning a weekend or composing a playlist.

It's a guide to Brooklyn bands. And it's a guide to Brooklyn *by* bands.

To clarify, this book isn't designed to help you stalk your favorite musicians. As a general rule, follow artists online, don't follow them home. Instead, the primary purpose of this project is to help you sort through the noise and give you an original source through which to simultaneously discover your new favorite places and your new favorite bands.

At its core, this is both an artists' tribute to Brooklyn and my tribute to Brooklyn artists, specifically the ones I've personally encountered or worked with, whose music I've enjoyed and obsessed over. This book features many of the musicians who have defined both my sonic and social experiences in Brooklyn upon entering my personal orbit, whether that introduction was via internet or algorithm, through an organic meeting at a show or event, or sometimes just by chance at a bar.

While plenty of brilliant books, several of which are sitting on a shelf next to me as I type these words, do a terrific job documenting a specific period, I'm not sure exactly how you capture an era when you feel like you're still in the middle of it. However, this book is my humble attempt to describe my favorite artists, their favorite places, and a sample size of Brooklyn's multi-faceted, forever-changing music scene through my personal journey and local artists' eyes, ears, and experiences.

More than anything, Bands do BK is a love letter. So with that, I'll leave you to it. I really hope you have as much fun reading this book as I did writing it.

SECTION 1
DRINK ABOUT IT

In a city where living rooms are a luxury and in an industry in which offices are irrelevant, for bands, bars are where a lot of the living and working is done. And while there are thousands of bars in Brooklyn and most of their customers probably share a common goal, it's safe to say that no two spots are exactly the same.

Some bars serve as an occasional setting for shows, with smelly backrooms, secret basements, makeshift stages, or carved-out corners just big enough to fit a sad dude with a guitar. In others, the only music is the crowd-sourced song selection emanating from the jukebox in the back, or from the speakers blasting the Spotify playlist of the evening's designated bartender-DJ.

A good portion of them could almost be rounded up to restaurants, as they put real thought into their food with dishes designed not only to satisfy the stoned but to impress the sober. On the other hand, most have just done the easy math and realized that cheap chips, free hot dogs, or $1 personal pizzas are more than enough to keep boozed-up Brooklynites around and buying drinks for a few extra hours.

And though plenty of bars offer standard tools for tipsy entertainment with TVs, pool tables, and dartboards, there are a few that skew more towards adult takes on Chuck E. Cheese, with full-on Skee-Ball sections, walls packed with pinball machines, and occasionally even a bona fide bowling alley.

In addition to differentiating them, it's these very attributes, these *bar bonus features*, that can make classifying these places pretty damn difficult. So to keep it simple, we're going to define bars in the most basic sense as places where artists hang out and drink up, even if some spots also serve food, others host shows, and plenty offer some unique-to-Brooklyn combo of anything and everything else.

No matter where you go, in the middle of your booze bingo card there's Brooklyn consistency in the form of the almighty bartender, who is a friend, a therapist, and a master of ceremonies who has witnessed regulars' most embarrassing moments, knows their deepest, darkest secrets, and is busy popping and pouring their beer-shot combo before they've even made it across the room to the bar.

With all that said, it's no surprise that this is one of this book's biggest sections, and it's safe to say that no matter where you are, or who you're with, or what you drink, there's a bar in Brooklyn for you.

And you better believe there's a band there as well.

CHAPTER 1
SEE AND BE SCENE

"It has a bit of a Cheers vibe, but if everyone in Cheers decided to start a band and wear a leather jacket." - Kate Black (THICK)

Interviewing artists is a lot like going on app dates.

You fix your hair, check your breath, come up with a handful of just-in-case conversation topics, and practice your personal pitch. Then, upon arrival at the destination, likely too early and too sweaty, you hype yourself up in the bathroom, sit down with a beer, and scan faces as surreptitiously as possible while you try to figure out who in the crowd looks most like the photo on your phone.

Except the picture is from Bandcamp, not Bumble. And you're often going out with like half a dozen people at once.

On a September evening in 2019, I had arranged to meet Brooklyn band Yella Belly at the nautically named dive palace and popular artist hydration station The Anchored Inn, a punk bar with appropriately cheap beers and properly graffiti-drenched bathrooms, plus bizarrely lavish touches like a giant chandelier hanging from the high ceiling and a wall filled with framed paintings of ships, horses, dogs, and the occasional clown or wizard. Described as a "place to get fed and drunk," it's a destination for those on the come up and come down, where patrons can shoot pool and whiskey until 4 a.m. or sober up with startlingly delicious, way-better-than-standard bar fare. Like all of the bars in this chapter, it's also where you're sure to find a lot of two things. Artists and alcohol.

Either conveniently or very strategically located a two-minute walk from Brooklyn practice and production hubs Danbro and The Sweatshop, The Anchored Inn is perpetually crawling with instrument-toting NYC musicians on their way to, or from, or in the middle of rehearsal. But despite the gaggle of artists milling about and mingling on a Monday, it wasn't difficult to identify William Thompson. Yella Belly, a medley of original East Coasters and Texan transplants, describes their music as "equal parts Texas grit and Brooklyn grime," and Will? Well, he was wearing a pretty fancy hat.

On the flip side, I had parked myself at an open spot outside of the bar entrance on Waterbury, and I imagine I was readily recognizable by my sheer lack of swag. I was wearing an outfit totally devoid of studs or leather, I didn't have a sleeve of tattoos, and I was without key accessories such as an instrument case or a pack of cigarettes. So it's safe to say I was by far the least punk-rock person present.

After spotting each other and going through the universal, *Is that you?* process entailing eye contact, head tilt, and hesitant half-wave, Will, with smile on face and drink in hand, ambled over to my table like a very on-brand Brooklyn cowboy. He parked himself on the bench across from me, and almost instantly the three other Yella Belly boys on site that evening materialized, immediately aware of our coordinates via what I could only imagine were some sort of shared band brainwaves.

Now along with the anticipation and initial internet-to-real-life identification, the app-date-to-interview analogy also applies to chemistry. There can be some awkwardness during interviews, and occasionally the whole thing is just *hard*. My questions might not inspire, my jokes might not land, and I've even had to excuse myself for fake bathroom breaks, sometimes frequently enough to imply a serious condition, so I could rack my brain for ways to make the experience a little less painful for both parties.

But on the good days, like on a good date, the chemistry is there, and the artists and I just click. The conversation flows, the time flies, and I get so absorbed in the fun of the interaction that I have to remind myself that I'm there to ask questions and record answers, not tell my own stories, offer my personal opinions, or show off my Ozzy Osbourne impression. Which, come to think of it, I probably shouldn't do on actual dates either.

Of course, unlike Match dinners, Tinder drinks, and whatever it is that daters do on FarmersOnly, there's a lot less pressure when neither party is there to find love or get laid. It also helps when it's a group situation, wherein most of the people present already know, adore, and thoroughly enjoy hanging out with each other. In these instances, the meeting feels less like a formal interview and more like I'm playing the role of (bar)fly on the wall, just hanging out and bearing witness to an often-hilarious hour of on-the-record band banter.

This last scenario perfectly describes the evening I spent with the Yella Belly boys, who laughed and reminisced while sitting around a picnic table that became increasingly cluttered with beers, wine, and White Claws as the evening wore on. Both in conversation and closeness, the four musicians seemed more like brothers than bandmates as they dug into a mutual memory bank, weaving together stories and finishing one another's sentences as they answered hard-hitting questions that would've made any *60 Minutes* interviewer, or at least an MTV VJ, proud. Like, for example, whether The Anchored Inn was more often the band's spot for pre- or post-practice beers.

"We try to do more after rehearsal right now," answered Will.

"It's been a learning curve," added drummer Jake Hiebert.

"Yeah, I think our carpet is mildewed over twenty times from all the shot-gunning in the practice space."

Beyond a drinking destination, as part of their oral ode to The Anchored Inn, the guys also explained its importance to their origin story, the bar's booths serving as the setting where conversations first started and big band decisions were made. And as work on this book went on, I wasn't surprised to learn that Yella Belly isn't the only group who has this sort of intimate association with the bar. Similar sentiments and stories were shared by many artists about The Anchored Inn and places like it, which have all played a pivotal role in the lives of Brooklyn musicians who might come out for band meetings or show up just for fun, gathering to bullshit over beers and plot over shots.

Six months later, I headed out on another professional and platonic five-person date with the members of jangle-pop outfit Forever Honey, whose sweet songs make me want to shimmy and sob, sometimes simultaneously. In an ultimate example of the artist overlap found in this borough and this book, Forever Honey shares half a band with Yella Belly, but I met this ensemble at Freddy's Bar and Backroom, a different dive tucked in a more southwest slice of Brooklyn, where another crowd of musicians can typically be found.

To put it simply, Freddy's is sensory overload encapsulated. While no longer in its original Prospect Heights location, the bar's roots go back to Prohibition. With multiple rooms crammed with framed photos and a fascinating mix of antiques, tchotchkes, and home and roadhouse decor, it's like visiting your great-grandparents' house where nothing has been thrown away for approximately a hundred years. Assuming your elderly relatives had a little bit of a drinking problem and were also the specifically strange sort who might keep pet albino frogs named Bluto and Burley.

As a hub, Freddy's has a storied history as a haven for artists and activists, and these days the saloon still serves as a meeting point for creatives, frequently playing host to live performances and video and art exhibits. And for South Slope songwriters and roommates Aida Mekonnen and Olivia Price, and Fort Greene residents Jack McLoughlin and Steve Vannelli, Freddy's had become the go-to gathering point between the band members' apartments based on two important aspects, the culture and the convenience.

Much like with Yella Belly, Forever Honey's closeness was clear to me after just a few minutes spent with the four friends in the corner booth by the freaky albino frogs. And after previously collaborating across state lines, now that the musicians had converged in Brooklyn they could get together more often, coming out to Freddy's to enjoy holidays and hangouts with other artists and make major band memories within the bar's very weird walls.

"I don't know if we actually signed our lease here," remembered Olivia, "but I had the papers to hand off."

"The first July Fourth we were here," Aida said. "Olivia got hit by a firecracker in the street. We spent the last New Year's here, we spent Halloween here."

"I feel like every night ends here, in this area." Jack concluded.

From Freddy's to The Anchored Inn and beyond, the first chapter of this book is dedicated to these types of very important community spots, designated destinations where you'll find the same individuals posted up at the bar, familiar groups hanging in huddles, and liquor being poured while creative groundwork gets laid. These are places one goes to meet and greet and eat and *drink*. Where band bonding takes place as musicians pre-game for practice, regroup after rehearsal, and on show nights, take one more shot before bouncing down the street to make soundcheck. They're meeting sites for both business and pleasure, where tours are planned, collaborations are kick-started, and during occasionally communal bathroom breaks in grimy stalls, where real life is lived and all the in-between fun gets done.

The Anchored Inn

Madam West (Sophie Chernin, Will Clark, Jory Dawidowicz, Todd Martino, Mike McDearmon); Kate Black, Shari Page, Nikki Sisti (THICK); Cory Peterson (Hollow Engine); Kayla Asbell, Pouya, and Obash (Bipolar); Jake Hiebert, Connor Jones (Yella Belly); Amelia Bushell (Grim Streaker); Dane Zarra (Oil Bay); Lydia Gammill (Gustaf)

Madam West: Anchored Inn is the band's go-to spot in Brooklyn.

Kate Black: I always seem to end up at The Anchored Inn, aka A.I., aka Ankey.

Cory Peterson: When we discovered this place some years ago during a break from rehearsal at our new studio, it was a rock and roll oasis in the desolate post-industrial area of East Williamsburg with a quarter-pipe out front and a large, crusty mermaid precariously dangling above the entrance. We had to check it out. Since then, the area has grown more popular with cultural spots like art galleries, a radio station and rehearsal spaces sprouting up on all sides. And I can't help but wonder if this place is partially responsible for the cultural boom.

Shari Page: This spot was also a music venue, and I remember seeing a punk show here with my co-worker and her brother. It was so wild.

Kate Black: I got to play at their venue, The Acheron, once with an old band before they shut down that side of the business, but I was really just starting to play music then and started going there more and more frequently as I bounced between rehearsal spaces nearby. There are at least five practice spaces that I can think of within a five-block radius, so it's almost impossible to go there and not run into someone you know, likely with an instrument on their back.

Pouya and Obash: We've been to this bar for years now. It's right by our practice studio, and we go there before and after our practice and we get twisted on Mezcal, Sangrita and Tecate. The things that we've done in those bathrooms stays only between us and the toilet walls.

Kayla Asbell: Anchored Inn is the most fun black hole where you show up at 8 p.m. and leave at 5 a.m. every time.

Connor Jones: It's been a big starting point to a lot of nights, because our practice space is right down the street. And ending points, on that note.

Amelia Bushell: I feel like after every practice, we probably go for a drink, or beforehand. Like any time I've had to be waiting for anything, it's usually been when I'm at Anchored. It's like the waiting room, basically, for anything music related.

Kate Black: I stop there whenever I have time on my way to practice and sit at the bar with my favorite Buffalo chicken sandwich and a Tecate.

Cory Peterson: At first glance, it feels like a fairly standard hard rock bar, with Lemmy riffs on constant rotation and an ideal billiards setup, but the perfectly kitschy nautical theme and unexpectedly great kitchen elevate things considerably.

Kate Black: All of their food is bomb.

Shari Page: I'll never forget when I first went to Anchored Inn and I ordered the salad and I realized how bomb the food was.

Kate Black: They also have the best burger in BK.

Jake Hiebert: The burgers are the best.

Nikki Sisti: The Carmen Fries are amazing.

Pouya and Obash: Obash loves their Buffalo chicken sandwich and their burger. Pouya is a vego and usually just sticks to the liquid diet.

Kate Black: We also have THICK "meetings" there when we have a lot of non-playing stuff to go over. Discussions at that bar have spawned music-video ideas and a lot of tour plans.

Amelia Bushell: At band meetings, it's always Anchored Inn. Really, it's just an excuse to have mid-week shots and beers. Yeah, band *meetings*.

Dane Zarra: Mainly this lovely dingy hub was where we would go to coordinate our big schemes, which translates to us always ordering beer, burgers, and shit-talking whoever couldn't make the excursion. Sometimes shit-talking the members right to their faces even if they decide to come.

Lydia Gammill: With my old band that was a big spot. I remember having band practices, and we'd all go and get beer and French fries and have a lot of famous band arguments. That's where you go to talk about details and work things out, and by the end of the night, you're drunk and you're saying what you want to say to people you hold close.

Madam West: It's both hilarious and soothing to sit in a booth next to another band having an identical conversation about an upcoming show, recording, or that one booker that sucks.

Kate Black: There is always a great playlist going, and the people who work there are a huge part of what makes the bar feel special.

Cory Peterson: And this is the only metal bar I've been where I feel quite comfortable wearing either a black t-shirt and drinking a Busch or a Hawaiian shirt and sipping a margarita. Can't we all just hang out independent of genre classifications? The answer here is, "Yes!"

Kate Black: It has a bit of a *Cheers* vibe, but if everyone in *Cheers* decided to start a band and wear a leather jacket.

Bar LunÀtico
Katie Martucci (The Ladles)

I think I came here one of the first nights that I got to Brooklyn. They have music here every single night, and we came out, and I fell in love with it immediately. I realized sort of separately, if I'm looking at Yelp or anything like that for a place to eat or to go out, all I'm looking at are the pictures and what the lighting looks like. Then I got here and was like, oh my god, everyone looks so good here. It's incredible.

There are singer-songwriters that play here, there's a band from I think Mali that plays here often. There's gospel brunch. They just have great music, and you walk in, and it feels like a vibe. It's like it's so mysterious, anything could happen.

The Brooklyn Inn
Peter, Sahil, Sean (Glom)

Sahil: This place has a few draws, one being that it is very conveniently located in the apex of where me and Peter live, and where my studio is, which is right down the street, so it is the closest bar to where I live and work. But besides that, I think that it's not the oldest bar in Brooklyn, but there has been a bar at this location longer than anywhere else in Brooklyn, and I think that means that there's been a bar in this room for over two hundred years or something like that. But all of the decor in here is preserved from what it was back in the day. It's just like classic, vintage stuff.

There are also rumors that this place is haunted, that apparently there's a building inspector from the eighteenth century who will come in here late at night. He wears a trench coat and has a big hat. I've never seen it myself, [but] I've heard stories. They play great music in here, also. That's definitely a fact.

Sean: The jukebox has a wild, well, I don't know. What's wild anymore? It's a cool selection of music. Bob Dylan, some Pixies, stuff like that.

Sahil: Radiohead, stuff that other bars would be too stuck-up to actually play. They just play the stuff you wanna hear in here, and it's really nice.

Sean: There's a good selection of Wilco, too. It's like, deep, older Wilco stuff, stuff that we like.

Sahil: Sitting at this particular spot, at this particular time of day, is peak Brooklyn in my mind. Late afternoon, sun's comin' in. I feel like it's hard to find a bar in Brooklyn that's this size, and this peaceful, and has windows and good music.

Peter: Sahil will refer to this place as his office, and we'll have office hours here.

Sahil: I conduct all my business here.

Peter: We conduct meetings and celebrations.

Sahil: The official signing with the label that released the first album was at this very table, right here.

Carmelo's
Stephen Berthomieux (The Big Easy)

At first, I tried to think of some of my favorite venues or music spaces that resonate with me, but after some thought, I realized there are no such places. While I have played plenty of great venues across Brooklyn, I don't find myself frequenting any particular venue outside of the capacity of playing music myself, or seeing friends play. Not like how I frequent Carmelo's, at least. No place in my neighborhood makes me feel as welcomed and promotes good vibes like Carmelo's. Not to mention the cheap drinks! It really can't be beat, in my opinion. Long story short, as a musician, I have love for every venue around town, but after the gig, we head to Melo's.

The Commodore
John Zimmerman (The Muckers); Ethan Bassford, Felicia Douglass (Gemma); Razor Braids (Hollye Bynum, Jilly Karande, Hannah Nichols, Janie Peacock)

John Zimmerman: The Commodore holds a special place in my heart just 'cause my buddies used to live right around the corner from there, and right when I moved to New York, I was staying with them. And I would, at some point throughout the day, always end up at The Commodore.

Ethan Bassford: This has been a favorite of mine for years, and I have a lot of fond memories of beginning or ending a night here with assorted friends and love interests.

Felicia Douglass: I've had a lot of fun nights at The Commodore. It's close to many venues and often the preferred place friends would end up. Their cocktails are festive and good but this isn't just a bar that happens to have food. The fried-chicken sandwich is notable.

John Zimmerman: They have the best nachos you've ever had and the best fried-chicken sandwich in New York.

Ethan Bassford: The food is delicious, and if it were just a restaurant it would be a good one. Southern-style things like hot chicken, very good and very large non-meaty nachos for the veggie folks. Great vibes, backyard, solid beers on draft. If you're feeling fancy, you can get something slushy and tropical too.

Razor Braids: Us RB babes love some nachos and frozen boozy bevs! Hollye is not so secretly obsessed with Commodore. She has spent her past two birthdays there and goes there more than is normal. She has forced the other babes to go there as well. For our holiday hang this year, we got fairly stoned and opened presents at Hollye's apartment. When we got good and hungry, we thought of no other place. We headed our way over to Commodore, where we sat in a booth in absolute silence, stuffing our faces with burgers and mac.

It's also proven itself to be a great post-prac or post-show hang, as it's the best damn food to eat when you are tipsy or have the munchies. We live for the spicy white cheese dip, fried-chicken sandwiches, veggie burgers and the drink, The Commodore, which is basically a very boozy Pina Colada.

It's comfort food in a fun environment, and it has something for every mood. If you're in the mood to dance, it's perfect for that. If you're in the mood to chill and sit in a booth and kiss your crush, it's got you! It's a place for us to go and blow off steam. Who doesn't need that in NYC? The weekends draw a bit of a touristy crowd, but the more you drink, the more that doesn't really matter. We know this, because we've done the research!

Duck Duck
Eddie Kuspiel, George Miata, Kevin Urvalek (Color Tongue)

George Miata: My first time moving into Brooklyn, Eddie had already lived here for a year in Bushwick, and then we moved to a place off the Lorimer stop in Williamsburg. This was the local watering hole. We used to go there and play darts all the time. We were working on an EP and it was before Ray and Kevin were in the band, it was just me and Eddie. We were transitioning our sound from a reggae-rock band to, something else.

Kevin Urvalek: Thank God.

George Miata: Kevin hates ska. I wouldn't put us in that category, but we were heavily influenced by Sublime.

Eddie Kuspiel: We liked punk and Jamaican music. A lot. And yeah.

George Miata: But that's the only bar I've ever had where it was like, *oh, let's go to our patented bar!* That was the spot. If we had recorded something, we'd go there to celebrate. It was a cool thing to be living in the city for the first time in your adult life and having a place to go that's right around the corner.

Easy Lover
Satin Nickel (Sam Aneson, Nikola Balać, Morgan Hollingsworth, Ariana Karp, Andrew Shewaga)

We have a definite soft spot for Easy Lover, a bar on Metropolitan and Humboldt in Williamsburg. Some might remember its old name, Legion. It has become a second home of sorts, and it's also where we shot our first music video for "Just Keep Running."

It fluctuates from chill to super lively, and it's a solid neighborhood spot. We especially love the rotation of local DJs in the front room and spontaneous karaoke in the back when the owner is around. The best part about it, though, is that it has become a haven for art shares and performances. We've joined a community of artists there who meet and showcase new material. Love this place.

Freddy's Bar and Backroom
Jack McLoughlin, Aida Mekonnen, Olivia Price, Steve Vannelli (Forever Honey)

Steve Vannelli: Freddy's is kind of the hang-out spot. Just kick back, relax, for the most part.

Olivia Price: When me and Aida first moved into the neighborhood, it was one of the first bars that we went to. Every Tuesday night, they have a jazz band playing here in the front, so we would frequent it in the early months that we were here, and then, ever since, it's kind of been a staple. And you [Aida] kind of got more into the Freddy's crowd.

Aida Mekonnen: It was recommended by a musician, and the Tuesday shows are amazing.

Jack McLoughlin: I feel like every night sort of ends here in this area. And the frogs—

Olivia Price: There are two albino frogs that they have in a little aquarium in the back of the bar. They look petrified, and they don't really move, so you can't really tell if they're real or not. But they are.

Aida Mekonnen: It feels illegal, but it's not.

Jack McLoughlin: It feels illegal, yeah. My favorite part about the bar, though. Well, there are two favorite parts. The first part is the frogs. The second part is the little TV that's playing the cat drinking the milk on loop at the corner of the bar over there.

Steve Vannelli: Freddy's is just a package deal. Obviously, the atmosphere is great, [there are] enough things to look at on the wall. I discover twenty new things every time I walk in here. Great food, it's affordable, and it's right in between our places. It's the perfect meeting spot.

Hartley's
Hallie Spoor

Hartley's in Bed-Stuy for their Monday-night live Irish music jam. So cozy in the wintertime, with the candles, Guinness and great Irish soda bread and butter. Plus the audience understands the rules of the music jam. When the singer sings a song, since it's all acoustic and not mic'd, everyone shuts up immediately, stops their conversation, and just listens to the music. Then when it's just the fiddles fiddling away, the crowd perks back up and resumes their conversations.

The Levee
Dang Anohen (Sallies); Lydia Gammill, Melissa Lucciola, Tarra Thiessen (Gustaf)

Dang Anohen: The Levee rules, man. That's a cool-ass rock 'n' roll bar.

Melissa Lucciola: My boyfriend used to work there, and he's still friends with the owners, and they're just amazing, amazing people. Usually when the owners are amazing, it just trickles down into the whole thing.

Dang Anohen: The bartenders are really cool. They're musicians, and they always play rock and metal.

Lydia Gammill: And they have cheese balls.

Dang Anohen: They have those cheesy puffs. And they have that, um, what do you call that Gatorade and vodka drink? Something you can get and you feel good about it.

Lydia Gammill: And the jukebox our friends are on. We're gonna get on The Levee jukebox. I'm telling you, one of these days. I'm manifesting it right now. That's another music-business bar in my mind. I've gotten drunk there with some nice record executive people.

Tarra Thiessen: I feel like after one breakup, I was there with you drinking tequila.

Lydia Gammill: Probably. One of the breakups.

Tarra Thiessen: One of the early ones.

Lydia Gammill: I don't break up that often.

Lucky Dog
Paul Hammer (Savoir Adore); Tracey (Strange Neighbors)

Paul Hammer: For a few of my friends with dogs, that's the only bar they want to go to. It has this beautiful backyard. It's like a dog run, but the owners are getting drunk.

Tracey: It's all in the name. Pup-friendly bar, so you can knock 'em back next to your furry friends.

Paul Hammer: It's also one of the only bars that's consistently open 'til 4 a.m. All of the venues are still around this area. Touring acts play Music Hall, Brooklyn Steel isn't too far from here. So when I lived on South Fourth, I'd get a text message at 2 a.m. like, "Dude, we're closing down Lucky Dog. What're you doing?" And I'm like, "Nothing, sleeping. But I guess I can go do this." Those are some of the nights I regret, but they're memories.

Night of Joy
Richey Rose (Songs for Sabotage); Jared Artaud (The Vacant Lots); Emir Mohseni, John Zimmerman (The Muckers); Darren O'Brien (Wildly); Nico E.P., Sean Wouters (Deaf Poets)

Richey Rose: My favorite spot in BK has always been Night of Joy, a beautiful cocktail bar on the corner of Lorimer and Meeker. It can be very low-key but has also hosted some epic DJ nights over the years. It's like Cheers for those of us who remember Misshapes parties.

Jared Artaud: When you walk into this Eurozone-styled watering hole it's like being transported to some dimly lit Parisian cafe, the perfect place to crawl to after a show or to grab a few drinks and conversation with friends. Plus the best staff bar none.

John Zimmerman: It's kind of a cute spot. A nice, chill spot if you want to take a first date or something.

Darren O'Brien: There's a reason Night of Joy is the setting for so many app dates. The roof is beautiful, the inside is really vibey, the cocktails are good, and the unreasonably beautiful owner has her indie-rock musician friends DJ, myself included.

John Zimmerman: Me and Emir both DJ there.

Emir Mohseni: We're trying to make people dance if they dance. It's really hard to make people dance in New York.

Nico E.P.: Our friend Jared from The Vacant Lots, he DJs there. Well, when he's in town.

Jared Artaud: I DJ here a lot, and no other cocktail bar in the city comes close to the atmosphere they've created inside or up on their rooftop bar.

Nico E.P.: The roof is chill.

Sean Wouters: It has an interesting, really vintage feel to it.

Emir Mohseni: It's really cool. It's a really nice, beautiful spot, and the vibe is really good.

Sean Wouters: It feels fancy but it's not. I guess that's the vibe.

Nico E.P.: You feel high-class.

Sean Wouters: You're drinking a PBR in a fancy place, you know.

Jared Artaud: The owner is the real deal and the cocktails are to die for. Few bars have that I-don't-want-to-leave vibe that when you do and you can't remember how you got home but you keep on going back. It makes the hangovers worth it every time.

The Palace
Justin Buschardt (Sharkswimmer)

This old-new-school spot has continued to be one of the favorite places to grab a frosty drink or three along with a classic burger and fries that has proven to be perfect every single time. It's right around the corner from our rehearsal space and directly across from McGolrick Park, so you can find us there on a pretty regular basis. Bordering the dark vibes of a cozy dive bar and your grandma's living room, it's just the perfect atmosphere. They even host stand-up comedy nights! Great people and dog-watching, and owner Rita and their staff are just the best.

Favorite thing there, ice-cold, frosty mug of Bud and shot special.

Rocka Rolla
Michael Tarnofsky (Edna); Nico E.P., Sean Wouters (Deaf Poets); Lydia Gammill, Tine Hill, Tarra Thiessen (Gustaf); Aidan (Strange Neighbors)

Michael Tarnofsky: I feel like this has to be a really important place for everybody in how centrally located it was and how important that once was, like, before a Music Hall of Williamsburg show. You never used to want to hang out at Union Pool before the show, so you walk over from Rocka Rolla. Unless you were itching for a new STD.

Nico E.P.: I love that spot so much. When I first moved up, my friend said, "Yo, we're gonna go bar-hopping." He took me and he goes, "Dude, they have three-dollar chalices here." It was literally a chalice of beer.

Tine Hill: The beer goblets.

Sean Wouters: It's medieval!

Tarra Thiessen: Rocka Rolla has that coffee thing that we like.

Aidan: Divey, cheap drinks, chalices of beer, "that coffee drink" and eighties hair metal constantly. A dash of goth. Floors so dirty you wonder if you'd catch Hep C if you lost a shoe. That kind of magical place.

Nico E.P.: We actually did a video there.

Sean Wouters: We filmed ourselves bar-crawling, bar-hopping.

Nico E.P.: We ended up at Rocka Rolla. By the time we got to that place, that was like our fifth bar, it was such a blur. I remember having a cigar like, "Sean, just have a cigar, dude."

Sean Wouters: I don't even remember that.

Nico E.P.: It got me destroyed. I took an Uber home, 'cause I'm like, I cannot comprehend what is happening.

Lydia Gammill: Rocka Rolla is where I learned what a Mind Eraser is thanks to Tarra and Vram.

Tarra Thiessen: It's vodka, Kahlúa, and club soda and you have to stare each other in the eyes and chug it.

Lydia Gammill: Like, they seem fine.

Tarra Thiessen: I get angry and sad after those.

Lydia Gammill: Tarra's great 'cause she's like, "Vodka doesn't affect me. Good luck." Mayhem. Mind Eraser mayhem.

Tarra Thiessen: The first time Vram gave me eyes was there. I was like, oh, that guy's cute.

Lydia Gammill: I've had a lot of old band meetings at Rocka Rolla. They've got a jukebox. It's like a heavy-metal scene. It's a dual life, the regulars and the weekend crowd.

Tine Hill: It got super popular with the bros.

Lydia Gammill: It's okay. Any bro shall cast the first stone, you know. We all have a bro within us. We all can be an intrusive species, depending on where we are. So, it's easy for me to resent, but I also express love and kindness, towards them and myself. Sometimes it just means I don't wanna go in there, though.

Temkin's
Deep Wimp (Trevor Courneen, Kyle Jutkiewicz, Wesley Rose, Charlie Waters)

We practice in Greenpoint, and three quarters of the band lives there, so we wanted to shout-out our go-to local bar. Temkin's on Greenpoint Avenue is kind of on the newer side but has come in pretty hot to our "best in the borough" list. Genny Cream Ale on draft is about as near to perfect as a bar can get, the music always kicks ass, and the decor is top-notch. Plus, your options for bathroom walls are outer space or flamingos, which makes selfies a must. Come to think of it, we should probably do our next band photo shoot in the bathrooms at Temkin's.

Troost
Matt Caldamone, Colin Lord (HYPEMOM)

Colin Lord: I moved in there, not into the bar, into Greenpoint, a few years ago, and it's always been the closest bar to me, which is nice. But also, they've always got some really interesting music going on there. And I'll admit on radio, on record, that I've definitely recorded sounds there, some of the music playing inside the bar, and used it in music of my own afterward. It's just got like a really cool selection of different kinds of acts playing.

Matt Caldamone: You know, in this day and age, I feel like it's kind of rare to not have your plans made before you leave the house. And it's one of the rare places where we've walked out of Colin's apartment to go somewhere and do something and seen the musicians up in the front window there and stopped in and just been like, "That sounds cool, I don't know what instruments they're using to make those strange noises," or "That person's voice is beautiful. We were going to go have a beer, let's just have the beer here," and to just like, course-correct, based on some new interesting sensory reception is, I feel, rarer and rarer.

Colin Lord: Yeah, Troost has always been a really welcoming, cool spot.

Tradesman
Marble House (Gabe Friedman, Danny Irizarry, Nicole Pettigrew, Javier Vela)

"Tradesman or what?"

That phrase, name-checking the Tradesman bar in East Williamsburg, gradually became part of our post-rehearsal routine, whether we had just logged a few hours at the nearby Sweatshop rehearsal studio or the nearby room we now rent monthly for ourselves. The bar has become the anchor of the East Williamsburg world where we've put in the sweat at practice and played many of our early gigs.

But it's more than just our regular stop to recharge and relax after putting in that work, it's where we get candid about our ideas, creative about our visions and ambitious about our future. And it has played a big role in making the four of us closer friends.

From the outside, the bar is the definition of unassuming. Its façade looks like a slab of concrete that someone carved a couple of big dingy windows into. It's easy to pass by without a second thought.

Inside is a different story. It's cozy and rustic, if small, with a brick wall behind the bar and curated tool designs sprinkled throughout, tied to the trade worker theme. There's also a nice back courtyard with tables open in the warm months. Overall, it's a well-set-up, neighborhood-joint sort of hangout, with kind bartenders that attracts regulars.

Another huge plus, its drink prices are among the most affordable in Brooklyn. And they don't skimp on alcohol in mixed drinks like many other Brooklyn bars.

But what sets the bar apart for us is its very welcoming and creative atmosphere. There's just the right amount of darkness for the late-night drink. There's always open space at booths or tables, for our bulky gear as well as our butts. The bartender is never overloaded with requests, so it's not a process to get a drink. The regulars aren't judge-y or overly hipster-ish. It's easy to imagine other bands and creatives making the Tradesman their regular spot.

In our many nights there, we've talked about our goals for finishing full albums and touring, the bridge of a specific song, even what our EP cover art should be. We've aired the many disagreements and frustrations that come with being in a band, a mashup of four creative personalities with different ideas. We've listened to each other's relationship woes and toasted to the fun high points on our journey.

And we've also stopped in after birthday parties for our bass player Javier who lives nearby, and after shows with a few friends, and also for no occasion whatsoever.

When we were brainstorming locations for our first photo shoot as a band, the Tradesman quickly came to mind. The images of us from the shoot at a small Tradesman table holding cocktails are some of our favorites. Probably because we look like we're in our creative element.

CHAPTER 2
BEHIND THE BAR

"It makes working weekends a lot more appealing if I know that all my friends are going to show up anyway."
- Matt Bernstein (Wet Leather)

What came first, the bartender or the bands?

It's no secret that the stage and the service industry see significant overlap, the best sort of Venn diagram with a big, boozy center, so it's a safe bet that when the babe mixing your floral-infused whiskey whatever or the dude cracking jokes and beers at your favorite dive aren't serving drinks, well, they're probably making music.

A few years ago, I had arranged to meet Wet Leather at Golden Years in Williamsburg. Warm, wooded, with a true timeless feeling, the self-described "classic bar for experienced drinkers" offers burgers and fries with craft cocktails on the side, and because it was where singer and guitarist Matt Bernstein worked behind the bar, it was where his bandmates and buddies could typically be found on the other side of it. It was raining that night, and by the time I'd finished the five-minute trek from the Metropolitan stop, I'd already very much violated the second half of the band's (un)official motto: "Never wear leather, never get wet." Fortunately, they're nice guys and let me slide, dress-code violation be damned.

Wet Leather had been on my radar and their music on my rotation since their summer set at NYC's Northside Festival, when my friend and festival plus-one Mike had picked them off the schedule not because he was already a fan, or even familiar with their music, but simply because he loved their name. And while this is essentially the music equivalent of judging a book by its cover, Mike *is* the kind of guy who wears a leather jacket in June, so in hindsight, his selection was both pretty predictable and completely on-brand.

Lack of real rationale aside, both the band and the evening exceeded both of our uneducated expectations. The blue lights and breezy rooftop vibes, a few frozen drinks, and a hit or two of the vape pen that Mike whipped out of his pocket mid-set, combined to set the sensory stage for the show on all fronts, while Wet Leather's irresistible brand of "anxiety pop," as well as the rest of the Brooklyn bill, provided the perfect Friday-night music fix.

Now at this point, I'd like to offer you a formal warning. I'm enthusiastic, probably to a fault. I don't enjoy things casually. I don't admire things quietly. And along with the very cool shoes of that stranger across the street and the sandwich that the chef responsible *must know* is the best I've had since this panini in Portland back in 2015, the music of my favorite bands must be recognized, praised to their faces, and then *shared with the world.*

With Wet Leather, this official proclamation of adoration happened a few months later, when after stalking the band from stage to stage across the borough, I finally found an opportunity outside the Bushwick venue Elsewhere to express my love in the most professional of capacities, by shouting compliments at them from the sidewalk as they loaded up their van after a show. And a few days later, in slightly more official form, I followed up via email to arrange an interview with the group at Golden Years.

But away from the fangirling that's the basis of both my blog and this book, let's get back to the bars, where artists aren't just spending their beer money but making it. With musician mixologists at the helm, Brooklyn drinking destinations basically double as tequila-soaked clubhouses, with the smartest of owners embracing and even encouraging this phenomenon by letting artists have the run of the place, empowering them to arrange the entertainment they're naturally primed to provide, thereby establishing an automatic and authentic community, and drawing a naturally cool crowd.

On the evening of our post-ambush meet-up, both the band and bar were making good use of this mutualistic relationship. Wet Leather was capitalizing on a built-in venue and bargain drinks, perks of their frontman's employment, while the bar in ultimate win-win fashion benefited from a major boost to their Monday-night crowd.

The occasion was the live premiere of the band's psychedelic music video for "Party," a song Matt described to me as being "about the deranged claustrophobic feelings that come with being at a party in a cramped New York apartment."

While the "Party" party wasn't taking place at a third-floor walk-up or inside a loft in a questionably converted warehouse, it did in many ways mimic the positive parts of a home-thrown Brooklyn event, but with upgraded amenities like a better-stocked bar and a bouncer on hand to kick out stragglers come closing time. And as the room filled up, the musicians played the role of gracious hosts, greeting friends, fans, and likely a few misguided leather enthusiasts who were all equally stoked for the video premiere and a rock-solid excuse to extend the weekend.

During our conversation, as Matt and Wet Leather keyboard player Jason Katzenstein discussed NYC influences, the poison-penned *Pitchfork* critic they dreamed of being roasted by, and favorite Brooklyn venues past and present, Matt brought up an additional bartender benefit, revealing that he'd held an advance music-video viewing for a few lucky Golden Years patrons when test-driving the audiovisual equipment the evening before.

"Last night, I ended up screening the video for the bartender and the four German tourists who were here," he told me. "The tourists said, '*Oh yah*, it's good. *Yah*, it's nice.' I feel like they wouldn't lie to me."

Golden Years is just one example of a spot where you might order an IPA or Old Fashioned from one of my favorite musicians, likely while elbow-to-elbow with the rest of their band.

Bounce down to Left Hand Path and let Brooklyn drummer

Brian Del Guercio make you a martini.

Head to Pokito and roll some dice with Max Pain and the Groovies, whose lovable long-locked bassist Kallan Campbell is probably pouring shots and shaking things up.

Or grab a beer at almost any Brooklyn venue, where in Clark-Kent-turned-Superman super-star fashion, artists like MG Stillwaggon of Spite FuXXX, Leslie Hong of Haybaby, or Ethan Alexander of So and So might transition from manning or managing the bar to rocking the stage.

And because an employee's penchant for performance comes in extra handy on karaoke and trivia nights, you might find Charmaine Querol of Nevva crawling on top of the bar and diving into drinkers' arms at Heaven or Las Vegas, or catch Emily Ashenden of Ashjesus popping in to emcee evenings at The Broadway, or cracking wise while quizzing customers at The Sultan Room.

At these places, any Brooklynite can count on a good pour with a solid side of entertainment. And as for artists, whether a group is gathered at a bar because their guitarist is manning it or the singer slinging the drinks got the job because they were already practically living there, one thing is for sure. With a bandmate, best friend, or combination of both on the payroll, everyone is probably drinking for pretty much free.

Golden Years
Matt Bernstein, Jason Katzenstein (Wet Leather)

Matt Bernstein: My favorite thing about this place is that it's become a go-to for our friends when I'm working here. A lot of friends from college, friends from other bands from New York, our friends from Caravela, UV Rays. It's kind of a running joke that the first ten seats at the bar will be our people. It makes working weekends a lot more appealing if I know that all my friends are going to show up anyway. I don't have to worry about missing out.

Jason Katzenstein: We go, "Matt, play this song! Matt! Matt! Play this song!"

Matt Bernstein: If our musician friends come in, I'll play their music to torture them. That's a fun privilege that I abuse when I'm working here.

We tend to gravitate towards divier bars in general. That's a lot of where we've played and spent time, and where I tend to feel more comfortable. This is a great place because you have that casual, unpretentious atmosphere, but you can get a really excellent cocktail.

Jason Katzenstein: I actually have one complaint about Golden Years, which is that Matt has never screened *The Mask*.

Matt Bernstein: It's been requested multiple times, and now I have no excuse.

One Stop Beer Shop
Hayes Peebles

There's a lot of history here. It used to be my local. I lived for two years across the highway, across Meeker. My roommate and I would just come here on weeknights, and we got to know the bartenders and whatnot. It's just one of those bars where you could show up and actually talk to people, meet people, talk to the bartenders. I feel like everybody wants that bar in their life. Not like Cheers, but a social place to go alone and spend some time.

So I'd come here, and I was working on this Beer Society thing they have, and I guess I was showing up enough that eventually they asked me to work here. All the money I spent on beer, I just started taking back. All the guys I used to be on the other side of the bar from became even closer friends and colleagues. For a long time, it was where I spent a lot of my time, both socially and working. This was just sort of the hub for me for a while.

I've been out here when it's nice and you sit outside. I've been here in the pit of winter and, you know, you're drinking eggnog shots and playing Christmas carols. I've just had a lot of fun times here, a lot of late nights on both sides of the bar, in a lot of different capacities. This bar is a fun place.

Pokito
Kallan Campbell, Tcoy Coughlin, David Johnson, Shane Preece (Max Pain and the Groovies)

Kallan Campbell: It's a really cute cocktail bar in South Williamsburg. I just liked the vibe and ended up getting a job there when I was drunkenly talking to the owner one night like, "Let me work here, dude." Then a couple months later, he hit me up like, "Still want a job?" Like, obviously, yes.

It's a cool spot because a lot of musicians do hang out there. And it's a really fun, eclectic crowd of some artists, but also just other people you normally wouldn't mix with, but because it's such a small, intimate space, everyone ends up interacting. So that's really cool. And if there's shows at Baby's All Right, then you can kind of go back and forth because it's walking distance. And the owners are artists and young and just good people in general to hang out with.

Tcoy Coughlin: What's that margarita called?

Kallan Campbell: The hibiscus margarita.

Tcoy Coughlin: That'll get you.

Kallan Campbell: Tcoy came in the other day getting two of the larges. I was like, "Be careful dude."

David Johnson: I think everyone in this band has blacked out at Pokito.

Kallan Campbell: We're pretty liberal giving out shots and giving friends drinks. Or even if like, I like you, you're gonna get a shot. So that makes it fun.

David Johnson: I'll tell ya what, there's a lot of gamblin' that goes down at Pokito.

Tcoy Coughlin: I've rolled some dice. I feel like you roll dice so long and then you're standing on the chairs. The next thing you know, you're standing on the table rolling the dice.

Kallan Campbell: You get a lot of people, like randoms, that will just join in on the fun, too.

Shane Preece: It's a good vibe in there.

David Johnson: The locals, they carry dice on them. We actually are gonna release a song called "Street Casino" and that is because of the gambling that happened inside of Pokito.

Tens of dollars are made and lost a night, *tens*. Hands can be like twenty bucks a person. Just depends on the night, this and that. It just gets tempting once you start losing money to bet more so you can get it back.

Tcoy Coughlin: Well, also, we all know where the money's going. It's going to the bar. Whoever won the hand is buying the drinks, then whoever won the next hand is buying the drinks, ya know?

Kallan Campbell: Ideally. I mean, I've given out shots anyways.

Reclamation Bar
Nicholas LaGrasta, Brett Moses (Teen Commandments); Jake Hiebert, Connor Jones, William Thompson (Yella Belly)

Nicholas LaGrasta: Where we rehearse is like five minutes around the corner from here, and we share that rehearsal space with a couple of guys that work over here and are also in the music scene. We met them through coming here, this guy Will Thompson and Connor.

Connor Jones: Reclamation Bar. Best bar in Brooklyn.

Jake Hiebert: That's actually debatable whether we're welcome there.

William Thompson: The only reason is like half the band used to work there, some still do.

Connor Jones: I still do. It's the best bar in Brooklyn. Everyone should go every single night. Tip your bartenders.

Jake Hiebert: It is great. I don't work there, and I agree.

William Thompson: It's our after-party spot.

Connor Jones: That's our real party bar, for sure.

Jake Hiebert: Connor doesn't kick us out.

Connor Jones: I *have* kicked Will out.

Brett Moses: It reminds me of how some of the places that used to be in Williamsburg felt. It feels a little more—

Nicholas LaGrasta: Loose?

Brett Moses: Free and Wild West kind of feeling, an anything-goes-here kinda place. Some of our weirdest nights at some point stop by here.

Connor Jones: They've got a great bar. They advertise as the neighborhood living room. And it's a huge regulars spot. It's very comfortable, very welcoming. The people are great.

Jake Hiebert: It's very much a meeting spot. Like, of any bar that I've actually been to, I honestly think I could go in there any time, for better or for worse.

Connor Jones: There's a really cool community. Everyone's friends in there. It's just a good vibe.

CHAPTER 3
RAISING THE BAR

"It's one of the places you walk by, and you're like, oh, this is why I live in Brooklyn." - Laura Valk (Skout)

While community is key and price is typically paramount, there are plenty of other factors that come into play when deciding which bar you're going to spend your afternoon, evening, or maybe the occasional morning in.

Often, it's about proximity. It's the watering hole on the way home from work, the midway point between friends' apartments, or maybe just a favorite bar based on one special memory, a spur-of-the-moment stop that once topped off a near-perfect night.

Frequently the drinks themselves are the draw, and there's no shortage of bars in Brooklyn where trained and talented mixologists play the role of performer as they squeeze, stir, muddle, mix, toss, twist, and *light shit on fire* for a thirsty audience of professional drinkers and cocktail connoisseurs every evening. Some bars dominate the daiquiri, others have mastered the Bloody Mary, and certain spots are known for their selection, be it a global bunch of beers, an extensive menu of mezcals, or a lovingly curated collection of ciders crafted somewhere super quaint-sounding upstate.

And then there are the more elusive elements that lure you in and make you a lifer, at least for as long as that particular bar has a lease. Good vibes, good people, good music, all that *je ne se quoi* stuff. Unique attributes that combine to create an unshakable, unfakeable coolness that has the power to transform *a bar* into *your bar.*

For Paul Hammer, that would be Fresh Kills.

In the early 2010s, back when I was living in Austin and still knew how to drive, "Dreamers" by Savoir Adore was all over the Alt Nation airwaves, and I would actively disturb the same stretch of city twice a day as I blasted it with the windows down, singing along while creeping along the traffic-clogged downtown streets that comprised my commute.

Fast-forward to Brooklyn. It's seven years since the release, "Dreamers" is well on its way to ten million Spotify streams, and I can no longer be trusted behind any wheel. To my utter disbelief, I am sitting in the back booth of the Savoir Adore-approved cocktail bar Fresh Kills with the man behind the band, who has graciously agreed to meet me for an interview for a blog that, and here's the kindness kicker, *didn't even exist yet.*

Now, I recognize I'm not interviewing the Beatles or Beyoncé here, and all the artists in this book can walk down Grand, Broadway, or Bedford without fear of paparazzi and pop into Sweetgreen for a salad without donning a disguise. But as a fan, it's still easy to be star-struck by some of these musicians and a little intimidated by the true talent, city street cred, and captivating power of their performances.

After all, the rock-star stereotype does skew more diva than docile and more naughty than nice, with classic tales of trashed hotel rooms and gone-viral riders banning brown M&M's or outlining avocado requirements for the green-room guacamole. There's also the fact that, from the fan's vantage point, musicians often seem more God-like than mortal while on stage, if only because of the booming voices, the bright lights, and the fact that you're quite literally looking up at them. And for those of us whose musical expertise doesn't extend beyond an elementary school-engrained recorder rendition of "Hot Cross Buns," making music is even more impressive because it's largely a mystery. Watching band members play together is like witnessing an intimate conversation in a language we're not fluent in, while ripping a guitar solo might as well be rocket science, or perhaps more like pulling a rabbit out of a hat.

However, as anyone familiar with the individuals featured in this book is aware, this potential worry is largely unwarranted. In fact, one of the most delightful conclusions I've drawn based on my interactions with artists over the years can be summed up quite simply. *Most people are really, really nice!*

That's all to say that while in my eyes and ears and extended Spotify history, Paul Hammer might as well be Paul McCartney, and I'm sure I greeted him accordingly awkwardly, I'm happy to report that he just might be the friendliest of them all. Dressed casually in a sweater and plain black baseball cap, he didn't strut into Fresh Kills like he owned the place but strolled in like it was his living room. And while it was his favorite bar where we were meeting and not his actual apartment, much like the guys of Wet Leather, Paul still made me feel right at home.

Fresh Kills is the rare bar that feels elegant but easygoing, where you can get a cocktail crafted with made-in-house syrups and fancy ice but won't feel weird if you make less than six figures and are sporting Adidas slides. The kind of place where everyone looks hotter and seems cooler, but the bartenders won't laugh in your face if you need seven of a drink's eight ingredients explained. Where you can just as easily sip solo, get to second base with a second date, or, say, bring a Brooklyn blogger.

Once Paul and I were settled in and he and the barman had greeted each other like old friends, likely because they were, the artist ordered an American Trilogy with rye whiskey, applejack, brown sugar, and orange bitters, while I followed his creative vision, or just casual advice, and ordered the Bartender's Choice.

"That's the move," Paul promised. "I've already had everything."

In true indie-rock fairytale fashion, Paul met his now-wife at a music festival Savoir Adore was playing in Brazil after one of the band's songs went viral via video game, and the pair had recently moved up to Newburgh, New York in search of the one thing, aside from LA weather, that had the power to pull creatives out of the city. More space. However, having lived three blocks away on South Fourth for five years, this bar was still very much Paul's Brooklyn home base. It was also a haunt to which he always returned when he was back, whether he was visiting, playing, or working on other artists' projects such as *Lamplight Motel*, the stellar debut solo record from his longtime friend Michael Hesslein (HESS), which he produced and engineered.

"Fresh Kills is the Paul Hammer special," HESS told me two years later when I interviewed him for this book over FaceTime. "He and I would go there a lot if we were in the city together during the making of this record. And that's where he and I would always go. Like, after he would do a lot of DJ sets at Baby's All Right, we would always finish the night off at Fresh Kills."

When I asked Paul what he missed most about the borough, particularly the section of Williamsburg that he had ricocheted around in for half a decade, he offered a two-part answer that's perfectly in line with what I've also come to value most about Brooklyn in my own five years here.

"I miss the spontaneity and community," he told me.

That response perfectly sums up the common themes outlined by other artists in this chapter, where you'll find more picks like Paul's, a selection of other artists' Fresh Kills equivalents.

From the most welcoming gay saloon to a tavern with riveting tunes, a bar with hotel vibes and another where customers have literally slept in the booths, these places are home to memories, heralded for specialties, appreciated for the unique roles they play, and adored for the specific feelings they impart. They're distinct destinations with one-of-a-kind wow or weird factors, serving as the setting for those incredible, often fleeting, only-in-NYC moments.

Paul also perfectly summed up life in Brooklyn as he described a situation that my own body and bank account can definitely attest to, which serves as the ideal introduction to a list of bars that both sell and excel in our enjoyment.

"I was dangerously close to way too many things," he said. "This is part of what's dangerous about living in Brooklyn. There's an opportunity to spend all your money, but also you can enjoy yourself, let's put it that way, all the time, every night."

And then, right on cue, complimentary drinks arrived at the table, and we took whiskey shots served out of little glass boots. As one does on a Wednesday night in Williamsburg.

The Adirondack
Sonny Hell

The whole time I've been in NYC, I've lived in Brooklyn, always somewhere near the L train, so I have a lot to say about the cafes, bars and restaurants in Williamsburg and Bushwick, but this past summer I found a random spot I really like right off the G train down in Windsor Terrace called The Adirondack.

A good friend of mine and I would get off late from our job every Saturday night, around 2 a.m., and walk around the corner to "The Dack" for a few beers before we'd go home. It became a routine that I would really look forward to. The bar has a cozy kind of alpine vibe, the beer selection is very well curated, and the bartender, Kelly, is just the kind of music nerd I like to talk to. He really set the mood there with his great song selection, and he always made us feel welcome.

In the summer, with the door open to the fresh air, something just felt a bit magical about that place. So I'd say if you wanna try some really good beer, listen to some really good music, and be kind of transported out of time for a little while, check out the Adirondack really late on a Saturday night. It's chill.

Barcade
Sam R. (Glassio)

I'm not one for this spot when it is crowded, but I used to live really close by and go on off-hours or really late on a calmer night. I'd put headphones on and listen to music I was making at the time and play a bunch of games just to test out new material in the real world. I also wrote the melody to the final track on my new album.

It's called "Thunderbirds," and I started singing it to myself when I was imagining an arcade machine of the same name existing there.

Beer Street
Emanuel Ayvas (Emanuel and the Fear)

I got really into beer back when touring in Europe with Emanuel and the Fear because every country, particularly Germany, Belgium, the UK, has a lot of interesting beers, and we got really into trying all these beers that you just couldn't get here. They have these small-batch microbreweries, but they've been there like a thousand years. Like, old monks used to brew beer or something. Now it's this whole craze.

It's really nice people, it's super small and chill, and Cory [the buyer] is great. I think he has really good taste. There's a lot of stuff here that you can't get anywhere else.

Branded Saloon
Viktor Vladimirovich (Prince Johnny)

I think it won an award for being the best not-quite-gay gay bar.

There is a predatory-ness in a lot of gay bars, or gay clubs, especially in Hell's Kitchen. Brooklyn has the edge taken off a little bit, but you know, it's the male gaze. It can feel like it's hard to put your guard down, and it's kinda hard to be yourself, and you're always trying to prove something. Like hunt or be hunted. But in Branded Saloon, somewhere between the ox heads and the old-timey chandeliers, there's something about the vibe that decreases that. And it's very unpretentious. The food is good, there's burgers. It's kind of like, a mix of a Chili's and a gay bar. I love going there to watch *RuPaul*. Everyone knows the bartenders.

When I was sending off my second single and doing all the emailing shit, I did all of that at like 11 p.m. at the bar. You know, cafes close. Where do I go when I'm a night owl and I want to work on stuff? Bring your laptop, sit down there, and they won't bat an eye.

Call Box Lounge
Nicholas LaGrasta, Brett Moses (Teen Commandments)

Brett Moses: The Call Box is the dirtiest, worst, best place. It's like just the least put-together, least thought-out dance bar in the world. We went there one time and there was a DJ eating McDonald's and DJing at the same time. She was going between Hall & Oates and gangster rap and she had a button that played, like, a gunshot. She'd be like, Hall & Oates! And she'd be like, *pew-pew, ow-ow,* and then it'd be gangster rap.

Nicholas LaGrasta: While *Seinfeld* was playing on the television.

Brett Moses: The weird thing is that everybody there was acting as if this was their scene and they know that this is what happens. Another thing where I'm like, I don't know anything about the world. At all.

Captain Dan's Good Time Tavern
Nico E.P., Sean Wouters (Deaf Poets)

Nico E.P.: My favorite spot, it's literally like two blocks from my house, is Captain Dan's. That spot is sick. They have awesome food, good drinks.

Sean Wouters: The micheladas are on point.

Nico E.P.: The micheladas are on point, which is always a plus for a bar for me. If you have a good michelada, you're gonna find me there. A good balance of Clamato and you have to have the Tajín salt rim. That's crucial. Because some places just give you the salt rim, and it's not the same.

Sean Wouters: It's not the same. We're both michelada fans.

Nico E.P.: The size is important too. [Here] they have a good size. It tastes really good, it has a good amount of spice. I tally it up, and they take a chunk of my money every month. Every month, some of my paycheck goes to Captain Dan's.

FourFiveSix
Connor Gladney, Laura Valk (Skout); Alison Clancy

Alison Clancy: They have good food, drinks, chill vibes, outdoor space and live music, and it's right by my house. I basically consider it my backyard. I particularly like that they have big comfy couches. Reminds me of the nineties coffee-shop vibe.

Laura Valk: That's our favorite spot in Brooklyn, hands down. It's just a giant living room. You're sitting on couches, and there's live jazz.

Connor Gladney: The brunch is great.

Laura Valk: The brunch is amazing. It's the only bar that I've ever been to by myself. I've never done that, but I'll go and get a whiskey and sit and watch live jazz.

Connor Gladney: It's such a great place.

Laura Valk: It's one of the places you walk by, and you're like, oh, this is why I live in Brooklyn.

Connor Gladney: Actually, though! It feels like a one-of-a-kind place. It doesn't feel like a place in Manhattan that's cookie-cutter, shoved into some building because it's popular or whatever.

Laura Valk: You know those places in Manhattan have, like, Brooklyn lights or Edison bulbs, trying to be something.

Connor Gladney: This place looks like it just *has it*. It feels real. There's also great outdoor seating. And it's quiet. I don't like places where I have to yell to say nothing. I tell bad jokes, so the more I have to repeat the bad joke, the more I know it was even worse than I thought originally. I don't wanna do that. FourFiveSix is also cool because you can go there in any mood, and it fits. If you're feeling energetic, you can go there, and somehow it works. If you just wanna veg, and you're half-asleep and you want brunch, it works. If you're emotional, it *works*. And when you look around, you notice something unique and weird every time.

Laura Valk: Like, oh! There are suitcases on the ceiling!

Fourth Avenue Pub
Alex M (DD Walker)

I had just played Barclays Center with Bear Hands. We were on tour with Twenty One Pilots. Having Barclays be the "hometown show" of the tour felt pretty surreal to begin with. I promised myself years and years ago that if I ever got to play shows on the arena scale, that when it came to the Barclays Center show, I would take the subway from my Hell's Kitchen apartment to the venue the way JAY-Z did when he first played there. So that was a weird and cool box checked. No security detail with me, but still felt like the box was checked.

Finishing the show, leaving the venue, and walking over to Fourth Avenue Pub was a very float-y, out-of-body experience, and seeing all these people that had all gotten to share this experience together that I was a part of was rad. I don't remember much about Fourth Avenue Pub except they were playing eighties metal, and that they had an old-school popcorn machine and the popcorn was really good. It's also right down the road from Douglass Recording, where Andrew Maury and I made the first DD EP. I absolutely love that live room.

Anyway, how I feel about Fourth Avenue Pub is much more about the memories attached than the place. That said, the ambiance there is perfectly low-key and low-lit like an English pub, their drink specials are dope and that popcorn is perfect.

Fresh Kills
Paul Hammer (Savoir Adore)

I lived three blocks from here, on South Fourth, for five years. I come here every time I come to the city now.

My favorite environments are always the places that take their craft as seriously as possible, but also don't take themselves seriously. There's not this pretense, there's no snooty front, there's no separation. This is almost like a DIY space where your favorite band is playing. There's no separation between the performer and the fan, and I'm the fan, you know what I mean?

Here, I meet the bartenders, and I talk to them, and it's just chill. This is the best cocktail you'll ever get, but you don't feel like you're doing something wrong. And that's a thing! I almost never go to a restaurant with tablecloths, even if it's the number-one restaurant in the world, because I don't love that environment. [Here] it doesn't feel fancy, but the quality is fancy.

Left Hand Path
Ethan Alexander (So and So)

You know the opposite of the *Cheers* song, sometimes you wanna go where everybody *doesn't* know your name. That bar's really nice to just sit and vibe out. I call it my hotel bar because it's literally downstairs from my apartment. So I'm like, I'm gonna go hit the hotel lounge.

You know the feeling when you're traveling and you go to a hotel bar and you could end up talking to literally anyone, from any walk of life. I've had conversations with people and they're, like, political advocates that work for the campaign for AOC, and then old-ass dudes who went to Berklee years ago and now play in, like, the symphony orchestra. You know, I've met people who play in metal bands, all sorts of different kinds. It's one of the few bars that I go into that doesn't have a set vibe, so it's really inviting for anyone to go in there, in my experience.

It feels like you're inside of an old wooden cargo ship or something, but the cocktails are fucking incredible, and all the bartenders who work there know exactly what they're doing and have been doing it for over ten years.

Maracuja
Nick Cortezi, Quinn McGovern, Yuta Shimmi (Marinara)

Yuta Shimmi: I just really like that bar because the owner is really sweet. A husband and wife own the place and are the only people who work there, and they open whenever they want to be open and close whenever they want to close. They're just very hospitable people. You know, they'll buy you drinks, buy you a game of pool. It's a nice bar, and it's always low-key.

Nick Cortezi: You should check it out. It's really nice.

Yuta Shimmi: Shout-out to Charlie.

Quinn McGovern: Charlie's great.

Yuta Shimmi: Charlie, one of the owners, he's just one of the kindest dudes I've ever met. There was one time one of my buddies was too drunk and he was like, "You know what, you can just sleep at the bar tonight." He passed out in a booth, and [Charlie] covered him and came back in the morning to let him out. Just a nice dude.

Skinny Dennis
Frank Graniero, Stephen Graniero (Caravela); Aleksi Glick (Snack Cat); Kallan Campbell, Tcoy Coughlin, David Johnson (Max Pain and the Groovies); Jonathan Freeland

Jonathan Freeland: [It] looks like places I used to play open mics at when I turned twenty-one in Georgia. The American flag hanging on the wall, the jukebox with Merle Haggard in it, sawdust on the floor. Like that was transplanted right from Marietta, Georgia and they snuck it right into Williamsburg.

If you're from the South, you've been somewhere that looks like Skinny Dennis. And I think that's the genius of that bar. Anyone from the South is going to see this place and be a return customer. I took my parents there, and they were in heaven.

Stephen Graniero: I like Texas. We've got some friends down South. Skinny Dennis is a nice change of pace where you can rock out in a different way.

Frank Graniero: If there's a really good band playing, it makes you happy. I don't know, it's hard to deny that place sometimes.

Stephen Graniero: I've walked in there and instantly been in a better mood if the band is good. You're out, it's unexpected, and the vibe's awesome.

Aleksi Glick: I have a lot of friends that play there. And I love that crushed iced coffee. It's the best five-, six-dollar drink you can get. It picks you up, it tastes delicious and, uh, it has alcohol in it.

Tcoy Coughlin: On Skateboard Sundays, we skateboard on Sundays, we're always trying to get that coffee drink. The Skinny Dennis people have like the five bars, and they've got that Willie's whiskey drink. And so we're skating on Sundays trying to get that upper, and it takes us the rest of the way.

Kallan Campbell: We skateboard for a while, then we go to Skinny Dennis, get some drinks, and then go skate some more. Just get nice, cooled-down-slash-caffeinated drinks.

David Johnson: And a buzz.

Kallan Campbell: *And* a buzz.

Tcoy Coughlin: The journey to the coffee drink and back.

CHAPTER 4
DIVE IN

"It's probably the most unpretentious drinking experience you can find, which in my opinion is a dying art these days in Brooklyn." - Sean Carroll

While Brooklyn artists appreciate a craft cocktail, they love a good dive, so here's a short selection of social suggestions for the most, shall we say, low-maintenance of music fans.

Test your trivia skills with the punk band HYPEMOM over two-for-five High Lifes at Do or Dive, a cheap and chill Bed-Stuy joint where the bartenders wielding the remote are pro-*Jeopardy*, but firmly refuse the group's requests to watch *Wheel of Fortune*.

Bus or bike down to the water and hit Sunny's in Red Hook, where you might find indie-folk trio The Ladles hanging and harmonizing, and artists of all ages, stripes, and styles putting 'em back amongst knick-knacks inside the saloon or joining a late-night bluegrass jam in the bar's backyard.

Crush Tecates with alt-country crooner Jonathan Freeland at hipster-hillbilly hotspot Bushwick Country Club, where toxic cocktail combos make for Members Specials, and shabby backyard mini-golf serves as a tongue-in-cheek nod to the name.

Pull up a stool between the shoegazers of Sooner and your new punk-rock pals Sallies at George & Jack's in Williamsburg, which is the type of tavern where you can buy draft beers the size of Big

Gulps for about the same price, and the next morning you're still shaking kernels from the free popcorn out of your pants.

Or choose your own adventure. Wander into any bar lit by a neon Budweiser sign, where the toilet seat is mysteriously missing and the tequila tastes almost like gasoline, to enjoy the simple pleasure that is sitting alone in the dark with a drink and your thoughts while indulging your inner old man.

If the last chapter was largely about bars that are doing it right by virtue of *trying*, putting forth an honest effort to create a carefully designed, well thought-out experience, this is a continuation of that concept in one sense. There is a very specific vibe. But it's more about cheap beer and well whiskey than craft and curation, less how-can-we-cater-to-you and more what-you-see-is-what-you-get, even if sometimes it's not *exactly* what you actually ordered.

In a borough both marked by and mocked for hipster this, organic that, and artisanal everything, this chapter is where you'll find bars that are *bars* in the truest sense of the word.

Old-school joints, gloriously un-hip establishments, and intentionally dingy dives noted for their simplicity, authenticity, and a total lack of showmanship and (at least unironic) schtick.

Places where musicians go to enjoy the might-as-well-be-Midwest experience that is drinking domestic bottles off suspiciously sticky surfaces and contemplating the pros and cons of eating from that community bowl of questionable snack mix.

Some of these establishments were called out as an escape from the scene, the antithesis-of-hip spots where artists retreat for anonymity and to avoid anyone they've ever worked, played, or slept with. Some perhaps weren't intended to play this role but have become dives by default, attracting a hard-partying crowd who just happen to love to pound Prosecco.

And yet other bars have naturally developed legitimate, unexpected little scenes of their own, serving as gathering spots for a diverse cast of characters who wouldn't necessarily cross paths or clink glasses otherwise.

While not intentionally designed to cater to the artist community, the popularity of these places within this particular crowd makes sense. After all authenticity is attractive, crusty can be cool, and in the words of our professional Brooklyn bar-hopper Paul Hammer, "certain bars just attract musicians more than others, and often it's the ones that are the cheapest. It just works out that way."

Or as one member of the psych-spiked garage-rock group summed up his band's sipping style, "Max Pain and the Groovies is not a proud band. We'll drink the well liquor."

Boobie Trap
My Son The Doctor (Brian Hemmert, Joel Kalow, John Mason, Matt Nitzberg); Tracey (Strange Neighbors); Khaya Cohen (Moon Kissed)

My Son The Doctor: Boobie Trap has been a long-time fave.

Tracey: One of my go-to dives when I'm in Bushwick. Decently priced drinks and when the weather is nice, the window areas are wide open and you can people-watch.

My Son The Doctor: John lucked out and once saw the bartender (owner?) chop off a guy's man bun with a pair of hedge clippers in exchange for a free bottle of Georgi Vodka.

Khaya Cohen: Boobie Trap for the free hair ties and lighters and man bun bottle deal.

Brooklyn Ice House
Matthew Iwanusa (Caveman)

There's a place called Ice House in Red Hook which I love. I actually don't drink anymore, which is kind of crazy, but when I did that was kind of my area. We would go there at all times of the day. Right when it opened, last person there at night, whatever. I think that place is really special. Red Hook, in general, I think is special.

The bartenders, they've been there forever. You can kind of talk to everybody who works there. They're all a little different. There are people who are from Pioneer Works, the art studio, and then there's guys you feel like are truckers coming in. It's such a cool mix of all these people.

It's funny, the dynamic is so different. If you were in Manhattan, everybody would be looking at everybody differently, you know? You can kinda go into Ice and not talk to anybody, which you see people do a lot, they sit in the corner. And it's like you can be in the Midwest or something.

I love Sunny's. Everybody talks about Sunny's. But Ice House to me, there's something special about it. That's probably my favorite place in the neighborhood.

Bushwick Country Club
Jonathan Freeland

I remember one night just being like, I want to find some cool, out-of-the-way place, and I found the website for Bushwick Country Club. Like, a dive bar that calls itself a country club? This sounds absolutely hilarious. I'm gonna go check it out.

They have the Members Special up there. It's literally one of those "Okay, what do we need to get rid of?" [things]. I was sitting at the bar, and the owner was here, and we just came up with this absolutely disgusting mix of stuff.

I love the fact that it is not pretentious at all. I ended up working on the Lower East Side down on Bowery. I loved the people I was working with, I loved the restaurant I was working in, but a lot of the clientele was just young, with money, pretentious. So coming here, I was like, it's divey, it's dingy, it is what it is, and nobody is here for fancy shit. And I love that.

Since I worked in the service industry, I do love trying out new cocktails and high-end stuff, but that whole lifestyle was never me. Obviously everyone wants to move up the ladder, but I'm never gonna turn into that guy that I remember waiting on, who was telling his date how he had his kombucha shipped in from Portland.

That's just a whole thing here, money dictating the whole way that you live your life. Everyone puts on a persona based on the situation they're in, that's just what we do. But this is me, and I have kind of a thing for Tecate.

Capri Social Club
Digo Best (Colatura); Steele Kratt (Steele FC)

Digo Best: Okay, maybe it's just me, but sometimes I need a bar where nobody knows my name. Where nobody wants to be my friend and where I can just be alone with my dark-ass thoughts, and when the mood is right, Capri's my haunt.

Steele Kratt: If no-frills was, like, a billing of a bar.

Digo Best: The owner Irene is a legend in antisocial bartending, a dark art I deeply admire. She usually sits perched on a stool behind the bar and when asked for anything out of arm's reach she'll emphatically announce she's all out, which is fine, because cheap Polish draft beer and underpriced Jameson, almost certainly refilled with bottom-shelf whiskey, is all you need.

Steele Kratt: It's literally just a room essentially, with a tiled floor, and everyone there is old and Polish.

Digo Best: Most of the regulars sit at the bar leaving the back room empty to sulk in. I particularly love the jukebox, which likely hasn't changed in fifty years and is perfectly unhip. Most nights I spend singing along to Sinatra and Elvis in full voice, never once drawing the attention of anyone else.

The Charleston
Nico E.P. (Deaf Poets)

It was my first birthday in New York City. I went there and had an awesome time, because it was non-stop drinking and pizza constantly. It was just a rotation. My friend's just like, "Shot! Shot! Shot! Shot!" And every shot you bought, you get a pizza. Anyone that's visiting, I try to take them.

Do or Dive
Nico E.P. (Deaf Poets); Lincoln Lute, Gordon Taylor (Plastic Picnic); Colin Lord, Luke Santy (HYPEMOM)

Nico E.P.: Around my house is [a] cool spot called Do or Dive that I go to. One time I got locked out of my apartment and didn't have a key. We came back from a late-night show. We went to Do or Dive and just spent a few hours there. Hanging out at three in the morning.

Gordon Taylor: We literally wrote a song called "Do or Dive." The name I think started out as a joke, because we were writing it during the summer, and where we live, Do or Dive is pretty much right in between our houses. So anytime we were biking home from the practice space, we would just end up there. There was some week where at least Emile and I were there like ten days straight or something like that. We started joking, all the lyrics were stories or things that we talked about while we were there, and the whole song ended up just being about that, we should call it "Do or Dive." We'll change the name later. And then, like usually happens, the name kind of grows on you and you don't change it.

Lincoln Lute: I always say that bar is so loud. The music's great, but it's so loud that you can't talk that much. And so you kind of just end up being like, "Yeah, totally!" and then drinking, and you're like, "Yeah, right?!" and then drink. You end up drinking so much more because you can't just stop and talk for a long time with someone.

Luke Santy: ABC Power Hour has been going on for a minute now. I guess if we're all getting together for *Jeopardy* at seven, we have to start watching like, David Muir at six-thirty and see what's going on with America, and then afterwards you might as well do *Wheel*.

Do or Dive will turn on just *Jeopardy*. Like they have a couple of old black-and-white TVs in there. And most of the time, they're just doing the jukebox or playing loud music, but from seven to seven-thirty, they turn on *Jeopardy* way too loud so no one can enjoy themselves unless they're there to watch *Jeopardy*, and we love it. It's just so fun. Really cheap beer-and-shot deals, but they do not let us watch *Wheel* there.

Colin Lord: It's a pretty hard line.

Luke Santy: I mean, they have, like, laughed in my face. I went there on my birthday, I think. I was like, "Please, can we watch *Wheel*?" and they were like, "Get *out* of here." They really don't mess with *Wheel*.

George & Jack's
John Farris, Andrew Possehl, Tom Wolfson (Sooner); Dang Anohen (Sallies); Sean Carroll

Sean Carroll: The reason I love George & Jack's is, first of all, it's probably the most unpretentious drinking experience you can find, which in my opinion is a dying art these days in Brooklyn. You know, I'm cool with everything being a scene, but George & Jack's is literally a bar with a popcorn machine in back.

Andrew Possehl: It's just a bar. It's not themed. It's just a regular bar.

John Farris: It's right off the L, it's obviously in the heart of Williamsburg, which is usually insufferable, especially during happy-hour time, but here it's not full of people.

Sean Carroll: It's owned by the same people who own Skinny Dennis, Horses and Divorces, Do or Dive, Rocka Rolla. Every place that I've spent way too much time, way too late at night.

Tom Wolfson: I think they're all great bars, and they're all really cheap. In Brooklyn? Rare and appreciated.

John Farris: The happy hour is like three dollars for a well drink, or something ridiculous like that.

Andrew Possehl: 'Til like 7 p.m.

Sean Carroll: Me and Hayes [Peebles] call it Darts Alley. I want to say that I am one of the worst darts players in the world, and Hayes is as well, but George & Jack's has been the perfect place to hone my craft. You just go there, you throw darts around for a little while, drink a Miller High Life, eat some popcorn.

Dang Anohen: I think my number-one thing to look at when I visit a bar, or any kind of venue, is the music has to be really good right off the bat. The jukebox is one of those old-school jukeboxes. They're kind of dying out, so if you can find a place with one of those, that's where you go.

Sean Carroll: They've got James Brown on the jukebox. I go in there and I just ruin everybody's night by playing ten straight James Brown songs. Those people wanna hear Blondie and only Blondie, which is cool. All I'm sayin' is they've got two James Brown albums on the jukebox. I'm going to play as much James Brown in that bar as I can. So I love that about it. When I'm not in the mood to be in a bustling, youthful environment, I go listen to James Brown and throw darts at George & Jack's.

The Graham
Scott Martin (Scott Martin and the Grand Disaster)

The Graham Bar. The holiest of unholy places. I mean, The Graham is an institution. It's like the degenerate version of Cheers. Everyone knows your name, and probably a whole bunch of other stuff about you too. I love it.

I've been living in Brooklyn for well over a decade, but when I moved into East Williamsburg several years ago, it felt like I was starting over, and I was looking for a spot where I could chill, have a drink, and maybe try to un-fuck myself a bit. I came home after a show one night, walked into The Graham for a beer and never left.

It's the epitome of a dive bar, and as such, an extremely classy affair. It's warm and kind of dim inside, lit by a multitude of lanterns hanging haphazardly from the ceiling. A photo booth and some arcade games from the early nineties lurk in the far corner, and there's a basket of condoms beneath a chalkboard that says either "Don't Fuck With Us/Don't Fuck Without Us" or "Con-damn You Look Good." A few objects behind the bar stand out. A neon pink flamingo, a sign that says "Soup Of The Day: Tequila," and a mysterious record from the sixties cryptically titled "You Don't Have to Be Jewish."

The place is usually filled with a rotating cast of characters, and it's nearly impossible not to strike up a conversation and make an acquaintance if you're so inclined. The marketing analyst, the tattoo artist, the art dealer, the reporter. Musicians, comedians, the burned-out sound engineer who just got off the job, all my fellow creatures of the night, all there. There's even the Irish bartender from the joint down the street who will, without fail, invite you outside for a cigarette and then proceed to tell you several hilarious tales concerning living in the McKibbin Lofts alongside an elderly woman and her talking parrot.

Sometimes there's a dance party in the back room. Or a drag show. Or a think and drink, or a drink and draw. Sometimes I'd go down there just to break the monotony of whatever day it was. I'd go to the Graham, order a drink at the bar, and wait. Something would happen. There are always shenanigans, there is always a story, and they always read like episodes from a sitcom. The Concert. The Photo. The Standoff. The Necklace. The Fire.

You know those places that are officially open 'til 4 a.m., but that you always seem to wind up leaving only well after the doors have been closed? Yeah, that's The Graham.

For the longest time, I only knew the owner as a shadowy figure named Tov. Upon inquiry, he always seemed to be "somewhere in Brazil." I finally met him one afternoon during the early days of the pandemic, selling to-go cocktails from the doorway of the bar. "I know who you are," he says. Of course you do. Damnit. Cheers for degenerates.

Honore Club
Dallin Smith (Max Pain and the Groovies); Michael Tarnofsky (Edna); Elliah Heifetz

Elliah Heifetz: Honore Club in Bushwick isn't some hidden speakeasy in the closet of a bodega. It's just a damn good bar. Wood paneling, wooden bar, wood everything. Vintage signs and lights transplanted directly from a run-down bar in the Midwest.

Dallin Smith: You go there on weekdays. The bartenders are always super badass, super cheap drinks, they play good music.

Elliah Heifetz: The sound system is pumping old country music most of the time, and warm, toasty seventies rock deep cuts the rest of the time.

Michael Tarnofsky: They play so much Merle Haggard and Tom Petty and sometimes the Eagles.

Elliah Heifetz: Beer is cheap, and you can add a shot to any beer (not just PBR cans!) for $2. There's a big ol' backyard, and you can buy Chicago-style hot dogs with all the fixins at the bar. I literally, and I mean literally, haven't felt more comfortable in a bar, restaurant, coffee shop or whatever since moving to New York. Nowhere better for a game of cards with my girlfriend, a Miller High Life, and a little Waylon on the speakers.

Pinkerton Wine Bar
Lydia Gammill, Vram Kherlopian, Tarra Thiessen (Gustaf)

Tarra Thiessen: Pinkerton's fun. It's like a dive wine bar.

Lydia Gammill: What's fun about Pinkerton is that it has like two completely separate lives. Like to most people, it's got a great happy hour and they do oysters, so if you're going there on a first date, it's like a money spot to be like, "Hey, I'm cool." And then there are the regulars who are just like, "This is our trash palace!"

Tarra Thiessen: A brunch bomb is like a mimosa in a rocks glass with a shot of tequila, and you have to chug it. Lydia has a story about throwing up in a cup afterwards.

Lydia Gammill: Yeah, I threw up.

Tarra Thiessen: In a pint glass.

Lydia Gammill: My partner at the time was like, "It was terrible, because I heard the sound of you vomiting, but I also heard the sound of a glass filling up." I contained it. I took care of myself.

Vram Kherlopian: Oh, you're responsible.

Lydia Gammill: I'm every woman. We also had Halloween parties there.

Vram Kherlopian: Yeah, water shots.

Lydia Gammill: Water shots!

Tarra Thiessen: Lydia makes the best Halloween speeches.

Lydia Gammill: Two years in a row. Because we did "Sober October."

Tarra Thiessen: And then we would break it at Halloween at Pinkerton at midnight.

Vram Kherlopian: And everyone would be very well behaved, ya know.

Sunny's
Caroline Kuhn, Katie Martucci (The Ladles); Lincoln Lute, Gordon Taylor (Plastic Picnic); Tracey (Strange Neighbors); Tcoy Coughlin (Max Pain and the Groovies); Gabriel Birnbaum (Wilder Maker); Aleksi Glick (Snack Cat); Elizabeth Wyld

Katie Martucci: It's right on the pier near the water, and the sunsets are insane. You don't get that in other places. It's so vibrant.

Gordon Taylor: That's just a magic spot for us. Personally, it's my favorite bar in the world, probably. It's really wild that a place like that with so much of its own character exists in Brooklyn and it's just hidden.

Lincoln Lute: It's funny 'cause it's not a place that we've spent a ton of time, but every time we go, it's so memorable. We usually bike there. It's always just this huge experience, then you get there and then you drink for a while, and you meet a million people, and then we bike home, and it's like, oh my gosh, I feel like [we] went on this journey.

Elizabeth Wyld: It makes me feel like I'm completely out of the city in this foreign paradise.

Lincoln Lute: And it kind of transports you to another time and place and feels like a mini-vacation.

Tracey: It's got this wicked old-school charm. It's been around since the 1890s.

Tcoy Coughlin: Sunny's is like the same owner from back in the day, so she's like a hundred-year-old woman and she hasn't changed the place a bit. You're gettin' a fuckin' shot and a beer, and that shot's gonna put some hair on your chest, you know, because that's how it used to be.

Katie Martucci: It's been around for a real long time. It's a little divey, and just very quirky, and they've got a back room for music. It's a really nice place. I'd heard about it from other musicians for years before moving here. It sort of got built up in my mind and then met its expectations.

Caroline Kuhn: I think a lot of the time it has to do with the crowd. We have our friends who are very supportive and nice, but I just love the vibe of what seem to be the locals coming in and out.

Elizabeth Wyld: It's all these people that don't seem like New Yorkers in that they seem really authentic. They're just wearing whatever the fuck they want. You walk in and you're just like, who *are* these people? There was this one night I went and there was this bluegrass music, all these old dudes playing mandolin and banjo.

Gabriel Birnbaum: When I was talking about not liking Bushwick because every single person was within like a seven-year age range, Sunny's is exactly the opposite. Every time I go to that bar, there are people in their sixties getting drunk, there's people that look like they might not even be twenty-one getting drunk. It's everyone. All the weirdos. People of all stripes. There's like, crusty old locals. It's just a pretty welcoming spot.

Gordon Taylor: The people there are just the nicest. You either have to live around the corner or it's people who like the bar enough to make the journey to go down. A lot of times in New York you find places where people are trying to impress each other, be cool, standoffish almost or something, like outdo one another, but at Sunny's it's just like no one's trying, everybody's just really friendly and they don't mind being silly. People are dancing and having fun. It feels really down to earth, and it feels really not pretentious.

Aleksi Glick: It's a really no-frills dive bar. This is a city where I feel like people are pretty real, but you definitely have a lot of bars that are just trying to be part of the scene or whatever, and [Sunny's is] just kind of a place where what you see is what you get. Here's a beer with a bug in it, and that's cool. I'm gonna drink it.

Gabriel Birnbaum: It's an iconic bar for me. It just represents everything a bar is supposed to be.

SECTION 2
EDIBLES

In this, the age of the internet, it's definitely not difficult to find a place to grab a bite.

You can search based on Michelin stars, *Times* reviews, or Reddit threads. You can follow the recommendations of a seasoned critic or Elite Yelper, find inspiration via food blog or Instagram account, or let the intern writing some website's ten-best-whatever clickbait be your guide.

But if you don't have a finance bro's budget, the sleuthing skills to determine whether that one-star review was for salmonella or spite, or the energy and ambition of Anthony Bourdain to traverse the borough in search of Brooklyn's best noodles sold out of a window in the back of a shoe-repair shop, you could bypass those methods entirely and just ask an artist instead.

The argument could be made that asking a musician for dining tips makes about as much sense as following a chef on Spotify, and the starving-artist stereotype doesn't exactly *scream* eating expertise. But taste is taste, and there's something to be said for experiencing Brooklyn through the mouths of your favorite musicians.

Sure, there will inevitably be plenty of evenings when, either for pure convenience or in a desperate, definitely-too-late attempt to sober up, you'll wind up dining by default on whatever cheap or free food is available at the bar. A bag of chips, a fistful of cheese balls, or a PB&J slapped down with your PBR. But when coffee, brunch, or dinner is the destination, and it comes to quality, atmosphere, and authenticity, this is Brooklyn. And you better believe there are plenty of options.

CHAPTER 5
JUST BREW IT

"I'm a creature of habit, so my first order of business in any new place is to find a cafe where I can feel at home."
- Jeremy Neale

What they don't tell you about sex, drugs, and rock 'n' roll is that the second is frequently referring to caffeine, and along with obvious and extensive bar experience, musicians have revealed themselves to be coffee-shop connoisseurs, experts on where to go for survival, revival, and, in the case of artists like Viktor Vladimirovich, coffee with a grande side of community.

Viktor performs under the name Prince Johnny, a solo pop project that the artist has snappily summed up as "St. Vincent hitting on Regina Spektor at David Bowie's funeral." As a convenient change of pace, the Brooklyn musician didn't live in Williamsburg, Bushwick, or Bed-Stuy, but right down the street from me, and when they sent over their list of favorite places so we could determine a location for the interview, I was delighted to spot a mutual favorite, the queer-owned coffee shop Cafe Eloise, right on the border of Crown Heights and Prospect Heights.

Now, just like bar loyalty, Brooklynites pledge allegiance to their coffee shops, skipping the Starbucks in favor of unique neighborhood shops with real local flavor. These can range from gleaming, Apple Store-like spaces with crisply aproned staff who have made latte foam into an art form, to charmingly cluttered joints run by occasionally hostile, often braless baristas, who know their beans like drummers know their beats.

However, the vibe at Cafe Eloise was neither sterile, intimidating, nor hipper-than-thou. Instead, the owners had intentionally fostered an atmosphere of inclusiveness, and friends and fans of all creeds could be found hanging out in the sunny space with plant-filled windows, where rainbow and Black Lives Matter flags flew above a door that was open in every sense of the word. Here, make-yourself-at-home was taken to the next level when the owners' tiny pup Diego would curl up for naps in customers' laps, and as a true testament to both romantic and coffee-shop commitment, I once witnessed a wedding officiated by the owner within the walls, with the "I Do's" toasted with Prosecco poured into paper cups.

Viktor had told me over email that Cafe Eloise essentially served as their office, and when I arrived, the artist was at work, perched outside on a sidewalk stool and sipping an iced coffee. True to their name and "glam troubadour spilling secrets" self-description, Prince Johnny boasted a silky white shirt, Disney Prince-level locks, and limbs and digits adorned with chunky jewelry. Most importantly for a songwriter, Viktor was in possession of some very solid storytelling skills, and once I'd pulled up a seat and we'd introduced ourselves, they wasted no time opening up and diving into their personal journey, beginning with the true goal that had inspired their move to NYC, a transplant tale old as time for a creative who had fled a landlocked, lackluster hometown for beautifully complex life in the big city.

"All I dreamed of, coming to New York, was having a life where I was surrounded by other artists," Viktor told me. "To get inspired by, to learn from, to mentor and be mentored. To find my tribe."

Earlier that summer, likely fueled by the same coffee we were sucking down that Sunday afternoon, Viktor had not just found their tribe but founded it with the creation of The Troubadour Lounge, a monthly showcase featuring queer singer-songwriters and raising money for charity. The artist had also found a home-away-from-home where we were sitting, right there at Cafe Eloise:

I just think that it's so important to have somewhere around you where you feel safe to be yourself, that also has an intimacy to it. The whole thing with New York City is that you're sacrificing the intimacy, until you find it. That's the whole journey after getting here. You have to fight for the intimacy. Anywhere else, Oklahoma, you'll have it. You'll know everyone, whether you want to or not. So that's what [Cafe Eloise] represents to me.

The last time I googled it, I was devastated to find that Cafe Eloise had been digitally slapped with a red "permanently closed" label. But that isn't the only coffee shop being claimed by artists, and Viktor isn't the only musician who has traveled to New York and found community around the corner.

As the 2017 winner of the Grant McLennan Fellowship for songwriting, Australian indie-pop artist Jeremy Neale had traded Brisbane for Brooklyn, traveling 9,600 miles to spend the summer of 2018 working on music in NYC, where we met at a stranger's SoHo loft during a Sofar Sounds show. He was performing, I was volunteering, and almost immediately I came to essentially the same conclusion that I would later read in headline form on the Aussie online rag *The Brag*. "Jeremy Neale is the nicest bloody musician in Australia." And it wasn't just because he spent fifteen minutes listening to me talk about "my friend who *also* lives in Bristol!" without once interrupting to tell me that I not only had the incorrect city, but the completely wrong continent.

It might seem odd that one of my first Bands do BK interviews was with an Australian artist and temporary resident, but unless you're born here, everyone is new at some point. As for the exit, well, everyone either leaves or dies eventually. And as Jeremy's Brooklyn experience was a concentrated case due to the limited time he had to work with, the artist's acclimation was accelerated by necessity. While he'd traveled from the other side of the world, aside from catching a few big shows like SZA, Janet Jackson, and Billy Joel, hitting the requisite tourist attractions, and making trips to Trader Joe's to get his friendly fix in the form of Hawaiian-shirted hospitality, Jeremy largely did as all New Yorkers do. He found hangouts he loved right in his neighborhood.

When we met in August 2018, the artist had already scouted out and discovered a handful of favorite places, mostly within a half-mile radius of his Bushwick Airbnb. One such spot was Dweebs, a cheery, sun-soaked coffee shop on Dekalb, where he was spending his days writing songs, a process he described as "panning for gold."

While the artist was enjoying his experience abroad, as well as the tinnitus relief offered by the honks and hollers of the Brooklyn streets, he did admit that some of the songs he was working on were about missing his friends and family down under. However, he'd found a sense of place and peace by settling into city life, developing a routine, and like a true local, establishing himself as a regular at a few select places.

"My immediate instinct is to make myself at home," he said.

Together, these anecdotes perfectly illustrate one of the primary themes that permeates these pages. As we all chase our dreams in this city, we're constantly trying to find places to call our own, where we can fulfill and refill our human needs for closeness, community, and connectedness. Along with, in the case of this particular chapter, the absolutely crucial cappuccino.

As touched upon previously, this book is based on the idea that in NYC the waking two-thirds of our lives typically takes place outside our apartments, although in the city that never sleeps and an industry not exactly known for R&R, two-thirds might be a conservative estimate. Within this model for a life lived primarily in public, coffee shops typically take the morning shift, with counters as breakfast-sandwich fuel stations, and cafe tables as cubicle equivalents where creatives clock hours working on the administrative side of their art. Whether it's the go-to shop for an Americano en route to rehearsal, or the spot with the most comfortable seats and quickest Wi-Fi, ideal for mass-emailing private SoundCloud links and EPKs, this chapter features artist-approved destinations for perking up, camping out, and getting shit done during the daylight hours.

And as a potential bonus, or maybe cause for major mortification, let it be known that if you're a musician and a regular who expresses an allegiance even stronger than the espresso, your music might just end up serving as the soundtrack at your favorite shop. Such was the case for Harper James (Eighty Ninety, Middle Youth) at his go-to Kensington cafe, where the owner had added the musician's solo album to the rotation.

"Apparently they still spin the record at Der Pioneer," Harper told me. "Poor employees."

Cafe Madeline
Katie Martucci (The Ladles)

Cafe Madeline is a really, really yummy cafe around the corner from my place in Ditmas, and the food is all just really, really freaking well made. Ditmas Park is just full of so many working musicians. If you go into Madeline regularly, you see someone walk in with a guitar case, and people are just super friendly. I feel like I've met a lot of people that I've started playing with in different capacities just by saying hi at Cafe Madeline. It's just known. It's like, "Oh, you must live in the neighborhood and you're a musician." I've met a lot of people that I'm now friends with there.

Crema BK
Sarik Kumar (Mars Motel)

My favorite coffee shop for the last few years happens to be right down the street from me on Driggs Avenue near McGolrick Park. Crema is a small little operation owned by this super cool local Greenpoint couple. The shop used to be a candy store back in the day and they have kept a lot of that old-world charm to it. They play great music all day long and are always super happy to see us when we stop by. This is going to sound strange, but I dig that they close down between Christmas and New Year, and for other specific holidays throughout the year. They are local, hardworking small business owners living their lives, and I respect that they take a much-needed break from the grind. I just have to make my own coffee during those stints!

CUP
Josh Inman (Oil Bay)

On Sunday mornings, I take the one-and-a-half hour walk from my apartment in Flatbush to my rehearsal space in Bushwick. I put my headphones in and trek north through Crown Heights and Bed-Stuy taking in the sights and sounds, trying to shake off the night before. As my weekly sojourn approaches its end, I am greeted by the welcome sight of CUP on Montrose Avenue, knowing that my ration of caffeine will fuel my creative process that afternoon.

I get coffee orders from the rest of the Oil Babies (this isn't a typo, this is just what we call each other) who are in the same desperate need of a strong cup of coffee to burn away the fog of Saturday night revelry. Some of my favorite memories are of the cold, grumpy mornings that turn into joyful jam sessions, thanks in part to the single greatest legal and widely available drug, dealt to me by the friendly baristas at CUP.

Cup of Brooklyn
Connor Gladney (Skout)

Cup of Brooklyn [is] right across the street from my apartment, and the people who run it are just so nice. It's usually quiet, it's the perfect place to go and work. Great prices, great coffee, great pastries, great sandwiches. And I get to walk across the street in sweatpants.

Daytime
Gabriel Birnbaum (Wilder Maker)

It's owned by a guy named Joey, who used to be my boss when I worked at another coffee shop which I will not name, because I might talk a little shit. Joey was awesome, and I got him to hire a bunch of musician friends of mine. It was all my friends working at this coffee shop, so it was really fun.

Joey opened his own spot, Daytime, and it's all of the good parts of that previous coffee shop (which I worked at, it was a big part of my life), but it's without any of the bad parts. So he got everything right. He roasts his own coffee in Red Hook. It's got a great menu. It's simple food. It's sandwiches and oatmeal, basic cafe stuff, but really well done.

The street-facing windows are all floor-to-ceiling, so there's tons of natural light, really beautiful, and there's tons of huge plants. [It's a] place where everyone is happy to be there, and it's just a really comfortable spot. It feels like being in a living room for me. All the local people come through, everyone's already adopting it as their spot.

Der Pioneer
Harper James (Eighty Ninety)

Der Pioneer [is a] European-style pastry shop and coffee spot in Kensington, Brooklyn. This is one of those places you go expecting to have a decent croissant and a small coffee, but you wind up having the best meal of your life instead.

Dweebs
Jeremy Neale

I'm a creature of habit, so my first order of business in any new place is to find a cafe where I can feel at home. If you're here in this town on your own and from a strange land, it can get lonely, but it's nice to be around other people working independently. Together, alone, y'know? Anyways, I've been putting in the hard yards to endear myself to the baristas, but yesterday I knocked over a potted plant, so I'm probably starting back at square one. Great place, great vibe. An ideal spot to stare at your to-do list and occasionally cross things off it.

Fiction
Peter Wise

I always appreciate an aesthetically pleasing, multi-purpose coffee shop, and Fiction in Williamsburg meets all the requirements. As a musician my hours are a lot different than the normal nine-to-five, so to be productive during free mornings, I like to get up and go somewhere to start my day. Fiction is a really cool hole in the wall. Coffee shop by day, bar at night. Great coffee and drinks, they have donuts (say no more) and an equally perfect place to get some work done, meet up with friends, or bring a date.

Jessi's Coffee Shop & Stella Di Sicilia Bakery
Davey Jones (Lost Boy ?)

My favorite spot is Jessi's, a coffee shop off the Montrose L. They close early and they're a family-owned restaurant. I appreciate them just because their prices are reasonable, they're not trying to rip you off for an egg sandwich. Literally spend five, six dollars and you're gonna be good, probably 'til dinner time.

There's also Stella's around the corner. They have the same thing. They're a bakery. You can get cookies, they have fresh rolls. They just do everything really nice there. That's also a family-owned business.

Jessi's has good food, good people. If you're a regular, that's also nice for them too, they appreciate that. If you're short a dollar and they recognize you, because I've been short, they're like, "Just get me next time," which is also nice. Stella's too. They're the same way. If you're short a quarter, a dollar, whatever, just make sure you bring it next time.

Jessi's opens early, because I feel like it's one of those spots where the construction workers come in the morning, and that's why they close at six on the nose. There's no fifteen minutes there, even five minutes. You can walk in, they'll be like, "Sorry." Okay, well, I tried. That was my fault, I had a really long Friday night and didn't wake up 'til 3 p.m.

In March or February, I was with some friends of mine and we were recording at Danbro, and I was like, "You guys have to come here." We start early, like ten. For them, that was early. We got to Stella's and I was like, "You gotta get the sesame roll." The sun was still kind of coming up and I just remember seeing my friend bite into this sandwich and just be like, *yes*.

Stella's and Jessi's are the hot spots for me. I see everybody over there. You know, initially when I was moving, I was really stoked that I was gonna be right by Shea [Stadium], but you know, Shea was obviously going through a lot of stuff. So it was bittersweet, but I was like, well, I still got Jessi's and still got Stella's.

Marcy & Myrtle
Viktor Vladimirovich (Prince Johnny)

So this is harkening to my depression days. I lived in Washington Heights for nine months, and then I moved to Crown Heights, and then to Bed-Stuy, then somewhere else in Bed-Stuy. All in a year. It was like the plague [with] different punishments. I had a crazy neighbor in Washington Heights, then bed bugs in Crown Heights, then I lived with film guys in Bed-Stuy. The worst.

In Bed-Stuy I was right at the cusp of admitting to myself who I am and what I should be doing, and going through a lot of fear, and taking off layers of trauma and all that bullshit. And right down the street was a cafe called Marcy & Myrtle. Great coffee, [it's] cute, baristas know what they're doing.

I think artisanal comes with the connotations of being small portions and pretentious, but keep out those connotations and [focus on the] good connotations of artisanal. Nuanced food. Go there [and] get an iced coffee, or if you're feeling fancy get yourself a chai and one of [their] sandwiches and have a ball. Sit there all day, and you can make friends with the person that will sit with you at that table because they're probably interesting.

Parlay
Felicia Douglass (Gemma)

Parlay has quickly become one of my favorite places to stop into in Sunset Park. It's family run and incredibly inviting with lots of natural light. They also have their record collection on display featuring classic hip-hop and R&B, which helps it feel familiar to me. I can't get down with irritable music at coffee shops, so I really appreciate their good taste in musical selection here. I'm a tea person so I usually get a matcha latte and a small treat, but the stand-out dish is Mum's Malaysian Curry Chicken, made by (you guessed it) the mom. It's a coconut-based curry with roti and cucumbers on the side and I always want more. I told them they should bottle the sauce.

Partners Coffee
Anthony Azarmgin (The Muckers)

I used to work there. It's a cool spot, just a spot to chill, do work. It's owned by Australians, so they've definitely got a good playlist. And good coffee. They're not pretentious. They know what they're doing. They're not trying, you know what I mean?

I loved working there, too. And it's really rare for someone that works in coffee to say that I really liked working there, because usually you hate your job, but I never hated my job.

Sunrise/Sunset
Jonathan Freeland

It's one of those very Brooklyn things. It's a coffee shop during the day, it turns into a bar at night. It's truly a neighborhood spot. Beautifully decorated. It's very minimal, not pretentious at all. They have a full kitchen there, so you can get an actual breakfast. It's just such a chill spot.

Before I had the capital to invest in a workspace, I would show up at a coffee shop at like noon, drink coffee, do the thing, get lunch and then right around three, I would pack up and go to a bar at like four for happy hour. That place was great, because I was like, cool, I'll do a beer with that next coffee. Let's go.

It's extremely reasonably priced, everyone there is very friendly, they have good coffee, they have good food. It doubles well as a hangout spot and a place that you can work.

CHAPTER 6
SOUNDBITES

"I love being in the studio, so I have very good associations with being in that neighborhood and having lunch, taking a break from something you love, knowing you're going to go back." - Hayes Peebles

Let it be known that being a musician is definitely a job, even if it's not always a paying one.

While corporate stiffs might scoff, I'd wager the work ethic of many artists I know is on par with what you'd find on Wall Street. And much like suits have day-to-days featuring depressing desk salads and takeout consumed in conference rooms, artists have their own schedules, often the kind of nine-to-fives that start after sundown featuring fries as rehearsal fuel, nachos as post-practice provisions, and pizza, *so much pizza*, as between-sets sustenance.

This brings us to another one of this book's most prevalent themes and a concept that contradicts the chaos that one likely associates with purveyors of punk-rock. *Routine.*

Now, if you still have some semblance of hearing, you probably haven't seen Venus Twins live. The Brooklyn bass-and-drums duo is *loud*, a fact that anyone could deduce like a scenester Sherlock Holmes given key pieces of evidence like *Fuzzy Sun*'s pitch-perfect description of the band as "sonic mindfuckery", or a photo of a wide-eyed audience member jamming his fingers into both ears, or the fact that even in MP3 form their music will still shake your succulents and rattle your living-room walls.

But whether or not you've heard this killer cacophony in real life, there's one thing that's obvious. Creating it definitely requires some serious carbs.

In perfect punk fashion, the Venus Twins are vegan twins, their project rooted in and reflective of the band's beliefs, projected through "Meat is Murder" merch and their fast and furious record *Eat Your Dogs*, a reference to the hypocrisy of claiming to love animals while simultaneously packing your plate with them. Along with warning me, their fellow vegan, about potential cream-cheese cross-contamination at a certain Bushwick bagel joint, Jake and Matt Derting shared a few of the spots that had defined their Brooklyn experience.

They told me about Champs Diner, their go-to spot for vegan pancakes, where after practice they can often be found recovering and refueling. They also mentioned Loving Hut, a cruelty-free cafe where Jake spent time hanging while Matt was working, the drummer screening Venus Twins videos while the bassist hustled to bring home the plant-based bacon.

Beyond the places provided by this literal band of brothers, Laura Valk and Connor Gladney of indie-folk dream team Skout perfectly illustrated the pedestal on which some of these businesses sit. Over beers and the buzz of the crowd at The Gutter, a Williamsburg bar, bowling alley, and music venue rolled into one, the artists explained the end-to-end experience offered by the wrap stars at since-shuttered Brooklyn burrito joint, Lucha Lucha, where the pair would often go to grab a bite after practice sessions.

"After rehearsals, I used to go [there], take a burrito, get in my Uber, hold it until I got home," Laura said.

"You feel like it's your baby," Connor added. "It's literally a sacred thing."

"It's ceremonial."

Rolling Stone-lauded harpist, guitarist, and overall folk phenom Lizzie No released her sophomore record *Vanity* in August 2019. Ten months before that, we sat at a high-top at 61 Local, a

Cobble Hill gastropub with a small second-floor space for performances, and over a pint of draft kombucha she told me that the ongoing recording sessions for the album were being capped off by band trips to Taco Bell.

When citing the Flatbush branch of the fast-food chain as one of her current favorite places, she didn't talk up the Gordita Crunch or sing the praises of cinnamon twists. Instead, it was the context that made it relevant, and when sharing what made this and the rest of her go-to spots so special, Lizzie offered a short and sincere explanation that's stayed with me, a thought so perfect that I began this very book with it:

> Every place that is dear to me in Brooklyn is dear because of how I choose to live my life.

This chapter features eateries that were mentioned in similar ways to what Lizzie, Skout, and the Venus Twins described, places and plates chosen for convenience, tradition, and maybe some superstition. Spots that the artists frequenting them will forever associate with this point in their lives and the work they're putting in, the music they're making, and the people they're doing it all with.

Whether the girl slinging slices around the corner from Baby's All Right or the guy moving midnight tacos outside the Morgan stop know it or not, the grub that they're dishing out while clocked in is more than just a meal to a good portion of their patrons. In fact, it's more than a routine. It's a true reward. It's a real *ritual*. And if a musician were to go missing, let's just say the people working at these places would likely be the first to notice and to get that artist's face plastered on an oat-milk carton ASAP.

Champs Diner
Venus Twins (Jake Derting, Matt Derting)

A favorite place of ours is Champs Diner. We're vegan, so it means a lot to have somewhere to go and absolutely destroy some pancakes. Also it's on Meserole Street, which is so close to our practice space. Sometimes when we have an intense four-hour rehearsal we'll hang there and book some shows or just relax.

Joe's Pizza
No Swoon (Tasha Abbott, Zack Nestel-Patt)

Joe's Pizza. No question. It's the best example of the best food. Between work, rehearsal, shows, and life, our eating schedules are pretty all over the place. We would often find ourselves needing to eat quickly before or after a show or rehearsal, and Joe's Pizza is always what we went for. We inevitably got Joe's on our way home from Alphaville or after soundcheck at Baby's All Right. Every time we decided to do something else, we were disappointed or took too long walking around trying to find something. Plus, everyone likes pizza so it's an easy thing for a band or a couple bands to do together, eating outside late at night or walking back to a venue.

A note on toppings. Tasha says, "Pizza has crust, cheese, sauce, and pepperoni. That's it. No more, no less. Fight me."

Other acceptable options are Best Pizza, Paulie Gee's Slice Shop, or Williamsburg Pizza.

La Isla Cuchifrito
Digo Best (Colatura)

I had just moved to Bed-Stuy, and my new commute home from working at Lake St. Bar in Greenpoint took me biking down Graham Avenue to where it met up with Broadway. Most nights ended with too many ciders and shots of Fernet with anyone I could convince. To try and head off the hangover, I would always stop at La Isla Cuchifrito on my way home. Cuchifritos are all over NYC, but La Isla is my spot for beans and rice, blood sausage and mofongo, all for under ten dollars. It's definitely one of the New York mainstays I will truly miss if I ever leave here.

Loving Hut
Jake Derting, Matt Derting (Venus Twins)

Matt Derting: I worked at Loving Hut, the vegan spot.

Jake Derting: That became a hang-out. Sometimes there wasn't a crowd there at all. They have a TV, so I'd go there. I didn't work there. I'd go hang out with him and put our music videos on the TV.

Matt Derting: There was only the owner and the owner's husband. We didn't have managers, there was only one server that worked at a time. It was never really that busy, but when it was busy, there was one of me and phones to answer, I had to pack to-go orders, I had to go wait all these tables. I had to make drinks, smoothies, and juices. So much stuff and it was insane.

Jake Derting: Sometimes I would help.

Matt Derting: You'd refill waters.

Jake Derting: I watched the front room because you had to get ice.

Matt Derting: I had to run across the street to the bodega to get ice, or to get change for a twenty.

Jake Derting: Thank god you have me.

Matt Derting: Thank you. So I don't work there anymore.

Jake Derting: Such a sweet owner, though.

Matt Derting: So sweet. I'd literally have nightmares, though.

Jake Derting: But all in all, great place to hang out. For me.

Matt Derting: We'll definitely be going back.

Luigi's Pizza & Giuseppina's
Matthew Iwanusa (Caveman)

I always think about my favorite Brooklyn places, and [Luigi's is by] far my favorite Brooklyn pizza.

When we started recording our second and third record [with] our friends who own the studio [Rumpus Room], I tried it once, and I remember walking in and being like, "Did you guys try this? It's so good." And they're like, "Yeah, it's the best pizza in town." So for the last, like, seven years, it's been my favorite place to go.

The way they make it is so good. If I think about going to a pizza place, I usually get like one slice. My limit is two slices. Like, you get two slices, maybe you eat one and a half, throw it away. But my friends and I talk about how there's the birthday-party pizza, where you can have so much of it. I don't know why Luigi's is like that. I'll get two slices, and then I'll get one to go. It's so good, I keep eating it. It's almost like it won't be there next time. I have to get another slice.

But then right up the block, there's Giuseppina's. You have Luigi's on Twentieth and Fifth Avenue, and then you can walk up one block to Sixth Avenue. It's sit-down, also really amazing pizza. They only sell calzones and pizza, and they're always playing Sinatra, and there's something cool about that, too. That's a really good pizza block.

My friends and I, we would go to Luigi's and then, okay, we're gonna start our night. We'd go to Giuseppina's, sit down, eat, get a bottle of wine. It was definitely pizza twice sometimes in one day, and if you're going to two separate places, it kinda doesn't feel as bad.

Nam Nam
Kevin Olken Henthorn (Cape Francis)

Nam Nam is the best Vietnamese banh-mi in the city, in my opinion. They're cheap, like they should be, and they're so good. They do two things, banh mi or noodles. Either or, it's fucking great.

My old producer used to live right next to there. We were also in the same band together. We started going there so much. Then my friend moved, and we ordered takeout from there, and the guy came through like, "Oh shit, this is where you guys are now!" Like okay, we've been eating too much of this. But they're great.

Newtown
Kegan Zema (Realworld); Kalen Lister (Death By Piano)

Kegan Zema: For quite a while, the countless musicians with practice spaces around the Montrose L stop had a pretty limited selection of food options. There's Danny's Pizza, the iconic Bushwick Pita Palace and of course everyone's favorite watering hole, Anchored Inn. While all these spots are great in their own right, when Newtown arrived it was a game-changer for my vegetarian palette.

Kalen Lister: The owners are all musicians, and there is such love baked into the food. I always run into musicians I know there, and the place has a really relaxed vibe. The hustle of the city can't reach it. The halloumi sandwich is my go-to.

Kegan Zema: Regardless of its location, it's easily one of my favorite spots to eat at simply because the food is so delicious. My go-to, the seitan shawarma, is a warm, tangy, spicy blend of flavors that has fueled me for many rehearsals. Its cozy atmosphere and charming staff make it a sanctuary amidst the industrial squalor.

Peaches Shrimp and Crab
Shari Page (THICK)

This is my favorite neighborhood spot in Brooklyn, and not just because they would play a ton of Anderson .Paak. This is the kind of place where you befriend everyone that works there. It's a really cool vibe inside and outside, and it really has the best brunch food. Of course, also seafood. This has been a second home for my partner and me. I used to eat here before weekend band practices. Drummers need a full breakfast and three cups of coffee.

Pies 'n' Thighs
Michael Hesslein (HESS)

I lived right across the street from Pies 'n' Thighs, so that was like one of my first places in Brooklyn that I would go all the time. Mail the Horse, two of our members worked there. I would just go there at all hours and drink coffee and eat fifty donuts and spend time, and that was a super great place and a super great community. Even though I didn't work there, it felt like I did at times, just because I spent so much time there. And that whole community of Pies 'n' Thighs was super solid, and it was a lot of musicians at the time. That's how we kind of met Homer Steinweiss, who produced our record *Planet Gates*, who did Sharon Jones & The Dap-Kings, and

Amy Winehouse. He was just, you know, hanging out there.

There's a rehearsal studio across the street from Pies 'n' Thighs called the Music Garage. I don't even know if it's still there, but I was playing piano for a band called Hollis Brown at that time, and it was a typical night for us to eat dinner at Pies 'n' Thighs until they closed, go across the street and rehearse. We were, at that time, rehearsing for an album that we would go and record with the Deer Tick guys and that whole Nashville crew. We would rehearse starting at midnight, be there until like three in the morning, and then we'd go to Lucky Dog and close that down until like 5 a.m., and that was like every night for a full summer. So that neighborhood, you know, definitely holds a place in my heart for sure.

Taco Bell
Lizzie No

My current favorite spot is the Taco Bell across the street from the studio where I'm recording my album, right by the Kings Theatre. [It's] a lot of long days, a lot of late nights. If you're singing all day, you're going a little crazy, you can't hear the sound of your own voice anymore. *Should we hit the cantina?* It's one of those fancy Taco Bells that sell booze. It comes out of a machine like a slushie, and they put Skittles in there. You can feel yourself getting hungover as you're drinking it.

I shouldn't be advertising for free for a chain, but that's my current moment right now: Hanging out with my band, recording, working super hard, then letting loose at Taco Bell.

Taco Rapido
Elijah Sokolow (The Living Strange)

One of my favorite spots in Brooklyn is this food cart called Taco Rapido. It's typically parked on Bogart Street around the Morgan L stop in Bushwick. The burritos are totally awesome. I would always run into friends there. That food usually reminds me of memorable nights when I would end up there after hosting a house show or I was hanging out with friends on my roof, and we got food from the cart to have up there.

Last February, I was on a schedule of working on music from 11 p.m. to 5 a.m., and the cart was one of the few options that was still open that late, so I went there truly all the time. The thing that really made it great was not only the food but whatever was going on around it, be it running into someone unexpected or feeling stoked on whatever stupid beat I made. I find that creating during that time is more conducive to getting out of my own way and allowing my intuition to make the calls because I'm a bit tired and removed from everything else. Heading to the cart at the end of that process became a solid part of that routine.

Tacos, Twins and Trains Taco Cart
Bandits on the Run (Adrian Blake Enscoe, Sydney Shepherd, Regina Strayhorn)

Owned by a pair of twins who love nothing more than listening to bachata, dancing and throwing down for good time, the taco truck on Bogart Street right above the Morgan L stop is a spot we've frequented after many a late-night busking or recording session. The clientele, composed of any old oddball getting on or off the L Train, is top-notch, and if you're good to the twins, they will sometimes invite you into the truck for a shot of tequila.

Vamos Al Tequila
Hayes Peebles

That is where we almost always get lunch when we're in the studio. I record at Transmitter Park Studio on Greenpoint Avenue. My producer [Abe] lives like a block from there, and so we spend a lot of time in that zone. Within that slice of Greenpoint there are a lot of things, but a lot of those are expensive or bougie, and Vamos is kind of the total opposite of that, a kinda corny Mexican cantina. It's got the fake kind of tile roof inside, it's pink and purple and they have margaritas. It's just very no-frills. Abe and I would always get the same thing. It was the lunch special, and it was the chicken quesadilla and a soft drink for like ten dollars or something.

That was always a place where we'd hang out. I love being in the studio, so I have very good associations with being in that neighborhood and having lunch, taking a break from something you love, knowing you're going to go back.

CHAPTER 7
GOOD TASTE

"I saw [my friend] build this place with his bare hands, and I know how much love and care went into every detail." - Adeline

With almost two hundred languages spoken and a population that's nearly forty percent foreign born, Brooklyn is home to countless cultures and their creations, and this diversity is deliciously reflected in the food scene, where you're sure to find food to please every palate. It's a melting pot, one you might throw dumplings, pasta, or perhaps pierogi into, and whether you're craving Caribbean or Korean, BBQ or Burmese, a specific specialty or just a unique space with a kick-ass atmosphere, there are plenty of high-quality options for anything and everything scattered across the borough. Not an ocean or plane, but just a few blocks or train ride away.

One such spot is Cafe Erzulie. Named for the Haitian Voodoo spirit of love, beauty, and dance, Erzulie is one of those Brooklyn-as-an-adjective establishments that's impossible to classify because it seems to do everything and do it well. Imagine a bright and chic flower-shop and cafe serving coffee and cocktails while moonlighting as an event space and music venue. But impressive multi-hyphenated mania aside, I'm throwing this community hub in the food-forward section for one of its biggest selling points, Haitian-inspired fare served with a side of undeniably good vibes.

Cafe Erzulie is the kind of day-to-night spot where people come both to work and to work it, to kick back and turn up. And on the afternoon that I met Olivia K for an interview it was already a scene, as some of Brooklyn's most beautiful people flocked to the backyard to soak up the last seconds of summer with friends, lovers, and laptops, savoring the soon-to-be-unfamiliar sensation of sweating while ice cubes in beverages across the patio fought a losing battle for survival.

As a performer and as a human, Olivia K possesses the rare kind of charisma that functions almost like a magnetic field. I first caught the "self-boogie enthusiast" at a Sofar Sounds show taking place in the organization's SoHo office, where the soul-fusion artist's equally powerful voice and personality were on full display as she combined song with motivational speech for what could almost be described as a musical sermon. While getting a group of New Yorkers to do anything is one hell of a Herculean task, the artist had no problem winning over the room and convincing the initially hesitant, inherently skeptical crowd to let go and sing along to her song "Good Things." A feel-good track, the anthem serves as a self-affirming reminder that you, me, she, we deserve the best, and Olivia's empowering lyrics were still echoing in my head weeks later as I walked into the cafe on the border of Bed-Stuy and Bushwick and ordered us two iced hibiscus teas.

A Brooklyn native, Olivia naturally navigates the city like a pro. That afternoon, seated in a patio chair under the shade of a tree with her middle-school-classmate-turned-manager Eric nearby, she drew on a lifetime of borough knowledge and referenced her Caribbean-American roots as she dropped recommendations for the mom-and-pop restaurants serving the food she had grown up eating, from Dominican to Trinidadian fare to the "crazy pastries you've never seen before" at Guyanese spots across Crown Heights.

Along with rattling off restaurant recommendations, the musician and DJ also shared her influences, describing the music she grew up immersed in while being raised by her artist mother in a multi-generational household in Brooklyn:

As a kid, I didn't listen to hip-hop directly. I wasn't like, *I'm gonna go listen to Biggie!* My parents didn't listen to hip-hop, but there was always the music around me. [And] on a Saturday morning, you can hear what everybody cleans their house to. Everybody cleans their house to different stuff. That's when you hear what they really are about.

I realize that a big part of what I'm drawing from when I'm DJing is that childhood of listening to so many different kinds of music all the time. The salsa, the bachata, the soca, the dance hall, the hip-hop, the old-school hip-hop, the R&B, the old-school R&B, the blues. There was all this stuff happening at once, and it's all natural for me. It definitely adds a global vibe and feel to it. And also, the old boom bap. That, in and of itself, is a beat and rhythm that's inside of me that I never think about, but it's always there.

While obviously in reference to music, this quote from Olivia also perfectly encompasses a bigger idea, the sheer variety that defines city life, illustrated by the different people, passions, cultures, and of course, cuisines you'll find across the borough. Just like art, Brooklyn delivers on the food front with deep roots and real love, and this chapter is dedicated to places at the top of their game, featuring restaurants that weren't mentioned so much in the context of music, but simply because the artists doing the picking have a real fondness for what these establishments have to offer. A taste of the South or the sea, of Trinidad or Tokyo, or in some cases just above-and-beyond service, unbeatable ambiance, a solid booze selection, or a really sick soundtrack.

In other words, this is food that tastes good, served at places that feel good, one-of-a-kind restaurants that fill you up in every sense of the word.

A&A Bake and Doubles & Ali's Trinidad Roti
Ethan Bassford, Felicia Douglass (Gemma)

Felicia Douglass: My mom is from Trinidad, and although I grew up with curry and stew chicken wafting through the house, I have yet to master most of the signature dishes. Crown Heights has great options for Caribbean food, but A&A is the one I keep coming back to. It's fast, no nonsense, and you know what you're getting into.

I'm always shouting out affordable places in NYC because it's important to know there are still some places out there who aren't charging an arm and a leg for something just because it's on a lovely plate. Doubles and bake are comfort food for me, so I leave there full and happy.

Ethan Bassford: A doubles (singular and plural, "I'll have a doubles" or "I'll have two doubles") is one of the most delicious foods out there, and A&A is the place for it. This is always where I take someone from out of town to eat, and I'm shocked there isn't a mediocre fast-casual version of it in every mall. Doubles are Trini street food, basically a messy taco of chana masala on an amazingly fluffy fried bread with contrasting sauces. Get all the chutneys on it and pepper (hot sauce). Sweet and savory and spicy and filling, cheap, plus it's vegetarian.

Also a big fan of pholorie, fried dough balls with the same sauces, and saheena, a sort of fritter of spinach and chickpeas cut in half and filled with sauces and/or more chickpeas.

A&A is one of the few places remaining in the city where you can really stuff yourself for like five dollars. Bake is a protein, generally fish, on a fried bread. More filling than a doubles but not as exciting flavor-wise, I like the smoked herring one personally. Conveniently located right near an open street where you can sit and eat.

A&A has roti now and it's good, and Ali's has doubles and they're good, but you gotta go to Ali's for the best roti and A&A for the best doubles. The roti is wrapped up like a burrito filled with potatoes and chickpeas and pumpkin and an optional meat.

I usually get a buss-up, which is more of a platter, just the richest most buttery flaky bread there is, with veg and/or meat. Get extra pepper on the side if you can handle some spice, theirs is top-notch. I usually do A&A for lunch and bring home Ali's for dinner. Bake and salt fish [are] also real good here, and their homemade drinks are a nice complement to everything.

Brooklyn Crab
Brandi Thompson (Brandi and the Alexanders)

Brooklyn Crab is this amazing place down in Red Hook. You need to get a group of friends, go down there. You're gonna have drinks, you're gonna have snacks, and you're gonna play cornhole and other games. It's a very cool adult playground with drinks and seafood. It's almost where I had my kids' second birthday because I was like, you guys are still young enough that it's really for us, right?

My husband and I actually went down there for a date night not too long ago, and I wish that we'd known how much fun it is, how many things there are to do there. There's a sandbox for kids, which is great, but there are so many things for adults to do, and the drinks aren't cheap, but they're not too expensive. It's just a fun atmosphere, and a good view of the Statue of Liberty.

Cafe Erzulie
Olivia K

I love being where the people are, where people are being authentic and fun and having a good time.

This particular cafe is really awesome in the summertime. It's like the whole world comes out. [Eric] introduced me because all his homies go here, and I ended up going by myself and I was running into people I knew. Like, "Girl, I haven't seen you since middle school, college."

It's just a random hot party. Hotties all over, hanging out, being friends. The DJs here are awesome. I've been here at all times of day, and I can get some work done if I don't run into anyone. And there's food, it's authentic Haitian food.

What I also love is this is a very beautiful place for Black Brooklyn, well-to-do Black Brooklyn, you could say. For Young Black Brooklyn to be out together in a small way. I love small venues, I love that intimate, cozy vibe. This place kind of has that. It can be very homey, and at the same time, it can be a turn-up covered with people.

Cheryl's Global Soul
Lizzie No

The best post-Brooklyn Museum lunch spot is Cheryl's. It was one of the first places I went when I moved to Brooklyn. You go in through that curtain and you feel like you've just walked into a tent or a camp mess hall, but a very elegant camp mess hall. It's teeny and warm, they have a beautiful backyard. I don't really fuck with brunch, but to get very great pancakes, waffles, your breakfast stuff, I do that at Cheryl's.

Chinar
Adam Holtzberg, Zack Kantor, Eric Nizgretsky (Loose Buttons)

Eric Nizgretsky: [It's a] Russian restaurant, a more nightlife type of thing. They have singers and dancers.

Adam Holtzberg: It's like a nightly bar mitzvah.

Zack Kantor: Lots of hats.

Eric Nizgretsky: Lots of hats. We dress up in ridiculous outfits. We overdress. We'll wear ridiculous suits with turtlenecks with our chains out.

Adam Holtzberg: Usually our chains are tucked in.

Eric Nizgretsky: Another cool thing about Chinar is that they allow you to bring, like, suitcases' worth of liquor, and there's no corkage fee. We showed up, no joke, with suitcases' and duffel bags' worth of liquor. We had like, twenty-something people, celebrating [a] birthday. We got so hammered. It was great.

Adam Holtzberg: It was really fun. Dancing to Top 40 music from like, ten years ago.

Eric Nizgretsky: There's a lot of *She bangs, she bangs, oh baby*. They take turns. There's a guy who sings American songs, and a guy who sings traditional Russian songs. It's so New York.

The Empanada Lady
Olivia K

It's not something you can go to. It's a phenomenon that can happen to you if you're lucky.

The park near our house is called Highland Park, and it's such a beautiful place, first of all. It's got tennis courts, basketball courts, handball courts, pretty much everything. I was there the other day, and I was on my bike and stopped for a break, and the Empanada Lady walked by. And the Empanada Lady was the *littest* woman on Planet Earth.

Oh, my god, it was fresh! It was poppin'. The crust was still crunchy. It was amazing. So that's not something you can *go to*, but if you're lucky…

La Loba Cantina
Gabriel Birnbaum (Wilder Maker)

That's my favorite neighborhood spot. I always go there when I have the chance. I had my last two birthdays there. It's a really nice space, which is really important to me. It's full of plants, [with] big windows. It's a mezcal bar in addition to serving Oaxacan food, and the mezcals are really good and there's a hundred of them.

I feel very comfortable there. I've worked in the service industry forever. I still feel like I do, even though I guess I don't anymore. And I feel like I'm so tuned in to the small emotional charges in the air of a restaurant, how the people seem when they're working and how they feel, and that place almost always feels great. People feel like they wanna be there.

All that contributes to the feeling of a great neighborhood place. It just feels good to be there.

Le Paris Dakar
Ethan Bassford (Gemma); Laura Jinn

Laura Jinn: Le Paris Dakar is my favorite spot for a relaxed and scrumptious breakfast. It's a French-Senegalese cafe with a few locations, and each is as lovely as the other.

Ethan Bassford: The best coffee shop in Bed-Stuy in my opinion, not just for the coffee itself, which is great, but for bissap, a tart and sweet and spicy Senegalese drink. It's sort of like Jamaican sorrel or Mexican *Agua de Jamaica*. Get a large one, it's the perfect accompaniment for all the other stuff you gotta eat in this neighborhood.

Laura Jinn: I always get crepes. I would normally come with a pal and split one sweet and one savory. The apple and goat cheese is particularly mind-boggling. They also have a creative selection of smoothies and fresh juices for when you need to inhale some nutrients, and the pastries are amazing as well. You really cannot go wrong here.

Momo Sushi Shack
Kate Black (THICK)

I fell in love with this place around when it opened. I was *so* excited to have such an amazing sushi spot right near my apartment. It became my spot where I go on "Kate Dates" and treat myself to dinner alone. It's my way of unwinding and getting to enjoy a crossword (I'm addicted to the NYT app) over my favorite food and wash it down with a glass of sake.

People say it's weird or intimidating to eat alone in New York, but I absolutely love it. You can tell I'm having a rough week if I've already decided to treat myself and it's only Monday night.

I usually try and stop by when Mark is working. He's an extremely talented artist and knowledgeable about pretty much anything you can think of, music or otherwise. I learn something new every time I talk to him.

Ponyboy
Zoochie

While we're based in Jersey and Manhattan, when we make our way out to BK, Ponyboy in Greenpoint is a favorite. It may be a sushi spot, but we just go for the disco-ball vibes in the back and a late-night cocktail. A good disco ball can really make or break a space, and this one sets the tone perfectly. We've considered getting a portable disco ball to bring around to gigs, so this is some pretty serious stuff to us. Also, the gin gimlet is *chef's kiss* and the cozy yet chic dance space is ideal for a great night with the homies.

Red Hook Lobster Pound
Raycee Jones

I come from a family of food lovers. We usually give the credit to the Italian side, whether that is scientifically true is TBD, but I'm gonna keep running with it. Moreover, [as] a gal from CT, lobster rolls have always been a family favorite. So when I moved to BK, I discovered Red Hook Lobster, and I've literally never even wanted to explore a lobster roll anywhere else. It reminds me a little of home, and I love to go with people and debate over Maine or Connecticut style. It's also down in Red Hook which is a wonderful neighborhood on the water, near a cute li'l view of the Statue of Liberty. One of those things you see and remember, "Holy shit! I live here!"

Risbo
Adeline

My favorite restaurant in BK is Risbo BK. Most delicious food (rotisserie, best chicken in NY hands down), great vibes (always good music), beautiful backyard. And the fact that my best friend owns it probably helps! I saw him build this place with his bare hands, and I know how much love and care went into every detail. We spend most birthdays, gatherings there.

Sushi Noodle
Nikki Sisti (THICK)

This is my favorite spot to dine in Bushwick! It's a cute, tiny BYOB sushi restaurant with a great ambiance. The place holds about five tables and has a tiny little Fender guitar amp that plays K-pop music in the background (the music may vary). It appears to be a "mom and pop shop" as the same server and chef are there every day and have been for over the past five years. Even though it's tiny I have never felt rushed to get out for the next customer. It's always such a relaxing environment. It's always a great spot for a date night or an intimate catch-up with a friend.

Sweetwater
Sean Carroll

Sweetwater is probably the most soulfully gratifying place for me in all of Brooklyn and in New York. It's the place I go when it's raining. I sit at the bar at 5 p.m. [and] I have a French onion soup and fries and a beer.

I have never left Sweetwater feeling worse than when I walked in. I feel like it fulfills this really, whatever's lacking in me on that rainy day, and I love the rain, but whatever's bringing me down, Sweetwater solves that with literally a French onion soup. And having gone there every single week for the last four years, I happen to know the folks that work there in a way. I look forward to walking in those doors.

Sweetwater, I cannot say enough about how emotionally and soulfully restorative that place is for me. I strongly urge you to go there someday and sit at that bar, say hello to Patrick, and get yourself a French onion soup.

Together
Sal Garro (Mount Sharp)

Somehow, it's hard to find Burmese food in New York City. Luckily, the one place you can get it is in Brooklyn, tucked away inside a tiny Bensonhurst storefront. The owner, Oscar, is a quiet gentleman who clearly has a lot of pride in his food. He's never been absent during all the times I've been to his restaurant, and he always checks in to make sure his food is to your liking. He also does me a personal solid of meeting me at the door whenever I pick up food to-go so that I don't have to lock up my bike. What a guy!

Televisions playing Burmese music videos are often playing in the background while you dine. The restaurant doubles as a sushi takeout place but, admittedly, I've never tried it. Instead, I focus on the foods that I think make this place shine. They serve a fish noodle soup, mohinga, that is like nothing I've ever tasted. Couple that with any of their curries or salads (the mango variety is a personal favorite) and you've got yourself a deliciously memorable meal. This is pure comfort food.

Wei's
Sam R. (Glassio)

Wei's is a wonderful dim-sum and cocktail spot in Williamsburg that opened up right around the corner from me when I first lived out in Williamsburg back in 2014. I've grown to know the owners there, and they feel like family at this point, [and] I think I speak for all of the regulars when I say that. One of the folks at Wei's is a brilliant DJ, William Robbins. He has great taste and plays a bunch of wonderful music. I'd often go to Wei's to just sit there and hear music that wouldn't usually reach my ears. It's a great source for finding new stuff to be inspired by, and I've gone away being really inspired by records I'd listen to there.

Yolanda
Olivia K

If you text me, I will come over in a heartbeat. It's a couple blocks from my house. It's a Dominican restaurant, and you know how Boston Market has the rotisserie chicken? They do that, but they have like five kinds of meat and all kinds of potatoes and yucca and yams, and then they have their special two kinds of rice.

They're like the neighborhood heartbeat, because there are so few places to order food over where we're from in East New York. It just has this homey thing. It's the same ladies always who are just like, "Hey, what's up!" and I practice my Spanish with them. They know me.

CHAPTER 8
OLD-SCHOOL EATS

"It's not like a place that time just forgot. It's more like you walk inside and it just IS the 1970s."
- Mike Borchardt (Nihiloceros)

While living in this city means constant exposure to the new, there's still nothing more New York than nostalgia.

In music, that manifests as a longing for venues past. Glasslands, Shea Stadium, Death By Audio. 285 Kent, Goodbye Blue Monday, Big Snow Buffalo Lodge. All are spaces that were frequently mentioned by musicians who had lived in the borough for years and had spent night after night sweating, singing, screaming, and careening within their walls.

There was often a notable difference in tone during interviews with the more seasoned artists who had been whipping and ripping around Brooklyn long before I had arrived. Those who spoke of the glory days, the golden years, the times that were less plastic and polished, more free and wild and raw. These individuals often focused more on reminiscence than recommendations during our conversations as they dreamily described not just a place, but a period of time, sharing nostalgia-drenched stories of experiences that could no longer be replicated, in places that no longer exist.

Much like many music fans wish they'd been in NYC for the rockin' and romanticized age of CBGB, the fact that I missed my window and never made it to the locally legendary venues that previously defined the Brooklyn DIY scene haunts me. But unfortunately that's just something you have to reckon with when you live here no matter when you arrive. The fact that missing out, both on the past and in the present, is a phenomenon that's baked into Brooklyn life. And those who come bounding into the borough a decade from now will surely experience the same sensation, wishing they'd arrived in time for whatever musicians and movements ultimately come to characterize the 2020s.

But rather than wax poetic about the dreamy days of yore, let's look at the High Life half-full. Maybe we can't take the subway back to a different era to relive a certain sweaty show at a now-extinct venue featuring a famous band before they got big, but we *can* go back in time and a hell of a lot further via taste. And best of all, we can do that *today*.

While it's getting increasingly easy to hop off the train and partake in whatever small plates, seventeen-dollar cocktails, and engineered-for-Instagram decor some shiny new spot has to offer, when you want something more traditional than trendy, more classic than "creative," there are still restaurants across the borough where the sauce is secret, the servers don't take your shit, and the photos decorating the place and maybe the gallons of grease they're frying things in might date back to before you were born.

While growing up in the suburbs meant my personal diner experience was limited to smiley-face short stacks at IHOP, and far more formatively every episode of *Seinfeld*, diners are a crucial constellation of the restaurant universe in NYC. They're places for gearing up and winding down, where you'll find early-bird patrons starting their day, partiers ending their night, and a handful of blurry-eyed stragglers stuck in a sedated zombie state, living their best lives in some strange limbo.

It's worth noting that these aren't always super memorable meals on the food front. Instead, these are often spots for conversation and contemplation, and for small, intimate gatherings with your inner circle, where secrets are spilled like maple syrup and stories are shared like an order of fries. These are the fluorescent-lit, vinyl-furnished havens where Ben Thornewill of Jukebox the Ghost does business, where The Muckers head for cheeseburgers and photo shoots, and where members of Hearth, Moon Kissed, and more might order 3 a.m. waffles with a free side of weird.

Along with the signature city staples, this chapter includes other traditional and beloved types of Brooklyn establishments, from a retro sandwich shop to a pilgrimage-worthy pizzeria, and long-standing Italian eateries focused on specialties rather than novelties.

Whether we're talking white-tablecloth restaurants with real wine lists or twenty-four seven spots specializing in scrambled eggs, no matter where they fall on the cuisine, price, and quality ends of the dining spectrum, what the following places have in common is their role as tasty time capsules. If these spots were songs, they'd be oldies, places preserving the borough's past, or at least offering a similarly satisfying sense of nostalgia, and serving up slices of old-school Brooklyn in both food and ambiance form that these days you won't find anywhere else.

Bamonte's
Keith Kelly (Jelly Kelly); Matt Caldamone (HYPEMOM); Steele Kratt (Steele FC)

Keith Kelly: A true old-school Italian restaurant set in between apartments on a residential street in Williamsburg. Established at the same location, it's still owned by the same family.

Matt Caldamone: I think it's been around since like 1890, so they advertise. It is a little white-tablecloth, tuxedo-wearing-waiter old Italian joint. They did film a couple episodes of *The Sopranos* there.

Keith Kelly: I first went there years ago with my family, my Aunt Midge and Uncle Santo to be exact. The place is truly real, the waiters are like ninety years old, the walls are a weird pink salmon color and decorated with family portraits, boxers and baseball players.

Steele Kratt: It's got the best bathroom in New York City, I think. It's got old Yankees and Mets portraits on every bathroom stall.

Keith Kelly: Chandeliers and actual waiter buttons on the wall. Gaudy as hell and lovely.

Matt Caldamone: It's best for the classic old red-sauce pasta dishes. They make a mean martini. If you order an espresso at the end of your meal, they might leave the bottle of Sambuca just sitting on your table and walk away.

Keith Kelly: The eggplant rollatini is my go-to move, followed by the baked ziti. Classic shit.

Matt Caldamone: There was a time when like, every friend gathering, every birthday party, every time we had a friend coming into town, we would go there, because you can call them at like five o'clock on a Friday and be like, "Hey, I've got fourteen people, we're outside. Will you be able to seat us?" And they'll be like, "Yeah, no problem." Like, nothing's ever a problem. They're such pros there.

Keith Kelly: (*Insert old-school Brooklyn accent here.*) They don't make 'em like they used to, know what I mean, my friend?

Di Fara Pizza
John Farris, Andrew Possehl (Sooner); Aleksi Glick (Snack Cat)

John Farris: I moved down to Midwood, which is real deep South Brooklyn. I'm a pretty close walk to the legendary Di Fara's pizza place. It's been there since 1964 [and is] run by the same guy and his children now.

Aleksi Glick: It's a New York institution. It's the best pizza you'll have, period. It's this one guy who's literally like, in his late eighties, who doesn't even let any of his family members make the pizza for him.

John Farris: He goes out of his way to get the top-of-the-line ingredients. The best flour, the best tomatoes, the best cheese.

Aleksi Glick: You'll have to wait an hour or two to get a slice, at least, but it's the best fucking piece of pizza you'll ever have.

Andrew Possehl: It took like two hours to get our pizza, but it was worth the wait, worth the experience.

John Farris: It takes forever. Like, everyone's in there just razzing each other, giving you a hard time. But the pizza is phenomenal.

Aleksi Glick: Di Fara's is, without a doubt, as soon as you taste it, worth it.

L&B Spumoni Gardens
Mike Borchardt (Nihiloceros); Raycee Jones

Mike Borchardt: On thick summer Sunday afternoons, we'd occasionally wind our way south down New Utrecht under the shade of the Coney Island-bound subway lines. Every so often, a train would rush high overhead and create a nice breeze, cooling us just enough to convince us to continue on our journey, 3.8 miles from our door to L&B Spumoni Gardens. So by the time we made the hour walk, we felt like we earned our square slices of pizza.

Serving up the authentic Sicilian square pies in Brooklyn for four generations now, L&B Spumoni Gardens was literally built brick by brick by Sicilians who came to Brooklyn and settled their families in Gravesend. The community came together, laid the cement, and stacked the bricks and the lumber to help Ludovico Barbati get his fledgling spumoni and Italian ices business off the ground, which quickly grew into a full-service pizzeria grounded in the old-world style and recipe.

Raycee Jones: This is a family favorite. I grew up touring what felt like the world, but was really a two-state radius, for pizza and ice cream. Deep in Brooklyn, a real original pizza place that I think everyone should go visit just to understand and appreciate what some real OG Italian Brooklyn life is.

Mike Borchardt: For us, nothing beats sitting outside on the patio. On any given summer day, families pack into little picnic tables under little Pepsi-Cola umbrellas, Italian and American flags flapping overhead. One such summer Saturday a few years ago, while enjoying a cheesy and sweet tomato-sauced pepperoni square slice and an ice-cold fountain soda pop, my wife paused for a moment, looked at me as though straight out of a Frank Capra film and said, "We really have a great life."

Raycee Jones: No frills. That was always my family's style. Good pizza, a how-ya-doing moment and a nice drive home.

Little Purity
Ben Thornewill (Jukebox the Ghost)

This is a classic Brooklyn Greek diner that I've been going to for my entire stay here in Brooklyn, and I love it.

I'm from Kentucky originally, and you know, there isn't that sense of like, truly local places, where you walk in and you know everyone's name, and everyone knows your name. That's always felt like the most New York-y thing ever. It's like *Seinfeld* or *Friends* or whatever, you know. It's like, that's where you go to find your spot. And this became my spot.

I started going there, I remember I had just gotten back from a European tour, and we'd been over there long enough that my sleep schedule was totally out of whack, and I was waking up at 6:30 a.m., which is pretty unheard of for any musician ever. I didn't want to cook, and I didn't want to do anything. And so every morning, like five mornings in a row, 7 a.m., I go to this diner, I order the exact same thing and become friends with everyone.

It's become the place where I bring people if they're in town. If we're meeting with a producer, or an engineer or a songwriter, I'm like, "Why don't we just go to Little Purity?"

We don't have living rooms in Brooklyn, right? There's no place where you're like, "Everyone come to my house. It's super cool and cozy!" And granted, we have a great apartment, but I wanna go to a diner where you walk in, and they know what you're gonna get, and you know what to recommend, and everyone's you know, smiling and friendly, and if they're grouchy, it's cool, because you love them.

So for me, it's a place I bring family. It's a place I bring musicians. I'll go and bring my notebook, and I'll sit down and write. It's the place I go after a long tour if I've been just getting my ass kicked by the road, and I need to wake up and go somewhere that feels comforting. It's the place I end up going to.

Paulie Gee's & Paulie Gee's Slice Shop
Jessica Leibowitz, Danny Ross (Babetown); Sean Carroll

Sean Carroll: In our two-square-mile town [Pelham, NY], we have like thirteen pizzerias and twenty nail salons. That's about it. That's pretty much the whole town. It's a good place, but those are really the two things we have going for us, and ya know, I was only using one of those things. But growing up there was fun. It really is assumed that you're going to have at least one slice of pizza a day. That is an absurd thing.

Paulie Gee's Slice Shop reminds me of those [places] in such a beautifully authentic way. You walk in, you've got the New York Yankees on the TV, they're yelling your name out on a way too muffle-y microphone.

Jessica Leibowitz: Paulie and I go back to probably 2010. He always remembers you, but his thing is talking to everyone at every table, no matter if he knows you or not, so it's just a welcoming space.

Danny Ross: It gives [Paulie Gee's] a real neighborhood feel. He walks around with a baseball cap and a cup of coffee.

Jessica Leibowitz: He always has a different hat.

Danny Ross: And he schmoozes with you. It's very classic.

Jessica Leibowitz: I do like the personal connection. He'll be like, "Why haven't you been in here recently?" And it also has a nice atmosphere.

Danny Ross: I pick places for the music.

Jessica Leibowitz: They have good music there.

Danny Ross: He's got a classic-rock thing.

Sean Carroll: I think it just brings me back to eleven years old, after a rec baseball game, going to Pelham Pizza, watching Mariano

Rivera win the game for the Yankees. While New York is full of pizzerias, I miss that small-town, you're-in-our-pizzeria kinda feeling a lot of the time, and Paulie Gee's Slice Shop fully provides that for me.

Roll N Roaster
Mike Borchardt (Nihiloceros); Matthew Iwanusa (Caveman); Tall Juan

Mike Borchardt: I'd never been on a roast-beef tour, though I definitely wasn't averse to the idea. Our friend, Anthony, was one of the only other people we knew who lived in Southern Brooklyn, and he had a car. Anthony had lived in the Brooklyn upside-down his entire life, and he'd suggested taking us around to every crazy and weird roast-beef spot he knew of. We couldn't say no.

Matthew Iwanusa: It's like Arby's, but it's like it never franchised. They just made one, but it looks like it's from the seventies still. It's really cool.

Mike Borchardt: It's like walking right into 1971 with absolutely no explanation. Even from the oversized parking lot, which in itself is a rarity in most of Brooklyn, you just get the feeling that they haven't changed the decor inside or out since originally opening their doors. It's not like a place that time just forgot. It's more like you walk inside and it just *is* the 1970s.

Everyone working there and everyone eating there just goes about their dining experience like everything around us isn't completely and absolutely bonkers.

Completely lined with tiers of wood paneling framing a palette of mustard browns and yellows, it's as though your grandparents' station wagon transformed into a restaurant.

I think everything on the menu is just a handful of bucks and comes covered in cheese. Everything is crispy and soggy and either made of roast beef or smells like roast beef and tastes amazing.

However great the food though, the second you roll up to Roll N

Roaster, you're far too distracted with the total insanity of where you are to pay much attention to what you're eating.

Matthew Iwanusa: I went to the beach, and we were looking for food, and I realized we were right next to this place which I've always wanted to go to. We get there, and it happens to be like the fifty-year anniversary. So we went and they gave us all free shirts and all this free stuff.

Tall Juan: I used to go there every birthday, my friends' birthdays, too. If it's your birthday, they let you spin the wheel and you can win something. If you spend more than, I don't remember how much, they give you champagne for free. So if you go with a big group of people, it's a really cool place.

This friend of mine was celebrating his birthday there, and he picked us up in a limo, and we all went in a limo to Roll N Roaster. My first music video, we have shots from that day.

Mike Borchardt: To this day, people ask me the story of our Great Roast Beef Tour of Southern Brooklyn, and often the only thing I can immediately recall is dinner at Roll N Roaster, and I can't even remember what I ordered to eat that night.

Sunset Diner
Emir Mohseni (The Muckers)

This is like one of the most fun for us on tour, to go to diners. So it's like all diners. It's just shitty food, but I love it. We went to Sunset Diner, and I fell in love because it's such an old-school diner and sometimes dark because the TV's on, and it's always news and the news is always bad, but we just had so much fun there and some really good conversations. Even the first photo shoot that we had [was there]. Chris wasn't even in the band at that time, it was me, Tony and John.

We used to go to that place a lot, but not anymore. They changed the whole design and everything, so kind of sad about that. I don't know, I love that place.

Tina's Place
Hearth (Sara Horton, Melanie Rose Wiggins); Steele Kratt (Steele FC); Emily Sgouros (Moon Kissed); Brett Moses (Teen Commandments)

Hearth: Tina's Place is hands-down our favorite restaurant in Brooklyn. Maybe "restaurant" is too formal of a word. It's the perfect greasy diner for classic comfort food.

Steele Kratt: You know, it's like they open at 3 a.m. and close at 3 p.m. It was originally built for truck drivers to go eat breakfast and then lunch when their shift finished, and then it became a place for drunk people to go eat after a night out or like a hungover brunch. It's just the perfect window for both of those things. And I'm not a trucker, so I usually will go there if it's late at night.

Emily Sgouros: I think I've only been to Tina's hungover, but it is definitely the best place for breakfast.

Hearth: No matter the time of day, I [Melanie] always get breakfast when I go.

Brett Moses: You can go get a full breakfast for like five or six dollars. And it like, has not changed since the seventies. The prices are the same, the wood paneling is the same. Tina's there. The regulars have been there decades and decades.

Hearth: It has been around for over seventy years, and it doesn't seem like they've changed a single thing about it since the day it opened.

Brett Moses: Highly recommend it. It's an institution. It's got that good, bad taste. Like, everything is so good now, you know? Food is so good everywhere, it's incredible. [Tina's] is a version of good that's endangered. You go there and you're like, oh yeah, this used to be good. And it's still good. And nobody does that anymore, you know?

Emily Sgouros: Every time I'm there, *The Price Is Right* is usually playing on one of the TVs, which is kinda soothing.

Hearth: They're cash-only, play courtroom dramas on the TV in the back, and have pictures from over the years covering the walls.

Brett Moses: It's so weird because everything there is very vintage, and then there's this poster that has a picture of a penguin sitting on an avocado. Like, that's the egg. It looks like it was drawn in Microsoft Paint. It just says "Avocados, they are here." Like, who on…? Somebody designed this! And someone bought it! And it's at Tina's!

Steele Kratt: Tina's has on two occasions been the most bizarre experience in my life. That's an overreaction. Not most bizarre, but a bizarre experience. It was probably like 4 a.m., and I was eating pancakes with friends, and the TV was on. And I don't know what channel it was, but it was just showing a bunch of puppies running and playing through a field, and it was really, really cute. And then every time it cut to commercial, it was just a news report basically for missing children. It would just go back and forth between puppies playing in an open field, and children that are missing and presumed dead. I don't know what channel it was, but I've been there two times late at night and that's the channel it's on and that's the program. It's fucking bizarre. So if anyone else has seen that, reach out.

Tom's Diner
Sean Carroll

It's reminiscent of every diner I've ever spent a 3 a.m. in, which, by the way, is a lot. Diners are very important to me. I would say pretty much every song I've ever written is somewhat derived from some way I've felt in a diner, or something that happened in a diner exactly like Tom's. I will do anything for a milkshake and fries, and there have been weeks where I've drunk a milkshake every single day. Tom's is a beautiful, beautiful place where the milkshakes are a-flowin', the fries are great, but the reason I mentioned it is really because of just the importance of diners in general in my life. Someone once referred to my music as a diner, saying it's not that presentable, it's not that pretty, but it tastes so fuckin' good. And that's the greatest review I've ever gotten.

CHAPTER 9
HANGOVER HELPERS

"This is a hungover, three in the afternoon, first meal of the day." - David Johnson (Max Pain and the Groovies)

An undeniably notable part of nightlife, booze is naturally a not-so-subtle theme throughout this book. However, I do want to note that, unlike a gender reveal party, family Thanksgiving, or visit to the DMV, alcohol isn't mandatory for the enjoyment of live music. In fact, there are plenty of loudly and proudly sober artists within the scene who tear it up under absolutely no influence, proving you can still have a blast in Brooklyn while sipping soda bitters or swigging Red Bull.

But for those who *do* partake, it would be almost inhumane to throw you a long list of bars without offering at least a few remedies. So before we launch into some listings for the borough's best booze-absorbing bites, here's a small selection of cures and coping strategies from our bands of experienced experts.

First off, for short-term relief there's no denying the hair of the dog, and from bandmates and bar mates Zach Inkley and Zach Butler of 95 Bulls, we've got the most straight-forward of solutions.

"More booze," offered the former. "I just drink again," said the latter.

We've also got less alcohol-oriented options, featuring both natural and NYC-specific remedies. "Water, sleep, eat, repeat," advised Charmaine Querol of punk power trio Nevva, whose bandmates swore by ginseng (Molly Schoen) and a bodega bacon egg 'n' cheese (Jenny Palumbo). Meanwhile, the four rockers of Impossible Colors simply recommended a strict regimen of rest, suggesting you "sleep for two weeks straight."

And then there are more detailed hangover-busting blueprints, post-imbibing itineraries so specific that you can only imagine the anecdotes behind the antidotes.

After a sweaty evening spent dancing in the basement, the best buds of new-wave punk band My Son The Doctor prescribe "the largest cup of coffee and the nearest Indian buffet." Meanwhile, indie-pop duo Tallbird suggests "drinking margaritas and eating poutine at Smorgasburg on Sunday mornings in Prospect Park." Jim Hill of Slight Of swears by "blue Gatorade, coconut water, and a pumpernickel-everything bagel with tofu cream cheese, capers and cucumber," and keyboardist Kayla Asbell of 95 Bulls and Bipolar recommends you "Eat Good Chinese (the real name of the place) in bed and make a Bloody Mary."

And finally, one perfectly formulated prescription, a tried-and-tested solution from Brooklyn indie-pop dreamer Papi Shiitake: "General Tso's (specifically from Randy's Chinese Food), one Gatorade (regular), one Vitamin Water (sugar-free), two Advil, *90 Day Fiancé*, and blunts. If hangover persists, order Beef Brisket Pho from Lucy's with a Sprite and add more blunts."

While the aforementioned cures have not been evaluated by the FDA nor any other regulatory agency whatsoever, the next time you wake up without pants or the will to live, too scared to check your bank balance and even more terrified to revisit your outgoing texts, well, it's worth a shot.

Now onto our official listings for the roughest of mornings following the rowdiest of nights. If after a wild streak of bar-hopping and show-stopping, you're still physically and emotionally capable of leaving the house to forage, or at least rolling over in bed and cracking open a crusty eye to order Seamless, this chapter has you covered. Read on for a few spots serving food that's perfectly engineered to soak up last night's sins and help you feel, at least for a little while, a little bit more human.

Then, come 9 p.m., you'll be ready to get back out there and do it all over again.

He Cherokee
Luna Rose (Hannah Rose Ammon, Sam Parrish, Jö Wagner)

Below the apartment where two of us (Sam and Jö) used to live, right off the Halsey J-stop, there's a breakfast establishment by the name of He Cherokee. It's got everything you could possibly want from a morning haunt at the right speed, temperature, and price. I (Jö) went there the other morning and received a scalding hot Bacon Egg & Cheese (SPK obviously) for $3.25 in under four minutes, and it was exactly what the doctor ordered. The food and ambiance are certainly what draws the customers in, but it's the unspoken and wildly unexpected gratuity that every customer experiences which earned my lifetime loyalty. No matter what you order, and no matter what time of day, you are gifted a Sunny Delight with every purchase. I didn't question it the first time, and I began to expect it the second time. This little but very important amenity earned He Cherokee the affectionate nickname of The Sunny D Cafe to us and is the cornerstone of a balanced hangover breakfast. Ten out of ten for creativity, and vitamin C.

Mable's Smokehouse & Banquet Hall
William Thompson, Connor Jones (Yella Belly)

William Thompson: Good barbecue is kind of hard to find in New York. Honestly, there's maybe a handful of spots.

New York, I found out you can't have a smoker, which is obviously integral to barbecue. So these people actually smoke all their meat in Vinegar Hill. They'll actually transport it, and it's this whole ordeal. It's astounding that they keep that routine up. It's amazing and you can taste it in the food. It's incredible, it's so good. The music's awesome. They have Texas beers and cocktails.

Connor Jones: And they deliver. Fun fact. I've had some hungover days when I've had that delivered. It's been fantastic. Like a full barbecue meal. You have to clean your sheets the next day, but the hangover's gone.

La Mesita
David Johnson, Shane Preece (Max Pain and the Groovies)

David Johnson: This is a hungover, three in the afternoon, first meal of the day.

You get a giant burrito with the healthiest dose of guacamole with another dose of pico de gallo and chips, all for ten bucks. It's insane. So that is the food spot right now for me. And every time you go there, there's two little kids, and they run back in the kitchen and get their mom and dad, and their parents come out and fulfill the order. It's a super cool spot.

Shane Preece: You gotta understand. We're Mexican-food connoisseurs a little bit because we're from the West Coast where you can get some really good Mexican food. We were looking for a spot forever out here.

David Johnson: New York is lacking big time in Mexican food.

Shane Preece: Not greasy enough.

David Johnson: It's hard to find a good burrito.

Shane Preece: Yeah, there's good tacos everywhere, but burritos is something else.

Tortilleria Mexicana Los Hermanos
Tanner Peterson (Tanners); Dave Palazola (Evolfo)

Tanner Peterson: If you need to cure that hangover, my hands-down favorite spot for life-support food is Los Hermanos. It's a tortilla factory and a BYOB sit-down spot for some seriously delish Mexican food.

Dave Palazola: Tortilleria Los Hermanos in Bushwick has been the site of many a pre- or post-show taco over the years. I remember once folding some shrooms into a picada and scarfing it down there before going to see Deerhoof play an amazing set at Market Hotel.

Williamsburg Pizza
Hayes Peebles

That's just really good pizza! There's always a debate on these things, and I really love all pizza, you know. I really do. I'm really open-minded. I'll eat like, Domino's, whatever. But I think as far as the Brooklyn or Williamsburg pizza landscape goes, that is one of my favorite spots.

I also used to live for a year, one very precious year, around the corner. So it would become very much a part of my routine. I was working pretty late nights [at One Stop Beer Shop], and I'd wake up around lunchtime feeling like shit, so I would go there, and they would take care of me pretty well. So when people come and visit or ask me, I always point people to Williamsburg.

CHAPTER 10
MARKET RESEARCH

"Every so often when I find myself back on that block, I'll stop in for a bite and it still feels like home."
- Kegan Zema (Realworld)

Coffee, stamps, cigarettes. Shampoo, socks, scratch-offs. A box of condoms, a can of soup, a paper bag-wrapped beer. And, of course, two dozen different types of "gourmet" sandwiches. The word "gourmet" has never been applied more recklessly.

Whether it's a family-run bodega that's been around for decades, a Whole Foods-style market featuring vegan jerky and a legitimate juice bar, or a deli dealing serotonin in grilled and greasy form, what those who don't live in New York might not understand is that what these stores offer is far more than a 7-Eleven experience, and convenience doesn't even begin to cover it.

These are bright lights that, depending on your level of intoxication or caffeine deprivation, might feel more welcoming than Las Vegas or more miraculous than the Aurora Borealis. And for artists, as for anyone in Brooklyn, these places characterize a city life authentically lived. Not a hangout spot necessarily, but a frequently visited location that characterizes those in-between and on-the go moments at any time of day or night. The pick-up, the pit-stop, the swing-by for a pre-show sandwich or a few six-packs to get the after-party started. And of course, the late-night mecca for a munchies-satisfying shopping spree when, to borrow lyrics from NYC rock band Parquet Courts, you're feeling *so stoned and starving*.

While this is a short chapter, these places play a big role. There's even a Brooklyn band called BODEGA. And any guide to the borough would be incomplete without mention of these noble neighborhood institutions, snack-stacked spaces sometimes tinier than studio apartments, where both the man behind the counter and the cat prowling the aisles have seen you roll through at all different times, in all different states, and have sold you everything from rolling papers to toilet paper.

And while these mini-marts with tiny umbrellas dangling from the ceiling, dish soap and canned goods crammed on shelves, and racks packed with plantain chips, pork rinds, and thirty different types of Bazzini Nuts might seem nearly identical to the untrained eye, there are distinct specifics that make each shop one's own. And, just like everything else in this city, everyone is very much convinced that theirs is the very best.

Best Deli
Jim Hill (Slight Of); Kegan Zema (Realworld)

Jim Hill: Like its name, Best Deli on Bushwick and Myrtle is simply the best.

Kegan Zema: You wouldn't think that a place calling itself Best Deli would literally be "the best deli," but in almost a decade of living in New York, no other spot can compare.

From about 2015 to 2017, I probably ate at least one meal a day there, most often a veggie burger or their fries. This was mostly due to working as a sound engineer next door at the beloved DIY spot, Silent Barn. In fact, for many who were part of that community, Best Deli was essentially our personal kitchen. While there are many other great food options in that area like the late-night burrito hot-spot, Regalo de Juquila, or several others that have come and gone (RIP Little Skips), Best Deli has an undeniable charm and prices that can't be beat. On the surface there may not appear to be much that sets it apart from any other bodega, but ultimately it's the friendly staff, consistent quality, and sense of community that make Best Deli truly the best. Every so often when I find myself back on that block I'll stop in for a bite, and it still feels like home.

The Brooklyn G
Lincoln Lute, Gordon Taylor (Plastic Picnic)

Lincoln Lute: Our first practice space in New York was in Williamsburg on South 3rd between Wythe and Kent. I have all these memories associated with that area. At this crappy deli that we'd go to because we didn't have any money, the Brooklyn G, we'd get sandwiches and go back to practice. Then we'd stand around in the freezing cold air at like 1 a.m., and then Gordon and Marshall would get on the train for an hour and a half and go up to Washington Heights.

Gordon Taylor: Every single time we'd go to practice, Marshall and I would pick up a sandwich from there. Usually because we'd commute so far, we'd be hungry, but also because we couldn't afford any of the food like anywhere else in Williamsburg. So that was our favorite bodega, at least for the first couple weeks living here. We called it the Brooklyn G, because I think it says Brooklyn Gourmet Deli, but all the lights burned out.

It's one of those places that always smells like bacon. So every time we walk by, even if you're not hungry, it's like okay, now we have to go get a sandwich.

Brooklyn's Natural
Bandits on the Run (Adrian Blake Enscoe, Sydney Shepherd, Regina Strayhorn)

Look, we know Brooklyn is chock-full of bodegas turned overpriced organic food shops, but we'd be remiss if we didn't mention this place, because the employees are among some of the best people we've met in Brooklyn. They're all magnificent people with very interesting backstories if you can find a moment to chat with them between customers.

The grill there is also excellent and open late. A few sandwiches we recommend are the Mexican with pesto for a quick evening munch, or the 49 Bogart with a fried egg for a bangin' hangover cure.

Four Seasons Grill Deli
DAD (Jeremy Duvall, Jesse Fairbairn, Jon Murphy, James Watson); Papi Shiitake

DAD: One of our favorite places in NYC is a sweet little gem of an establishment on Wyckoff Avenue. Stocked with the finest Boars Head ingredients and staffed by friendly employees, Four Seasons is a wonderful place to go for a Lime-A-Rita or an authentic bodega sandwich after a long day's work. They have the entire Hana menu at nearly half the price! One time Jimmy and I [Jon] got locked out of my apartment in the rain after a warehouse party, and we went to Four Seasons because we didn't know where else to go.

Papi Shiitake: They cook their bacon right, and they sell beer. Get the onion rings and skip the hot wings.

Mr. Kiwi's
Ronnie Lanzilotta (Evolfo); Lexie Lowell

Ronnie Lanzilotta: If there were a place that might live up to an out-of-towner's imagination of gritty BK eclecticism, it would have to be the Myrtle-Broadway intersection. Sun streaking through elevated train tracks casts disorienting grids of shadow down upon the five-way intersection perpetually choked with traffic. Commuters, locals, gentrifiers, junkies, and immigrants collide here. The anchor holding it all together is Mr. Kiwi's. The glowing green awning of the twenty-four seven family-owned grocery store seems to supervise this unruly intersection.

Lexie Lowell: Conveniently placed directly underneath the rattling JMZ tracks near the Myrtle stop, drop in after seeing a show at Bizarre Bar or vibing the smoky dance floor at Mood Ring.

[It's] a twenty-four seven one-stop-shop with a secret. Freshly squeezed, customizable, and yes, appropriately priced juice, possibly the only one in the tri-state area.

Ronnie Lanzilotta: Come for the four-dollar fresh juices, stay for the discount produce.

There's a menu, but I've never seen anyone order from it. You just pick from what they have on hand and your cup will runneth over. "Drink some," they might say as I chug half my juice, just to have it refilled to the brim a moment later.

I'm probably the only person who ever thought it would be a good idea for Mr. Kiwi's and Market Hotel, the 450-cap concert venue directly upstairs, to do a cocktail collab. I imagine you exit the show, run downstairs to get a juice, and then run it back up to the bar to spike it with booze. Impractical, surely, but one can dream.

Lexie Lowell: The owners, while never exactly gregarious, know exactly what assortment of goodies a Brooklynite might need at any hour of the day or night.

Ronnie Lanzilotta: It never really mattered if I was starting my day and forgot to eat breakfast, or ending my night and trying to head off an inevitable hangover, the juice always hits.

Lexie Lowell: I have yet to discern who the real Mr. Kiwi is despite my many inquiries, all met with a mysterious smile and twinkle in their eye. So, freshly squeezed juice in hand, I ask will the real Mr. Kiwi please stand up?

SECTION 3
LIVE FROM NEW YORK

Clubs, apartments, art galleries. Bars, backyards, basements. Rooftops, train stops, coffee spots, thrift shops.

You can take Shakespeare's "All the world's a stage" literally in Brooklyn, where no matter where you are, there's likely one or more musicians in the vicinity, and every night of every week all kinds of art is being shared on established stages, at unconventional venues, and in literally underground spaces across the borough. There are shows of both the official and unofficial, the perfectly rehearsed and largely improvisational, the free and the ten-bucks-plus-service-fee varieties.

You just have to find them.

In June 2021, I was in a big no-sleep-*in*-Brooklyn phase, showing up to five shows a week with a brain so fried I could barely carry on a conversation, and a bank account so depleted I was doomed to drink some cheap beer called Medalla. While a year prior I'd stocked up on hand sanitizer, now I was focused on accumulating experiences, and over the course of just one of these weeks, I consumed live music at a wider spectrum of venues in a shorter time span than I ever had outside of South by Southwest.

On Sunday, I spent five hours at a Greenpoint recording studio being serenaded by Sean Wouters and showered with rose petals during a video shoot for Drunk Ex. Tuesday, I bopped and headbanged to Namesake and 95 Bulls at The Broadway, while I danced Wednesday away at Our Wicked Lady with Endearments, Fair Visions, and Color Tongue. And on Saturday afternoon, I headed to Putnam Palace, a DIY venue run by my drummer and photographer friends Cade and Michelle, where rain turned a backyard show into a sweaty basement rager featuring Nevva, Safer, and Beeyotch, and we all flashed our vax cards, shed our inhibitions, and went as wild as one can in a room with ceilings just over six feet.

And then there was what was set to be the grand finale, a Saturday night "roof battle royale" thrown by Spud Cannon to celebrate their new record, an appropriately unsanctioned event for the self-dubbed "good kids making bad decisions" who had reportedly snuck onto Vassar's on-campus squash courts to record their new album during secret all-nighters.

Ahead of the show, I had followed the band's Instagram instructions and messaged for the address of the venue. And that night around 10 p.m., after some post-Putnam recovery in the form of a noodle bowl the size of my head, I hopped in a Lyft and soon arrived at the supposed point-of-party, a dark destination sandwiched between a deli and liquor store. Where there was absolutely no show to be seen, heard, or found.

After circling the block on foot for what felt like forever searching for a hidden door or secret portal to enter that night's version of Narnia, all while confusing neither hip nor young nor particularly amused strangers with my confused inquiries, I finally shot a text to Spud Cannon superfan Tom Gallo of the blog and podcast *Look At My Records!*, who had arrived at the event an hour or two earlier. It was only then, when Tom responded to confirm the address, that I realized the mistake. Whoever had shot me the address had accidentally omitted a digit. It was *315*, not *15*.

While this is not exactly the kind of error that happens when you're buying tickets to a public venue through an established platform, it's an easy mistake to make. After all, these are humans, not robots, firing off responses to these messages, and those are just the risks that one assumes with the *fun-official*. Plus, for a free show with a skyline view in a secret spot, that slight detour was honestly a very small price to pay. When I eventually arrived at the correct destination less than a mile away, it was instantly identifiable by the audible buzz of the crowd above and the sight of crop-topped twenty-somethings filing in and out, smoking on sidewalks, and hanging out in stairways. And upon reaching the summit, a soccer field-sized roof, I found what I had been looking for and hoping for all along. What appeared to be hundreds of people drinking and dancing, some talking each other up, others feeling each other up, and plenty peeing increasingly unselfconsciously in, on, and probably off the roof's concrete corners.

Following rain delays and performances by the evening's opening bands, Spud Cannon's members, decked out in white, finally took the stage for an extremely stoked, no longer soaked, crowd. Formed in college, the band has claimed that all they've ever wanted to do is make people dance, and late that night they did just that, as in front of a bouncing ball of fans and friends, the artists played a joyful set under the stars. A long-awaited show, it was also a much-needed release. A celebration of Spud Cannon's new album, the triumphant return of live music, and the incredible feeling of being young and alive on a summer night in Brooklyn.

Then in true rock 'n' roll fashion, we all partied until the cops came.

While not every show is this unique or involves this amount of (mis)adventure, what the venues, DIY spaces, and music experiences outlined in the following chapters all have in common is authenticity. After all, while you can build a stage or book a band, you can't force these memorable moments and you can't manufacture this sort of magic. Love has to be at the heart of it.

That said, love doesn't *quite* pay the rent, so much like experiences are ephemeral, sadly many venues don't have the longest of lifespans. But you can't stop the music, and as latitude and longitude are always in flux with doors opening and spaces shuttering, and any space can be temporarily transformed (pizza shop by day, mosh pit by night!), live music isn't limited to location. While designated performance sites are obviously integral, other public and private places across the borough are constantly being transformed into venues, morphing for music and serving as sonic soapboxes where musicians show up and go all out for exposure and experience, for practice, a passion for performance, and sometimes just for a few dirty bills tossed in a guitar case.

To steal a line from *Jurassic Park*, much like "life finds a way," live music always does too. And while it might not always look or sound the same, you better believe it always, always feels good.

CHAPTER 11
STAGE RIGHT

"Performing is definitely the thing that I live for—that catharsis, that exorcism of all of the shit, and just letting it all go." - Gillian Visco (Shadow Monster)

    Before we break into our venues chapter, let's talk about one stage in particular and the crowd you might catch there.

    According to the six-degrees-of-separation theory, any two people on Earth are six or fewer acquaintances apart. However, when it comes to the Brooklyn music community, I'd wager it's more like one and a half.

    Those two guitarists live with that bassist, who dated that drummer, who just started a side project with a certain keyboardist, who is hooking up with one of those guitarists because they all went on tour with that one vocalist, who went to high school with this violinist, who's doing that weird Bach-meets-Blink-182 thing with the stepsister of the original bassist's half-brother. You get the idea.

    Brooklyn is a beautifully tangled web of wonder and weirdos, a community packed with people who are constantly creating and collaborating. And while within this shape-shifting scene bands morph and multiply like musically gifted gremlins fed mostly beers after midnight, rendering any comprehensive diagram I could commission for inclusion in this book instantly useless, the expansion and overlap make it extremely easy to discover new music in a way that's far more effective and organic than any internet algorithm.

As an example, let's start by dissecting a real-life Brooklyn supergroup of sorts. Take local artists-not-athletes 95 Bulls, a product of the pandemic, birthed over an unconfirmed number of drinks on the Our Wicked Lady rooftop. The band is composed of members of The Mystery Lights, Jelly Kelly, Bipolar, and Smock, and is fronted by boundlessly talented human Koosh-ball equivalent Emily Ashenden of Ashjesus, whose cropped platinum hair and even-more-cropped t-shirts, combined with her quick jokes and signature roof-rattling voice, make her both visually and audibly recognizable from a mile away.

Rather than break a band apart, you can also start with an individual and branch out from there to places, people, and projects past, present, and future.

I first caught post-punk poet Zach Ellis when he was playing drums in a friend's band at Ridgewood venue Trans-Pecos. At that point, I didn't even know about his roles in local bands Haybaby and WIVES, and it was definitely before I'd heard of Dead Tooth, the project he named after his own actually deceased top incisor. This encounter was also a full six months before his collaboration with aughts underground artist Darius VanSluytman (No Surrender) would make landfall with "I Hate the Precedent," the duo's debut scorcher of a single, in the fall of 2020.

Ready for things to come full circle? The night I met Zach, the bill also included Johnny Dynamite and the Bloodsuckers, whose mulleted multi-instrumentalist of a frontman plays drums in the aforementioned Ashjesus, and Jelly Kelly, whose bassist Dom Bodo is in 95 Bulls.

Head spinning? These are just a few examples of artist intersection, connection, participation, and proliferation. When I was emailing musicians to double-check projects and spell-check names, many individuals responded with resumes including bands I had no idea they were even involved in, a phenomenon that goes double for drummers, who often appear to play in like eighteen projects apiece. And to be honest, I still haven't quite mastered all the ins and outs of artistic incest responsible for this twisted and tangled family tree. However, I do remember the exact moment this particular slice of the scene first snapped into focus for me.

It was a January evening on the roof of Our Wicked Lady, which basically functions as Bushwick artists' home base, during a show that had been dubbed Dirty Jerz Fest. The lineup featured seven sets of Jersey jammers turned Brooklyn bands, and all the groups were embracing their Garden State roots, leaning hard and hilariously into the theme with atypical show amenities like a spread of Italian cuisine set up to the right of the stage.

While I didn't recognize every band on the bill that night, Gillian Visco of the self-described "angsty and loud duo" Shadow Monster had been my guest on the Bands do BK radio show a few days prior, so I decided to make the trek from Crown Heights on a school night to show my support and to hear the band's new record *Punching Bag* live. After the fifty-five-minute subway pilgrimage that involves crossing the same river twice, a now-routine journey that by this point feels less absurd than it sounds, I flashed my ID, climbed the stairs to the roof, and wove through a crowd of beers, beards, and beanies as I made my way to the bar. And it was there in line, while waiting to order a gin and soda, gazing absentmindedly out at the crowd and contemplating the concept of a concert with Caprese salad, that it hit me. *Hey, I actually know these people!*

Now up until this evening, I'm sure I had already encountered many of the artists, producers, and promoters in attendance on multiple occasions. There had always been bands and managers throwing back beers in booths behind me, waiting for the train at Myrtle, Metropolitan, or Morgan beside me, and smoking cigarettes in front of the venues I'd strolled up to and stumbled out of. I'd already spent time surrounded by the creative artists in this music community, and I had long been hanging out in the eye of the hippest of hurricanes. The thing is, I just didn't know it.

But that night, after a year and a half of bouncing around the borough and scouring the Brooklyn-shaped corner of the internet, something suddenly clicked. And with the grungy sounds of Shadow Monster blasting from the speakers and the smell of lasagna wafting through the air, I transitioned from a state of ignorance, afloat in a sea of hot, anonymous strangers, to one of hyper-awareness, in which I could suddenly identify individuals like a Times Square tour guide pointing out landmarks from the top of a double-decker bus.

"Don't look now, it's Zach from Smock! And on your right, hey! It's Rich from Bloodless Management!"

While it sounds a little crazy, I think this instant shift of consciousness might sum up the very nature of a scene. As an unassuming outsider, it's possible to be totally immersed in it physically, just a bar stool away from the borough's hottest psych-rock outfit as they discuss their dreams and drama, all while remaining completely unaware. But spend enough time in these places and go to enough shows in these spaces, and you realize that each little scene is kind of like a small town, or maybe even an ecosystem. There's intimacy. There's history. Everyone knows everyone, and they're all very much connected.

That night, after exchanging hellos and a few thrilling half-hugs with artist acquaintances who would later turn into full-fledged friends, I completely recognized the beauty of this special corner of the universe. And as I gazed out over a crowd of no-longer-strangers singing and dancing and consuming cannoli, I truly realized how tight this community is and how crucial spaces like Our Wicked Lady, where people gather to share art, support each other, and get a little weird with it, really are.

So, while subway platforms, park pop-ups, and semi-converted warehouses near superfund sites might be the greatest of grassroots examples, let's start with beloved public music venues like this. Those that are labeled and listed as such, zoned some specific way I know nothing about, and probably pay taxes and even accept credit cards. Establishments with real websites, addresses on Google Maps, and someone manning the door who doesn't literally live there.

Under this more "official" umbrella, there are, of course, a wide variety of venues.

First, the locally loved worn-and-torn spaces that offer artists who live down the street a home-field advantage and a safe space to experiment, sometimes for crowds in the single digits. Lower-stakes stages where you'll spot an ex in the crowd, your friends' bands' stickers on the bathroom mirror, and maybe that weird dude who lives above you on bass.

Then, there are the iconic clubs that New York musicians might make it their mission to play, a goal that's aspirational but also attainable. Venues where the bills are stacked, the sound is always on-point, and the day they do get booked, artists are sure to bring their A-game and maybe even their parents.

And, of course, you've got the bigger, flashier establishments. Cavernous, perpetually packed venues where you might drop a Hamilton on a hefeweizen, lose your buddies on the way back from the bathroom, and catch bands that even your high-school classmates back in Dayton or Dubuque are down with. All with two thousand of your closest friends.

These are all occasions where you might take an elbow to the ribcage or man bun to the mouth while enjoying the chaotic catharsis that is being showered in strangers' beer and sweat and fill-in-the-blank mystery fluid. Where, depending on the music, you might sing, scream, cry, dance, or maybe dry hump along in the crowd, moving and moshing together as a synchronized unit, like a boozed-up flock of birds, or an extremely emotional school of fish.

Of course, these venues are more than designated square footage, a sound system, and a stage. What truly makes these places remarkable are the individuals who choose to spend time inside them. It's the passionate people who are booking and bartending, in the booth and behind the bar, in the crowd and on the stage. Those who opt for nightlife over Netflix, and who show up to create, facilitate, and enjoy art all year round. No matter the venue, no matter the genre, music fans get up and go out to these spaces for the same reason. To enjoy the collective experience of being captivated by the music, enthralled by the artists, and one hundred percent absorbed in the action.

Be it a Tuesday or a Saturday, in the middle of a blizzard or at the peak of the most gnarly heat wave, these venues are places for community and congregation. They're sticky-floored churches where we worship, hallowed places we must protect. Keepers of electric energy, hosts to our most mind-melting experiences, and the setting of our most beautiful, often blurry memories.

In other words, it's never *just a stage*. This is where we band together.

Alphaville
Zach Ellis (Dead Tooth); Lydia Gammill, Tine Hill, Vram Kherlopian, Tarra Thiessen (Gustaf); John Farris, Andrew Possehl (Sooner); Natalie Kirch, Rosie Slater (Sharkmuffin); Patrick Phillips (Namesake, formerly known as Honduras)

Zach Ellis: Alphaville is always going through weird shit, but we've played there probably more than anywhere. It's always been a classic spot for us.

Tarra Thiessen: It sort of became a living room to me. I felt like I was playing at Alphaville like, twice a weekend. I feel like there was a six-month period where I was only playing at Alphaville.

Lydia Gammill: It's a big sort of staple Brooklyn scene venue. I remember it sort of, when it first was opened, it was like, the continuation of Alaska. When I was coming up as a young musician, Alaska felt very *people in the in-crowd*. People were obsessed with Alaska. It stressed me out because it felt like a high-school situation. There was nowhere to sit or stand. You had to pick a herd really quickly.

Alphaville sort of opened up as the venue brother or sister of that bar. And I think it had better seating, but it also sort of did serve to be like this quad for the Bushwick scene, for better or for worse. Sometimes you're comfortable, and you're like, I know everybody, and then other times you're like, I'm on somebody else's turf, and I just want to eat some tater tots in private. But it was nice. It was fun to sort of, as the band progressed, to feel more and more at home.

Vram Kherlopian: That felt like a weird home for us. We played a bunch of shows there, we have friends that work there. It's our own little concrete prison. It's just one of those places I feel like I have a lot of really positive memories. I've always liked it.

John Farris: It's a really cool space. A lot of venues aren't actually great places to hang out, but Alphaville is a bar you would go to whether or not there's a show.

I actually for a year lived like two blocks away from Alphaville, I think before I ever went to a show there. And then we started playing and got a show there and it just instantly stood out as the top venue for a band to play at. The staff there could not have been more chill. And sometimes dealing with sound and venue management as a band can be kind of painful.

Natalie Kirch: They have a nice staff, and most of the staff are also musicians. They always have really good sound engineers.

Patrick Phillips: I worked at Alphaville the last five years. So I spent a lot of time in there, and we played a ton of shows there.

It's a small operation. Before the place opened and I got offered the job, a couple of us were in there painting the place, so you really had a very hands-on experience.

I really like working in the venue aspect because it's all so connected. When the bands are playing, you can ask the other bartender to cover the bar for twenty minutes and go back there, and I just love that. I just loved being close to the music, and I loved the do-it-yourself atmosphere, and I really found joy in touring bands coming to town and, you know, hooking them up with some drinks or some food here and there.

Bands from out of town, you know, they come to New York, and they're like, "Holy shit, I'm in New York. Like, *we're here*," and you can just kind of sense that excitement. So I don't know, for me as a bartender, I would just want to be kind to musicians, because as a touring musician, you just kind of wanted that same kindness. You're tired, you're broke, you're showing up in Baltimore, whatever it is, and just like a couple free drinks, and a little food and a little kindness goes a long way.

Andrew Possehl: They always seem to bring in really great bands, too. You can go there any given night and see some great bands.

John Farris: I'm not sure what the top-tier is at this point, but they sell out that room with pretty big acts. I remember U.S. Girls, who's a pretty big band at this point, it was completely sold out. I wouldn't have expected that so deep in Bushwick, like at what's essentially kind of a dive bar.

Vram Kherlopian: I feel like that's one of those places where I've seen just three people in the audience and like two hundred.

Tine Hill: You never know what you're gonna get.

Vram Kherlopian: The shades of Alphaville. It's just really funny. I've gone to see my New Jersey friends' bands playing there. And I'll get there and it's like, me, and they're like, "Hey audience of Vram!" You know it's like, yup, we all have been there.

Patrick Phillips: I watched the band BODEGA, who are friends of mine, play their first shows there and just grow and get better and bigger crowds. Even on our new record, I wrote a song called "Hole In The Wall" about the Alphaville experience. Just being close to the music and being able to see bands just kind of come together and work out their kinks and grow. I liked being on the ground floor of that. That's just a very Brooklyn thing to me.

Rosie Slater: The first time I met Lydia was at Alphaville. New Myths did a show with Total Slacker. I remember seeing Lydia, like, she's so cool!

Tine Hill: The Public Practice record release show.

Lydia Gammill: That was our first big show. Public Practice were coming out of the gate swinging, and I was like, these guys are cool, I need to align myself with these guys. And they were nice, and they liked us, and they did us a favor. That was a big show that we really got in front of like, a certain part of the community and got to establish ourselves.

Natalie Kirch: There was also 2019, we released our EP *Gamma Gardening* and Chris from Future Punx was the sound engineer for that. It was really fun, we felt super supported, the place was packed out, the sound system was great.

Zach Ellis: We had a really good show there once, and Mark Brickman hit me in the face with his bass guitar and he cut my eye open somehow. I was bleeding all over. That was fun. Actually, that was the first day of our tour. Our takeoff show was at Alphaville, and then for the rest of the tour it was just like a big purple shiner.

Rosie Slater: Delicate Steve, we finished up a tour with two nights in New York. And I just remember the one at Alphaville. I don't know what was going on with the fog machine, but we couldn't see anything. It was just a wall of fog, and I look over and Steve is standing on an amplifier. And those ceilings are not terribly high, and he's a tall guy. I think it was Chris from The Muckers' amp, and it was on wheels, and Steve is just kind of skateboarding himself around on this amplifier on stage.

Patrick Phillips: I got arrested at Alphaville while I was working. I had an open-alcohol-container unpaid ticket from 2009 or 2008, and there was some noise complaints from an upstairs neighbor who had recently moved in. I think this person called 311 like thirty-five times over the course of a week.

So one night, I'm training this new employee, and probably thirty minutes into my shift, like sixteen cops from all these different precincts raid the venue. And I don't know what it was. I think they might have been sweeping the neighborhoods and venues and stuff. But I tried to contact the managers and the bosses and to no avail. And I was kind of stuck in charge of the situation, and a lot of the patrons were getting angry, and there's a lot of really crazy energy happening. So I tried to be as nice as I could, but it kind of ended up ruining me in the long run because they ended up taking my ID, running it, finding out about the unpaid ticket, and I ended up staying in jail for thirty-one hours.

It was Martin Luther King Jr. weekend, I had just sprained my ankle two days before, it was probably like fifteen degrees. It was a really eye-opening experience, but I came through the other side, I think, a little bit stronger. That was just a night at Alphaville I'll never forget. I showed up to work and then just ended up getting released from jail two days later.

Baby's All Right

Amelia Bushell (Grim Streaker); Alex Chappo (CHAPPO); Steele Kratt (Steele FC); Paul Hammer (Savoir Adore); Gillian Visco (Shadow Monster); Rosie Slater, Tarra Thiessen (Sharkmuffin); Kristof Denis (Deep Sea Peach Tree); Emir Mohseni, John Zimmerman (The Muckers); Michelle Birsky (Birch); Michael Tarnofsky (Edna); Ryan Egan

Amelia Bushell: Baby's All Right always just brings me to life.

Alex Chappo: They curate the vibe nice, the look and the feel of the place.

Steele Kratt: It's a really fun place to play.

Paul Hammer: I love Baby's All Right. I have a little bit of a problem with venues where it feels like you watch a show and you're immediately kicked out. Baby's, you play a show and then you hang out all night. It's about music, and it's about the community. It's a sweet fucking bar, and it's where everyone is hanging out, regardless of the show.

Amelia Bushell: When Baby's All Right first opened, that was definitely like a hub. It just always seems to have a built-in crowd, which is kind of cool as well, because I never really feel like I'm playing to an empty room there. It always feels like there's a lot of people there.

Gillian Visco: Baby's is one of my favorite places to go see shows. Any time anyone's like, "Oh, we're playing Baby's," I'm like, I'll be at that show. I love that place.

Rosie Slater: I think I've played Baby's with almost every band I've ever played in.

Kristof Denis: I got into playing music when I was around eight, but I never really formed a real band until I was in high school. At the time, my friends and I would go to shows as much as possible, most of which were in Brooklyn, and most of my favorites were at Baby's.

Steele Kratt: I think that they're probably the best venue in New

York, because they cater to both unsigned and independent bands and signed bands.

John Zimmerman: Tons and tons of bands have played there. Small bands through really good big bands.

Kristof Denis: As a young eager-eared boy, I saw bands there like Acid Dad, Larry and the Babes, Twin Peaks, Mac DeMarco. Seeing live music like that at that age really seemed to get under my skin. I started writing a bunch of music with plans to form a band of my own.

Ryan Egan: When I first moved to New York, I moved not too far from here, and within that first year, this was opening. It was the coolest spot to play, and hard to play. At least, it felt that way.

Michelle Birsky: Playing Baby's All Right, you need to make sure you're on your A game. There's usually important people.

Michael Tarnofsky: Over time, that place still feels like a barometer. It used to be the hardest place to get booked at.

Ryan Egan: I think it was a goal to achieve as a local band. I eventually headlined here. That was special. That really feels good when you're pursuing a certain venue for a while.

Kristof Denis: Over the years, we've played a bunch of shows and released more music, and it seems like people are finally starting to notice. Trying to be successful in something like this takes a long time if done honestly, without daddy buying features in Pitchfork or record deals, but the long journey makes the good moments immensely rewarding and satisfying.

Michael Tarnofsky: It always felt like getting an email back from Baby's All Right, it was like, oh my god, we're about to be Aerosmith. Which was obviously never true, but it felt like the ceiling before Bowery Ballroom.

John Zimmerman: It's a legendary spot. Before I moved to New York, I held that place in a higher, as like a, "Wow, I really hope I can play there some day." Now we've played there so many times.

Emir Mohseni: In [maybe 2015], I wasn't in New York at that time,

I saw on my Instagram that King Gizzard played a big show somewhere in Brooklyn and then, after-party, there was another show they played at Baby's All Right. That's how I saw Baby's the first time. I was like, wow, this is such a cool place. Then I moved to New York, and the first show that we played was at Baby's All Right. And that was a dream that just came true at that time.

Kristof Denis: I had always wanted to play there since I started going in high school, so it really came full circle for me when we got the offer to play there opening for Lunar Vacation. It was definitely one of our best shows to date. Baby's is just such a solid venue with great vibes.

Rosie Slater: The people who work there are super cool.

Steele Kratt: You know, everyone on the staff knows you and remembers you.

Amelia Bushell: Loved it, and I still love playing there because the sound system is so good.

Rosie Slater: The sound people at Baby's are some of my favorite people in the whole world. You walk in and you're like, cool, the gear is in great shape and even if we screw everything up, there's someone running everything that will make it sound okay. That's my favorite thing. As long as the sound person is good, I'm happy.

Tarra Thiessen: Sloppy Jane did a residency there that was amazing. I was blown away by it because they had a fifteen-piece band or something, and it sounded great. And at that level, when you're playing DIY spots and mid-size bars, it's hard to get everything sounding good, so I was really impressed. Gustaf played with Sloppy Jane, and at the end of it, I saw Haley from Sloppy Jane talking to Nick Zinner in the green room from the Yeah Yeah Yeahs. I'm a crazy Yeah Yeah Yeahs fan, and I, I didn't say hi. I'm awful at those things.

The Broadway
Jono Bernstein, Jessica Louise Dye (High Waisted); Ethan Alexander (So and So); Gillian Visco (Shadow Monster);

Zach Ellis (Dead Tooth); Nico E.P. (Deaf Poets); Connor Jones, William Thompson (Yella Belly); Gino Gianoli (Duke of Vandals); Dan Barrecchia, Joey Giambra, Ed Weisgerber (Shred Flintstone)

Jessica Louise Dye: A lot of these places that have left opened up room for new spaces to fill in. So I know we were one of the first bands to play The Gateway a bazillion years ago.

Jono Bernstein: Which is now The Broadway. It was Paradise and then it turned into The Gateway.

Ethan Alexander: Before it was The Broadway, it was The Gateway, a pretty infamous, trashy place.

Gillian Visco: I have a few fond memories of The Gateway. Some people have other types of memories from The Gateway. I always had a great time there.

Zach Ellis: I went there once, and the amp they had hadn't been turned on in a very long time and just sounded like there were bees in it or some shit. But The Broadway, they turned that shit around.

Nico E.P.: They've been having a lot of sick shows. One of the first times we checked it out, we came to watch The Muckers, which is a sick band. Sound is incredible, the vibe is awesome.

Gillian Visco: The sound system is amazing.

Ethan Alexander: The one thing that everyone always says about that place is that the sound for the musicians is incredible. So instead of it sounding like a garbled mess, you know, they really put in the extra mile to make the electronic side of it good, which I don't think many other places, even venues, think about. Even the indie soft-boi rock people who come in there are like, "Wow, it sounds so clear." If the prima donnas of the scene like it, I guess it's pretty good.

Gillian Visco: Since they opened, a lot of our friends have started bartending there. That just always makes it better. It's nice. It feels like home.

Connor Jones: One of my co-workers at Reclamation and a good friend of ours works there, so that's my new Monday [and] Tuesday go-to. Also, my good buddy Eric works there, and you should tip him.

William Thompson: We are all about the tipping.

Connor Jones: Yeah, that's how we survive!

Ethan Alexander: It's the best bar job I've ever had. The people who did the hiring, specifically Lance, you can tell he was trying to create a group of people that would actually get along with each other and enjoy working there. And I think that shows.

I also think that all the people that work at Broadway are kind of sassy people. I know that there's probably several people who've had a bad experience at Broadway specifically because all of us don't really put up with a lot of the same bar bullshit that a lot of other bars put up with, which is one thing I really like, and I know that when my friends come in, they kind of like that, too. You know, if there's an old man ordering a Manhattan with his wife, thinking they're gonna relive the glory days, they're probably gonna have a really bad time at Broadway.

Gino Gianoli: We played a few times there. We felt like every time that we were there, it was just a party.

Ethan Alexander: Getting gigs there isn't that hard as long as you can make sure people come out, which is one thing I always appreciated about Broadway, as opposed to other places. Like you really can play any genre of music. We've had drag shows there. It's not just a punk bar. Even though the staff would probably fool you on that.

Jono Bernstein: Paradise was around for so long in that area of Brooklyn. Whoever is holding that spot needs to understand that they're a big part of the community beyond just throwing like rock shows.

Ethan Alexander: I will say out of any of the places I've ever played in Brooklyn, The Broadway goes above and beyond to take care of the musicians. Especially in this scene, as a musician in Brooklyn, [everyone] understands at some level that they're never gonna make it. They're never gonna make any money. And at the end of the day, you're doing it because you love it, not because you're trying to make money. But it is really nice when the bar is not trying to screw you over.

Joey Giambra: They always treat us really good there. It's just really great hospitality, everything's really organized, they really help out the bands, making sure that they get the funds that they need.

Gillian Visco: There's tacos and they feed their musicians, which is really cool. They're like, "Here's your drink tickets and here's your taco tickets."

Ed Weisgerber: And the green room with the private bathroom. That's a major plus.

Ethan Alexander: It's like a choose-your-own-vibe adventure book. You can just have casual cocktails, play pool. Or you can sit at the bar, do beers and shots, or go upstairs and see a show, or go downstairs and sober up.

Gillian Visco: They definitely put a lot of attention into the aesthetic of the room. It's like this weird Quentin Tarantino vibe downstairs, retro, like the seventies.

Dan Barrecchia: It's kinda this old-fashioned spot. It's nice, but at the same time it has this old spirit to it. There's something really cool about that place that I can't put my finger on.

Ed Weisgerber: It's got some magic.

Dan Barrecchia: There's some magic there, like you'd see that place in a movie.

Brooklyn Steel
Leah Lavigne (Ok Cowgirl); Ryan Egan

Ryan Egan: I love Brooklyn Steel so much. The sound is probably my favorite in the city.

Leah Lavigne: I have so many favorite places in Brooklyn, primarily concert venues, but one of my favorites is definitely Brooklyn Steel. I've gotten into way too many shows there for free just because I know a bunch of people who work there. (Thanks crew, love y'all.) To me it's the perfect-size venue. Anything larger and you lose the ambience and the ability to see and connect to the artist as a person rather than some ant-sized demigod.

I love small intimate venues, but people [equal] energy, and being packed into an 1800-capacity room with professional-grade lighting and stage design can just make for such a rich experience. I also love that Brooklyn Steel manages to showcase a lot of new bands that are just blowing up as well as underplays of more established bands.

Ryan Egan: I went to an LCD Soundsystem show. A friend offered me tickets, and it ended up being one of the best shows I've ever seen, I think. I was stunned by how good of a live band they were. The gear on stage was unbelievable. Vintage studio gear, synths, in a huge venue, and they made it home because their team just dialed in that room so well. It sounded so good. That was a mind-blowing concert, nothing really lives up to it since. I've gone to a couple really good shows there, but damn, that's how you set up shop in this venue and nail it.

C'mon Everybody
Mitchell Parrish (Fever Dolls)

It was just one of those nights: Everything went right. We'd been pushing this show for weeks. After not playing for two months, I connected with Eric, the GM of C'mon Everybody, through a friend, and we put together a bill with our friends Ali Dineen and Record High. It was our first show in Brooklyn. And in a lot of ways, it felt like our first show as a band. Fresh off releasing our second single and music video "Adeline," there was a lot of momentum, both creatively and interpersonally. We crammed hours of rehearsal time in Battalion Studios during the coldest weekends in February, reworking arrangements, perfecting interludes and, of course, a few on-stage antics.

Sometimes, everything just goes right. Eric took a chance on us.

And having never played in Brooklyn before, we were rolling the dice ourselves. But at a place like C'mon Everybody, where the drinks are affordable, the sound is dialed, and the attitude is "Get in here and welcome to the team," the odds are in your favor.

A few days before, my mom confirmed that she was flying up from Charlotte to see my new band for the first time. Without pretense, during the band introduction interlude of the set, our frontman Evan bellows, "And Mitchell's mom is in the building!" The sold-out crowd roars in applause. That's the beauty of C'mon Everybody. Your mom is not only welcome but celebrated.

I really don't remember the set that well. I didn't even feel like I was playing the bass. I just remember looking out into a sea of smiling faces, singing along and dancing. Afterwards, Eric walked up to me and told me that it was one of the best sets he's seen at his little venue in Bed-Stuy.

You don't expect that kind of care or attention at your run-of-the-mill venue. C'mon Everybody is different. Every email, every text, even the settlement was a symphony of compassion and kindness. It's places like this that remind you why you started playing music and seeing shows in the first place.

The Gutter
Connor Gladney, Laura Valk (Skout); Meredith Lampe (Work Wife); Patrick Porter (A Very Special Episode); Gino Gianoli (Duke of Vandals); Scott Kodi

Laura Valk: I feel like The Gutter is kind of legendary in Brooklyn.

Connor Gladney: You can come in here to drink, you can come in here to drink and bowl, you can come in here to drink, bowl and play pool. Or any combo.

Meredith Lampe: The Gutter is one of my favorite spots in BK. Some of the first pals I made in the music scene used to take me out here for their late-night half-off bowling lanes. We'd shoot pool on their slightly off-kilter table in the front while we waited for it to get late enough, 1 a.m.? 2? I can't even remember, to get the cheap lanes. Ironically, I went there probably ten times before I found out there was a venue in the back!

Laura Valk: There's also a venue in the back. It's fun to wander in on any given Thursday, Friday, Saturday and see what's happening.

Patrick Porter: One of the coolest parts about the Spare Room is how going to shows, whether as part of a band or as a spectator, is always feeling like you're part of a secret club that meets in the hall out behind the bar's stretch of bathrooms. Always looking forward to the next night we can pack into that back room with our friends.

Scott Kodi: If I had a dream about a local show, it would probably take place in that dark, loud, invariably friend-filled room. And I always enjoy getting roped into bowling by bandmates who insist it's really not all that late.

Patrick Porter: So many memories have been made in their Spare Room, and it is an integral part of countless artists' stories, including our own.

The last time we put out an album we had our EP release show at The Gutter. It was where we had our first gig with Chayse in the band, where we played our first Brooklyn Drum Collective showcase, and where we kicked off our first extended tour. The Gutter's also where we usually look forward to Pizza Fest each year, where I almost died from a crowd-surfing incident during The Royal They's party for *Foreign Being*, and the spot where we first saw so many of our favorites.

Gino Gianoli: Gutter will always be a special place in Duke of Vandals' history. It was there, after a few rounds of Jameson shots, where the band came together, and after more Jameson, where we played our first gig as a band.

At the time, there was a practice place in the building next to Gutter. Missy, Danny and I had recently started jamming there and sharing the place with another band. The point of those initial sessions was to try out ideas and see how far we could take this.

After two, three hours sweating it out in a nine-by-nine room with a leaking AC, we would head to Gutter for beers and whiskey and a few rounds of pool. Sometimes the place was packed and loud. Some other times it was empty and loud. One night, after watching a band play in the back room, we realized we could do it better and louder. Duke of Vandals was born.

About four or five months later, we had become regulars. Beers and shots came and went. Discussions of how the practice went, or new ideas to try next time, were all we would talk about. One night one of the bartenders, who also happened to promote and book bands, asked if we were playing any gigs anytime soon. Instead of replying that we were still working on songs and our sound, I said that actually we had nothing booked for the rest of the month.

"Cool," he said. "A band dropped off the bill for next week's show here. It's yours if you want it."

We looked at each other.

"Hell yeah!"

Mind you, we hadn't played a single show yet. We hardly had our songs fully finished. But here was an opportunity, and we'd better take it and figure out the details later.

After a few shots to celebrate our unexpected first booking, reality set in. Oh shit, now we actually have to play a thirty-five minute set. Do we have enough songs? Do we actually know the songs inside out? We were about to find out.

That week was a whirlwind of rehearsals, reworking finished songs and finishing new ones. As far as everyone was concerned we were just another band on the bill. For us however, this was do or die.

The date arrives. The time is up. You guys are next. Step on stage and take your place. A quick soundcheck. The chatter in the room gradually dies and attention is redirected. Towards the stage. Towards you. One, two, three, four, the drum kicks, the bass booms, the guitar shrieks. The ruckus begins. It's a wave, and you gotta ride it.

After the show, we all ended up back at the bar doing Jameson shots, high on adrenaline and knowing for certain that this was just the beginning of the adventure. This was our very first gig, but only we knew that. Later that night, the promoter came to have a drink with us.

"Cool show," he said. "You wanna play in two weeks?"

We looked at each other.

"Hell yeah!"

Hart Bar
Mary-Louise Hildebrandt (Maladaptive Mistress); My Son The Doctor (Brian Hemmert, Joel Kalow, John Mason, Matt Nitzberg)

Mary-Louise Hildebrandt: Hart Bar in Bushwick is a Brooklyn gem.

My Son The Doctor: We're a broken record here, but Hart Bar is such an underrated venue in Bushwick. Shout-out to Dares, Pinkie Promise, Henry Black, and many others we've played with there.

Mary-Louise Hildebrandt: I first went there for a basement show not knowing I would discover my new favorite bar. The atmosphere is witchy and wholesome with great food and a staff so genuine that they didn't even mind when I ordered a soda without liquid spirits there!

Littlefield
Brandi Thompson (Brandi and the Alexanders)

This is the place where my professional music career began. It's a longer story, but right after I quit my job and needed to start finding paying gigs, I got offered a background vocalist gig here. It was this old-school soul revue they were putting on at Littlefield once a month or once every other month. You get up there with a bona fide soul artist from like the fifties. So, they're old, but they're still doing their thing. They're seventy, eighty years old, and performing. Like, some of them got moves, some of them would just sit in a chair. They all could still sing. It was just a really cool first foray into really getting paid for singing. It was nice to be able to be like, I'm getting paid to do something I really enjoy doing.

Muchmore's
Moon Kissed (Khaya Cohen, Leah Scarpati, Emily Sgouros); Vram Kherlopian, Tarra Thiessen (Gustaf); NAHreally

NAHreally: Other than my apartment, my favorite spot in Brooklyn is Muchmore's in Williamsburg. I've rapped there more than anywhere else other than my apartment. It somehow feels like a cross between your grandma's living room and a grungy music venue, in the best possible way. Shows at Muchmore's always feel extra organic and real, and even a small crowd can make the room feel full. The stage is small, and the room gets really hot, but the bartenders are good people, and I've never had a bad time there.

Moon Kissed: The live room is yours if you book Muchmore's for the night. Anything can happen. No bodies are being policed, but instead all are invited to sweat on the "dance floor" then chill on the dusty couches in the back. The stage is messy in the best way. The bathroom is spacious, filled with stickers advertising local artists, and rumor has it people fucked in there during the first party.

Tarra Thiessen: There's a hot tub on the roof of Muchmore's that leaks, which I've never gone into. There's weird stories about the hot tub, but the main thing is that it leaks, which is why Muchmore's can be kind of fucked up.

Moon Kissed: Muchmore's feels like it has zero rules. It's tiny and fairly hidden. They don't have a liquor license. The bartender, who we're pretty sure never blinks, will hook it up with beers, wines and shots of Soju all night long. There's an outdoor area with a few tables for smoking, belligerence, and striking up conversation with new friends. Then there's the entrance, the narrow front room with a bar on the back left and couches and tables in the front. Across from the bar to the right is the live room. There's sometimes a sound guy or door person, but usually you're running that shit yourself.

Tarra Thiessen: I did sound at Muchmore's for a while before I started bartending there, and [they have] laundry there, so I would do my laundry during my sound gig.

Vram Kherlopian: Tarra would do the Sunday bartending shift from like twelve-to-six, and then we'd all show up.

Tarra Thiessen: And do laundry.

Vram Kherlopian: Lydia would make Gustaf merch, t-shirts.

Tarra Thiessen: Drink and draw with like two people there and all my friends. This was like the kinda job I only had to give my friends free alcohol and do my laundry and like, get up before 12 p.m. one day a week. That was fun. Muchmore's is such a shit show.

Moon Kissed: One December, we hosted these three residency parties at Muchmore's called Can't Deny The Chemistry, named after "Muscle Memory," a single from our first album.

The idea and themes for the party were born from an intense desire to be a part of something bigger than us. In the LCD Soundsystem song "New York, I Love You But You're Bringing Me Down," James Murphy sings, "Take me off your mailing list for kids that think it still exists yes, for those who think it still exists." We are those "kids" he's referring to, and we wanted to prove him wrong because we *knew* that our community had the potential to unleash the amount of fire and electricity that the song claimed had faded from the city.

We sat down with our manager, Brian, who was around for the magic during the period this song is referring to, the late nineties and early 2000s NYC made famous by bands like the Strokes and the Yeah Yeah Yeahs. We asked him, what about that time made going out so exhilarating? Brian leaned forward and said, "Sex." Everyone was fucking each other, so it was all about who's gonna be out tonight, and who will I go home with tonight, and will my crush be at the show? You know, that giddy excitement that lures you out night after night no matter how tired or hungover you are.

We wanted to bring that energy back. Not the pressure to fuck at the end of the night, but the excitement of being in the same room with a bunch of beautiful, young human beings, meeting and bonding and feeling intense euphoria and giddiness. And Muchmore's was the spot to do it.

We themed the three parties Sex, Drugs, and Rock and Roll. They occurred the first three Thursdays that December, and we booked our friends Von, Sara Neal, and Muriel to perform accordingly. Each week was a special and unique blend of the same and new people, and by the end, I [Khaya] felt as if I had woken up for the first time in a long time.

Music Hall of Williamsburg
Abner James, Harper James (Eighty Ninety); Jon Sandler (Great Good Fine Ok); Alex Chappo (CHAPPO)

Abner James: Music Hall of Williamsburg is probably our favorite venue to see shows at and probably that we've played. It's the perfect size, where you feel like you're at an intimate show.

Jon Sandler: That was a venue where I always went, and I always thought the sound was so good before GGFO started.

Harper James: I think it's the best-sounding venue in New York. They have this excellent staff of sound people, and the room is perfectly designed for going to see a lot of medium-size bands. I don't know if Imagine Dragons would sound good in there, but—

Abner James: Probably.

Harper James: But probably.

Jon Sandler: Music Hall of Williamsburg is a place where we've had a lot of our most special shows. Our first big sold-out show in New York was there. It was the last show of a tour and I got really sick. I had laryngitis and bronchitis and a fever.

I was totally panicked. To me, this was like the biggest show of my life. I was so sick all day, making everybody else nervous. But you know when you hear about mothers lifting a car off their child? It was like adrenaline kicked in, and it was one of the greatest shows that I can remember.

Alex Chappo: That was like awesome to be able to play that place, just because I'd seen so many cool bands come through there.

Jon Sandler: It's really dreams-come-true kinda stuff. Even during rehearsal, you're standing on the stage and there's no one there, but you're like, wow, this is amazing. Performing is my favorite thing ever, so the stage is like my temple. I'm not a religious person, but that's appropriate. It's almost a religious experience performing on a stage you've seen a million shows on.

There's lots of great spots in New York that we've played, but for some reason that place, there's just a really good feeling about it.

The Nest
Superbloom (Tim Choate, Brian DiMeglio, Matteo Dix, David Newman); Annie Nirschel

Superbloom: The Nest is actually a dive bar and live venue in the basement of another bar called Bluebird. It has zero Yelp reviews and it's amazing. There really isn't that much to say about the venue itself. It has minimal to no seating, and insanely heavy bands playing ninety-nine percent of the time in a basement. But the folks who run the place, book bands and very importantly, run sound there, make it hands-down the best joint for a certain type of band, i.e. loud. A shout-out to Graham Fahey for booking us multiple times and generally just being a legend. More about the hero Sam Barna shortly.

Annie Nirschel: The Nest is an incredible independent venue on Flatbush that we've come to know intimately. Once as a headliner for a solo heavy metalist, once in the middle of a Halloween show with a local band Winner Camp and a screamo version of their radio hit "What do a egg do?", once as the closer at a local taping of the Bobby Bop show with host Bobby Bop, notorious Space Eel, and his corn-loving brother Doug.

We've also seen Hot Topic's favorite customers, Cara and Russ, play in their industrial death metal band, GLDN. We've seen big-time comedians, improv, burlesque shows, and have consistently been remembered by the Nest's dad, Karl, the legendary purveyor of underground Brooklyn's counter-culture goodness.

Superbloom: The Nest also has a special place in our hearts because first, it was the scene of the crime for our first on-stage, guitar-throwing rock-star moment. Second, it's where we met our spirit animal in the form of sound engineer and lights/smoke machine master of puppets, Sam Barna.

As any band can attest to regardless of where they live, the band vs. sound-person relationship can be a delicate and often fraught game. We have not always been totally fortunate in that realm, though definitely one hundred percent never for faults of our own. So when you meet someone like Sam, who not only encourages you to be loud, not only offers to help record your barely listenable set with your silly zoom recorder, not only is clearly very knowledgeable and also a very nice person, but who mid-set starts to play into your delusions of grandeur by improvising a spur-of-the-moment light show *synchronized to the beat of your songs which he has never heard*, and then proceeds to top that by firing off a fucking *smoke machine*, well, when that happens, then you know you're in the right place. And that place is The Nest.

Also, tequila shots.

Our Wicked Lady

Nick LaFalce (Atlas Engine); Shane Preece (Max Pain and the Groovies); Dane Zarra (Oil Bay); Gillian Visco (Shadow Monster); Kate Black, Nikki Sisti (THICK); Zach Ellis (Dead Tooth); Joe Dahlstrom (Hot Knives); Johnny Dynamite (Johnny Dynamite and the Bloodsuckers); Parrot Dream (Kiki Appel, Gonzalo Guerrero); Matt Bernstein (Wet Leather); Emily Ashenden (95 Bulls); Michelle Birsky (Birch); Kira Metcalf

Nick LaFalce: More often than not I'm at Our Wicked Lady.

Shane Preece: Our Wicked Lady, that's a favorite. I guess it was one of the first places we started hanging out when we came here.

Dane Zarra: We have deep, deep love for Our Wicked Lady.

Gillian Visco: I love this place because everyone from the owners to the staff, to all the people that play there, to the people that do the door, everyone is super sweet and nice.

Nick LaFalce: I remember just within the first few times I went I was just meeting so many people that were so just authentic and cool and playing in cool bands and doing interesting things.

Kate Black: You can tell that the bar is owned by people who are invested in and part of the music community in Brooklyn. They created a really welcoming place to play music. It's never stressful and always feels like you're just part of the fam.

Gillian Visco: We played there, and we were on the roof and Keith, one of the owners, is bartending in the back. It feels very homegrown. It's like family when you're there. *When you're here, you're family.*

Zach Ellis: Zach and Keith, they have been doing shows and going to shows forever. Zach's old band, they're called Bugs in the Dark, we played with them at Brooklyn Bowl once. And they were just always the sweetest people. When we found out they were opening a venue, we're like, that's gonna be the spot, that's the shit. Like, those people are just the coolest fucking people, they're gonna make this awesome. They were always just about shows, you know, and that's why I feel like a place like that will last.

Joe Dahlstrom: They put in their work. They worked really hard, and they're still working really hard.

Zach Ellis: I think Our Wicked Lady is just really like a perfect blend of professional and just cool people running it. Like, it's clearly a very legal and wonderful establishment, but you don't feel like you're in some snooty venue.

Johnny Dynamite: I've been so thankful for their presence in our little scene.

Parrot Dream: Our Wicked Lady is a great community spot. We'd often run into folks we knew there.

Gillian Visco: I'm there like, three times a week. Like, when I open my Uber app, it automatically suggests Our Wicked Lady.

Parrot Dream: We've been practicing at the adjacent studios for a while now, so we've spent quite a lot of time in that building. Many band practices and band drinks, hot toddies, Braven and Tecates mostly, were had at Our Wicked Lady, and a lot of the writing for our full-length album, *Light Goes*, was done there as well, so this spot is very much present on our band's timeline.

Matt Bernstein: It's right by our practice space, so we can just roll everything down the hill after.

Nikki Sisti: This venue is right near our practice space and something I bike past on a daily basis. I usually know people standing out front and get pulled in for a drink or ten. I find the venue to be really welcoming and it's open to a variety of different genres and groups of people.

Dane Zarra: We've had many hangouts on the rooftop, watching our friends and bandmates playing in their sidebands.

Emily Ashenden: It's where we [95 Bulls] were conceived like a big angry baby.

Johnny Dynamite: They have such a welcoming vibe, and their roof will always be my first choice for throwing a big show. I remember when I moved to Bushwick, I would pass the venue on my way home from work and hear all the noise bellowing from their rooftop.

Michelle Birsky: That was how I learned about Our Wicked Lady the first time. I heard music, and I was like, where the hell is that coming from? We ran upstairs and it was some weird night where they were passing out Jager shots. After that, I was like, we need to play this roof!

Johnny Dynamite: At the time I thought, damn, I hope I can play that roof someday, thinking it was some exclusive spot. But it's not, it's for the community.

Shane Preece: Playing there with fuckin' open skies and the breeze hitting you is just an epic, epic thing.

Nick LaFalce: Nothing beats that rooftop in the summer, unless you include a $4 Estrella and a $2 hot dog.

Zach Ellis: I love playing on the roof up there, but I think some of my favorite shows are right down in that bar area. Like, it's awkward as hell. People have to walk right in front of you to go to the bathroom. But it just feels so good in there when it's packed, and it sounds great, too.

Gillian Visco: Rich, who does sound there, is amazing.

Zach Ellis: He's a super pro.

Kira Metcalf: I first found myself at OWL for a Pom Pom Squad show in the summer of 2019, a time when it was wholly acceptable if not encouraged to throw yourself into a sweaty pile of strangers on a rooftop in Brooklyn with a tequila soda spilling down your arm. I loved the venue right away not only for its name or because the show was so good. Every room had an energy that was equal parts inviting and exciting, which can most assuredly be attributed to their killer staff.

Zach Ellis: Everybody that works there is essentially part of the community. Which is really cool. I'd imagine it's probably really fun to work there.

Joe Dahlstrom: A lot of Venn diagrams overlap at Our Wicked Lady. The Mystery Lights is sort of a bigger group and they had roots there, and then you look at Spite FuXXX. And Ethan [Alexander] is an incredible musician, he blows my mind.

It's a really friendly place, too. That means a lot. The bartenders have been nothing but generous with us and we were very grateful for that.

Nick LaFalce: They've got the best bartenders in town, consistently great booking, and they really go beyond with their weekly "Thursdays for the Cause" fundraiser shows.

Parrot Dream: Usually on a Tuesday or Thursday we'd head over for a drink after practice. Their show series, "Thursdays for the Cause," which raised money for a different organization each month, was always good to check out and did important work. If there wasn't live music at OWL, there would be comedy, parties, performance art and/or karaoke, and the energy was open and felt inclusive.

Nick LaFalce: I always like their vibe, what's going on any given night.

Nikki Sisti: They hosted one of the first Brooklyn Battle of the Bands, that I know of at least, and it was A LOT of fun to watch and support music that I would have not found on my own!

Kira Metcalf: This was the kind of place I needed to play. I got that opportunity a few months later when OWL hosted its annual Winter Madness battle of the bands-like tournament. We didn't win, but as they say at the Oscars, it was truly an honor just to be nominated.

Dane Zarra: We were picked as one of the sixteen bands to play in the Winter Madness tournament. This little addendum to our Oil Bay careers was an honorable and inspiring set of shows that we were so humbled to be a part of. The first night we won! We relished and enjoyed the victory! Sadly, in our second event we weren't able to make it to the third round. Honestly, it didn't matter. We had so much fun that the experience was all we needed and will never forget.

Nikki Sisti: My favorite memory is when THICK played a show there on the rooftop, before they had a canopy. We were headlining, and there was one more band before us. We saw the clouds above and knew a storm was on its way. The band before us was about to finish their set when it started to pour. The band continued to play their last song, and it was just really beautiful, all of us singing and dancing in the rain. Unfortunately, the rain was too much, and one of their amps exploded and *caught fire*! Rather than throw in the towel, the OWL staff kept the party going! They had the bands and the crowd help move all the gear to their downstairs bar. We were all soaked downstairs, and it felt like a house party. It was a *blast*, and I always really appreciated how the OWL staff was so easy-going and positive. They now have a canopy on their rooftop, so hopefully there will be no more exploding amps. Unless someone is rocking too hard.

Kate Black: *Yes!* That is one of my all-time favorite show memories. It was a sad day for OWL's new mixing board, but it was worth the scramble to pack everyone in downstairs. I vaguely remember shots being poured in our mouths while we were shouting our lyrics at the top of our lungs, standing on a table and not really being able to tell the difference between the rain and our sweat.

Michelle Birsky: We've had bad shows there, and we've had good shows there, and you know, it's just a community feel.

Dane Zarra: OWL will forever be in our hearts.

Gillian Visco: Our Wicked Lady is my home away from home.

Pete's Candy Store
Bandits on the Run (Adrian Blake Enscoe, Sydney Shepherd, Regina Strayhorn); Phantom Wave (Ian Carpenter, Rachel Fischer); Ben Thornewill (Jukebox the Ghost); Michael Hesslein (HESS); Hayes Peebles

Bandits on the Run: This place is a local music mainstay. For almost twenty years, this cozy but surprisingly ornate local joint has been a hub and a home for the off-kilter and under-the-radar.

Phantom Wave: We've played a couple gigs there, and even once with an old Ross Fame amp that Ian found on the street. It made for an interesting albeit skronky guitar evening.

Ben Thornewill: It is a little nothing venue of a venue. One of those stages that is like just high enough off the ground to make you trip and fall but not high enough to do anything else. And I mean, maybe standing you could get twenty-five people. Seated, it's just like fifteen people around the perimeter. And that's been a place that I've just loved going to and seeing my friends test out new songs or new material or play songs they haven't played before.

Michael Hesslein: I think my first solo show I ever played in New York was at Pete's Candy Store years ago, before I even thought I was going to ever release a solo record. It was one of the first places Mail the Horse ever played. Just like, squeezing a bunch of guys on that stage, which is insane. We had a pedal steel player and we had a full keyboard setup. It was totally ridiculous. But a couple of years after that, I played my first solo shows. I did like a once-a-month residency there, and I always loved to play that place when I felt like I needed to debut new material, or just kind of like a test venue for certain ideas. I loved how intimate it was, and it felt like you could pack thirty of your friends in there and it would feel like three hundred.

Hayes Peebles: I've been playing music and releasing music and performing since I was like thirteen. I always considered myself a musician and always thought of that being my primary goal in life, but for a while I just really didn't act like that at all. I got a full-time job as a copywriter and would occasionally write and keep music in the back of my mind, but maybe not actively pursue it. Then, once I started to lean into it a bit more and really wanted to play again, the first place I did play was Pete's, and Pete's would continuously book me.

I think a really important part of any music scene is getting a foot through the door, and whenever I try to book shows in different towns or cities, I always look for a place like that, where they have a lot of different artists every night and it's a small room, giving people the opportunity to just play. Because it doesn't really exist everywhere.

Ben Thornewill: For me, it's like a real return to what shows used to be like, which is like, kinda terrible, but in a great way. And by that, I mean like, no pressure. It's not this whole big thing, where half of the stress is selling tickets or, you know, it's the event. It's like, you're just gonna go to this place, you're gonna get a drink. They make great greasy grilled cheeses, and you can watch your friends play at a tiny little venue in the back.

Phantom Wave: It's a place to have a casual intimate gig with great beers on tap and delicious paninis. Also there's a decent roomy backyard that's great to hang in on a breezy night.

Ben Thornewill: It's a really, really cool space.

Michael Hesslein: It's like the perfect date spot, too. I brought dates there when I wasn't even playing. It felt magical to be back there on just like, a random day. Lifelong friends I've met at that place. One of my best friends, she was a fan at first. I met her at a show. That was like ten years ago. That's what Pete's can bring to you, you know, and I just love that place. Pete's is a special place.

Prospect Park Bandshell
Paul Hammer (Savoir Adore); Lucia Pontoniere (The Ladles); Ben Thornewill (Jukebox the Ghost)

Paul Hammer: The Bandshell in Prospect Park. That's the coolest fucking thing, a bucket-list thing to be able to play that. It's such a Brooklyn level-up achievement.

Lucia Pontoniere: You know, it's a free show, and you can get right up there and see the most amazing bands. And it's a beautiful park.

Ben Thornewill: They do concerts all summer long. Sometimes they're ticketed, and they're sold out and you can't get in. A lot of them are free. But there's a huge field right next to the stage, and so the other thing to do is just go lay out on a blanket, or kick around a soccer ball or just hang out. There's a whole community of people that are just mooching off the free concerts just on the other side of the fence.

Rough Trade
Kevin Olken Henthorn (Cape Francis); Nicholas LaGrasta (Teen Commandments); Jake Hiebert, Connor Jones, Jack McLoughlin, William Thompson (Yella Belly); Adam Holtzberg, Eric Nizgretsky, Manny Silverstein (Loose Buttons)

Kevin Olken Henthorn: I love playing Rough Trade. I just love that venue.

Nicholas LaGrasta: It kind of reminds me of Empire Records. You know, if it was a real place but it also had the addition of an amazing music venue. And that's certainly one of our favorite places to play.

And if we're not playing there, then it's also a great place to like, go have coffee and go record shopping.

William Thompson: I think that's one of our favorite venues.

Connor Jones: That's my favorite venue to play by far.

William Thompson: I like Rough Trade a lot because I feel like it's one of the last venues that actually kind of respects artists a little bit more. There's a hospitality person there. You would see them all the time, but I mean, that was the first position to get cut whenever venues would go downhill.

Connor Jones: I also think it was actually designed to be a music venue. Like, the sound in there is actually good. It was built properly.

William Thompson: A well-vetted sound person and a hospitality service. Artists can't get over that.

Connor Jones: They have beers! They give you pita chips and hummus.

Jake Hiebert: We actually got our rider accepted. We got pizza, a bottle of whiskey, and decent beer.

Connor Jones: But that was last time. We changed it.

William Thompson: We have chips and salsa.

Jack McLoughlin: Five-and-a-half Juuls.

William Thompson: Bon & Vivs.

Jake Hiebert: We changed it to Bon & Vivs?

Connor Jones: We talked about it.

Eric Nizgretsky: Rough Trade is an important venue for us.

Adam Holtzberg: I've seen great shows there.

Eric Nizgretsky: It's definitely a good room.

Manny Silverstein: It's just a good size. It's big enough that it's a real thing and you don't feel like you're just playing in some bar or something, but it's small enough that if you go to a show, it's really intimate. If you're playing a show, you're not like, how the hell are we going to get anyone to this gigantic venue?

Eric Nizgretsky: And when you're on stage, the way it's set up, it just feels more intimate.

Adam Holtzberg: At least for me, I think it was the first show we played at Rough Trade, it was a sold-out show, and seeing everyone, top tier and bottom tier, filled out, was just very, "We made it!"

Kevin Olken Henthorn: I think one of our last group of gigs as Stone Cold Fox, we played Rough Trade and sold it out, and it's a great feeling. It's just a great room. It's a perfect-size venue. I'll hopefully have a different perspective on that in a couple years, but right now it's the perfect size.

Saint Vitus
Proper. (Erik Garlington, Natasha Johnson, Elijah Watson); Ray McGale (Color Tongue)

Proper.: Saint Vitus has been an institution since day one. From the Nirvana tribute show with the surviving members, to Carrie Brownstein of Sleater-Kinney hosting a conversation with Questlove, this venue hit the ground running.

Ray McGale: It's the Greenpoint metal bar. It's really cool. They have the upside-down crosses and stuff like that. It's very tongue-in-cheek. The place has a great sense of what they are. It's such a fun bar to see a show at or hang out. It's a good time.

Proper.: You also never know who you're gonna see just hanging out there. Once I [Elijah] saw Björk at a show there that Queens hardcore band Show Me the Body was headlining. And I'll never forget my friend yelling loudly enough for Björk to hear, "Yo! That's Björk!"

Ray McGale: There's always very interesting shows there. After the Grammys, or whatever it was where they did that shitty bootleg Nirvana reunion with Paul McCartney, they did a secret show there. So they'll do big shows like that, but like, we played there one Monday night.

Proper.: Although they primarily lean towards heavier music, the sound is so good they can cater to all genres, and they make it a point to do so. I [Erik] once saw Bartees Strange perform with a full string section, and it was one of the most moving pieces I've ever heard.

I [Natasha] have been going to Saint Vitus for about as long as I lived in New York. Living in Bed-Stuy at the time, I would take the B43 which drops you off right in front of the venue. Whether it's risking my life watching The Suicide File to relive my early 2000s hardcore days, singing my heart out along to Red City Radio at a 2 p.m. matinee, or zoning out in front of about ten full stacks squeezed on a twenty-foot-wide stage getting physically blown away by Sleep. I can also count on great sound and a memorable time. It also doesn't hurt that the awesome staff recognizes me and my drink order only from going to shows.

Each one of us had unique experiences with the venue, and the first convergence was when Iron Chic reached out to us to play on February 28, 2020. This also happened to be the same day as Natasha's birthday, which she absolutely took to heart by wearing a pink prom dress the whole night. At the end of the set, the crowd started a "Happy Birthday" chant which Natasha until this day quotes as her favorite song. While we didn't know at the time it would be the last show we would play that year, we sure did play like it was. The sold-out show was a memorable experience that left a lasting mark with all of us. Saint Vitus is of the few existing places in Brooklyn where we can see friends play on the same stage as legends of their genre. Its quality in people, sound and event choices stands out among the rest.

The Sultan Room
Anthony Azarmgin, Emir Mohseni, John Zimmerman (The Muckers); Jono Bernstein, Jessica Louise Dye (High Waisted); Brit Boras, Marina Ross, Rosie Slater (New Myths); Melissa Lucciola (Gustaf); Blu DeTiger

John Zimmerman: The whole place is called Turk's, and it's like a restaurant on the first floor, a venue on the second floor, and a rooftop bar.

Emir Mohseni: Beautiful space.

Anthony Azarmgin: And the food! Oh, my god. The food, the drinks, the sound, the vibe.

Blu DeTiger: The Turk's Inn is my favorite spot in Brooklyn right now. The food at the Turkish restaurant is amazing, but they also have a beautiful rooftop and a venue for live performances. I tried some new Turkish dessert, which was amazing, then headed up to the roof to check it out, and everyone up there was listening intently to the artist performing up there.

John Zimmerman: That place is awesome. They did a really, really good job.

Jono Bernstein: I was brought on as a production manager, and from the start it was a crazy project, and I couldn't believe we were doing it. I feel like this is a spot where every person who was involved in it, they may have not been in New York that long, but they had this really clear vision of what they wanted for the restaurant, and then also for the venue. And it was really crazy to step into a place where they had enough resources to make this dream a reality.

Blu DeTiger: The actual venue has the coolest stage and lighting set-up. It's a psychedelic, kaleidoscope-looking backdrop, with a circular stage and a DJ booth in the corner. All the decor is spot-on.

Rosie Slater: It looks like you're sitting in a spaceship. A 1970s spaceship, which is my whole aesthetic.

Brit Boras: The lights behind, it's like you're in this crazy LED raver light show.

Marina Ross: It's absurd. It's so over the top and works so well. I just want to live there. I just want that to be my living room and the roof to be my roof and the hallway to be my hallway.

Melissa Lucciola: I love The Sultan Room. It was just an all-around perfect experience when I played there. They were nice. They fed you. The door people were nice, they didn't treat you like you were some animal who was trying to get on their stage or something, like I've been treated a lot.

Jono Bernstein: The way that it was booked from the start also was one of those things where we made sure that we were having top-notch acts coming in to do it. So, if it was a venue that hadn't been around for so long, how do you get that respect? You connect with the community. You know, you can have a local band, but you can also have a huge touring act come in, and it can be like a super intimate spot. So there was a lot of that going on. And you know, we played there. A few different bands that I played in ended up playing there.

Jessica Louise Dye: It became a clubhouse. We often, as a band, we just live there on those barstools and we take it over.

Emir Mohseni: The people that work there, they have this amazing environment for everyone to have fun.

Blu DeTiger: This spot is perfect for trying out a new Turkish dish, rocking out to your favorite band, chilling on the rooftop, or moving and grooving to some late-night disco.

Brit Boras: That's what Brooklyn needed. Brooklyn needed, like, a really great new venue.

Union Pool
Anthony Azarmgin, Emir Mohseni (The Muckers); Michael Hesslein (HESS); Darren O'Brien (Wildly); Khaya Cohen (Moon Kissed); Kayla Asbell, Dom Bodo (95 Bulls); Nico E.P., Sean Wouters (Deaf Poets); Emanuel Ayvas (Emanuel and the Fear); Aleksi Glick, Chantal Mitvalsky (Snack Cat); Alison Clancy

Emir Mohseni: My favorite place to play a show and hang out. Union Pool is one of my favorite spots.

Michael Hesslein: It's another place that I hold dear. I think that's the best place to see live music in Brooklyn, still. Was ten years ago, it is now.

Darren O'Brien: A sentimental favorite that, along with Passout Records, was my social HQ my first couple years in New York.

Emir Mohseni: The vibe, the design of that place, everything just looks cool. Union Pool has that vibe. Baby's All Right has that thing. They just have good taste.

Khaya Cohen: So many belligerent memories there with the courtyard and the taco truck, and the stage feels like an old magic show.

Anthony Azarmgin: They have this like, Prohibition, 1920s theater vibe.

Darren O'Brien: It has one of the best-looking stages of any small venue in the city, and lately the sound techs have been on point, so it's a great place to see and play shows. Even when there's a line of micro-minis around the block for the front room, the venue is an oasis.

Kayla Asbell: Union Pool looks good and sounds fabulous. You just gotta escape the twenty-one-year-old horny hoards hanging in the backyard.

Michael Hesslein: Because of the setup having the backyard back there, you just feel like you're going into a different world when you walk into that room.

Emir Mohseni: The room is beautiful. The vibe is really good, and the sound system is insane.

Dom Bodo: Union Pool has some of the most fun shows and the best sound and bartenders.

Sean Wouters: I love the vibe. I went there a few times for drinks and they always have random, good-ass bands playing outta nowhere.

Emir Mohseni: We had such a good release show when we first released the EP that we had just put out in 2018. That was a really good memory from that place. It's always good times, but that time was special because the show was kind of like, packed, sellout. The crowd was really good, and then we partied after with friends.

Union Pool is one of my favorite places to play.

Michael Hesslein: Mail the Horse had many a great show there, and I played there with a lot of other people that I play for as well over the years.

It's a legitimately special venue. I think it's the perfect size for a club show is kind of how I always felt about it. And that's why I started doing my annual Christmas concert there.

It started out in a basement in Bushwick in 2012. We couldn't afford to go home, so we were kind of missing our family, missing the Christmas spirit, basically. And we just like, got together in the basement and sat around the piano, and I played the Christmas songs that I knew, and everyone sang along. It was very endearing but also cheesy. Over the next couple of years, it got bigger and bigger and bigger, and we just turned it into a party, and then it eventually became a show, and then eventually it turned into a charity event.

And we still play Christmas songs, and I dress up as Santa sometimes and hand out beers. We have a couple of friends who write original Christmas songs, and we play those. We had our last one at Union Pool, and it was a sold-out special, special night. That's probably my best memory and most recent memory of playing there. But I've played what feels like a hundred shows there.

Anthony Azarmgin: I've seen really good acts there. I remember Yeah Yeah Yeahs did a free show there once and I just drunkenly stumbled upon Union Pool. We were passing by and we went in and I caught the last two songs.

Emanuel Ayvas: That's one of my favorite venues. I was just there and saw a great show. I hadn't been to a show where every single band was incredible in a long time, and they were all really good. I saw like six people I know there who are all badass musicians, and I was like, something good is happening. This is the right place to be.

Anthony Azarmgin: I think that's the cool thing about small venues. You stumble upon a really sick band that's driving through town or a really cool resident act. There's a gospel act that plays there.

Alison Clancy: I have friends who play there every Monday night for The Reverend Vince Anderson and his Love Choir. I like things that are regular. New York can sometimes be a hard place to build community because it's so big, but when there's something regular, where you know you'll see the same people, it's a nice feeling.

Aleksi Glick: I feel like this is often a post-gig hang, too. I always run into people I know. There's always a lot of artists and musicians hanging out here. You know, as well as some corporate douchebags, too. But it's just a place I feel at home. I feel my tribe is here.

Emir Mohseni: And then the DJ booth in the front when you get in. They have good DJs playing music there, mostly vinyl. I think it's a really cool spot to hang and chill with friends.

Nico E.P.: You go there, you have five bucks on you, and you just go down the list and see what's three or four bucks, so you can tip.

Alison Clancy: And they have a taco stand and a nice outside area. I think those are the common denominators I like. Food, a good outside area, and good live music.

Chantal Mitvalsky: This is the quintessential beer garden. I'm from Australia, where beer gardens are everything. They're probably everything here too, but I feel like this place has the most amazing outdoor area. It works in summer, it works in fall, it works in winter. Everyone's here. It's a great space, there's a taco truck. What more could you want?

Michael Hesslein: This sounds old-school in the world of Tinder or whatever, but if I was, like, a twenty five-year-old single guy, I would feel like I could meet someone at Union Pool or make a new friend there, which sounds super cheesy. I know I sound probably a thousand years old. But that's kind of how I always felt about it. It's like an intimate, cool place. Same reason why I love Pete's [Candy Store] is I felt like you could go there and like, change your life, even if it's just by meeting someone new, or I don't know, maybe it's too romantic. But that's kind of like how I feel about Union Pool.

CHAPTER 12
DIY, TOGETHER

"I think it's on us to just create our own reality, and to create the scene or the system that we want to see, that we think works for us and for our community."
- Jon F Daily (The Black Black)

It was the first day of spring, and I was sucking the foam off the Modelo I had transferred into a paper coffee cup for drinking discretion while a battery-powered bubble machine spewed soapy spheres into the face of latex-clad Madi Cox (Space Sluts), who was performing a synth-y cover of Britney Spears's "Toxic" on the sidewalk in front of the East Williamsburg Econo Lodge.

I was quite possibly the happiest I've ever been.

While this show was intended to be virtual via locally run streaming platform and online music and event hub bandNada, with the organizers' explicit instructions "don't try to find us IRL" delivered at the end of the Instagram promo video, I had opted to take the warning with a wink and had come not just running but *sprinting* to what is not actually a chain motel but a much beloved DIY space in Brooklyn.

That Saturday afternoon marked 374 days since my last real show, the sun was finally out after the longest winter of the longest year, and I was absolutely determined to be in the physical presence of music rather than separated by a screen, even if it meant listening and watching while waving awkwardly from across the street and down the block.

Fortunately, upon my arrival, I wasn't shunned but welcomed with open arms by the venue crew, though still from the requisite six feet away. And it felt so, so good to be back. Organizers lugged instruments, amps, and the namesake Econo Lodge rug, donated by an ex-girlfriend and actual motel employee, up and down the stairs. Musicians shuffled in and out. A handful of friends who answered my texts to "*Come tailgate!*" mingled on site. And while the audience probably didn't exceed a dozen that day, the enthusiasm was on par with that of a packed house, with the energy embodied by the artists and attendees, a thirst for art that can't be quenched and a spirit that can't be squelched, never more evident.

At this point in early 2021, no one knew exactly when live music would be back, in what capacity, or which bands would have first dibs on established stages when restrictions were removed, but it didn't matter. Live music at that moment looked like a group of masked friends and a sidewalk of coiled cords. It sounded like Sean Spada, Shadow Monster, Ilithios, The Planes, Ana Becker, and Kissed by an Animal giving it their all, while having a ball. And it tasted like cheap, warm bodega beer as sudsy as the bubbles that were somehow still being pumped out of that machine two hours later.

For the first time, in a long time, there was a feeling of real optimism about the months ahead, as one of the show's organizers told me matter-of-factly about the upcoming summer, "We're just going to do it ourselves."

Now, for the record, I'm mostly a good kid. I never syphon my neighbors' Wi-Fi, I don't top off my Diet Coke unless the free-refill policy is explicitly stated, and I call my mom pretty much every day, sometimes twice! However, I still have an intense desire to be, if not bad to the bone, at least edgy to whatever's just under the epidermis. And this is probably why I'm most excited and intrigued by what's going down in Brooklyn's unlicensed, underground, and off-the-grid spaces.

Obviously, I'm in the right place. While "official" venues like those in the last chapter are obviously places we know and love, they're only a fraction of the spaces, the *experiences*, that Brooklyn has to offer. After all, live music isn't limited to businesses boasting liquor licenses and indoor plumbing, and you don't need an official designation when you're DIY. As long as you've got a few square feet to serve as a stage, with actual elevation optional, and either a decent sound system or enough silence to allow for some acoustic action, you're basically good to go.

As for the audience experience, the vibe is just *different* in these unconventional venues. You're at bloodshot-eye level, tequila-spitting distance. Close enough to feel the bassist's breath and smell the synth star's shampoo, for the singer to steal your drink, or the drummer to impale you with a sweaty slip of the hand.

You don't just go to these places to watch a show; you go to *participate*. And by the end of the night, you could be sitting stoned and cross-legged on a living room floor, hypnotized by an acoustic set, or hammered with your hair down while crowd-surfing through a cloud of smoke in the kitchen, all before dancing out into the street in the early morning, drinking a beer of mysterious origins while wrapped in a jacket that may or may not actually be yours.

Rowdy vibes and loose rules aside, it is necessary to note that authenticity isn't at the expense of quality, and that DIY isn't synonymous with shitty sound. In fact, it's often exactly the opposite. Most of these spaces aren't just run *for* musicians, but *by* musicians.

This means that even though the buildings themselves weren't originally engineered for optimal acoustics, and even if the venue is not one hundred percent "authorized" in every sense of the perfectly permitted word, they've likely been macgyvered as much as possible to provide the best sonic experience for both the audience and the performer, ultimately earning what's most important for the credibility of any venue, the artists' real seal of approval.

And that's not all, because DIY doesn't stop at the stage and it's not just about throwing shows. It's also about building community.

In addition to serving as an accompaniment or alternative to the mainstream scene, depending on who you ask, the hustling teams behind DIY spaces across the borough go above and beyond, all while flying under the radar, to lend a hand and spread the love. By providing musicians with a place to play and sometimes sleep, operating with a Couchsurfing style of hometown hospitality, many crafty creatives are contributing to an expansive support network that benefits both local bands and outside artists passing through town on tour.

This exercise in paying-it-forward is exemplified by power pair Lily Reszi Rothman (Sloppy Jane) and Paris Andersen, who run a performance space called "hartstop" in their apartment. These hardworking producers roll out of their beds and right into the venue, harnessing their industry experience and cross-genre connections for shows where bands of all types tear it up indoors and out, and might just be found crashing in the living room afterwards.

More than a physical space, hartstop is an entity, its founders hosting events in other Brooklyn spaces as well as in the digital realm, while also compiling and sharing mental-health and mutual-aid resources, inviting local vendors to sell their wares, and engaging members of the community to promote each other through outsourced playlists "crafted with love."

Along with throwing shows and fostering community, DIY is also at its core rooted in the concepts of creation and innovation, real *Field of Dreams*-sorta stuff, the idea that when what you want doesn't exist, you have no choice but to build it yourself.

Take the friends of BK indie-pop act Zoos, a few of my favorite humans, who abandoned a music facility in soul-sucking Times Square to build out their own spot in Bed-Stuy. Each of the band's members poured in real love, manual labor, and a good chunk of change to transform a blank slate of a retail space into a Brooklyn hub for creativity and collaboration. In appropriate Zoos fashion, the studio also serves as a literal animal house with multiple aquariums housing the foursome's fish, Matt Damon, Ben Affleck, and Art Vandelay among them.

And then there's the trippy team behind Rubulad, who has created a one-of-a-kind Bushwick venue with creepy-cool carnival vibes, giving you the strong sensation via visual feast that *shit's about to get (sur)real*. Aesthetically, imagine the decor you'd find at a homecoming dance held at an art school, with stuffed animal-adorned walls, a backyard with funhouse-style installations, and other aesthetic elements that would either be even more amazing or absolutely terrifying if you were on drugs.

These spaces exist in all styles and sizes, and they're all different. But while DIY comes in a variety of funky flavors, there are a few things that all of these spaces have in common: organic magic, an anything-goes atmosphere, and a feeling of freedom that allows artists to bypass the bullshit, get down and dirty, and try out new material without worry or risk.

This concept of cutting one's teeth and honing one's sound was beautifully summed up by Kai Sorensen of psych seven-piece Evolfo as he described the role that Aviv, a former DIY venue, played in the band's journey:

> It's hard to catch a break in Brooklyn. Searching for a scene and community that would welcome what we were trying to say as a band took time and a lot of energy. We kept grinding though, and after some time, we found ourselves in the smoke-filled DIY venues of Bushwick, which lead us to Aviv.
>
> Playing those packed rooms on stages we barely fit on solidified our sound. Raw. Sweaty. Thumping. Can't hear shit. Aviv holds a special place in my heart for that. I'll always remember grabbing Marty after our first show and right there saying, "I think we made it to New York."

Street cred aside, when it comes to DIY, for music fans there is *one* catch. You see, when it comes to many of these spaces, where schedules aren't posted and addresses aren't searchable, the age-old necessity of knowing, or at least following, the right people still applies.

Rather than neon lights and red velvet ropes, there are unmarked warehouses and unlisted lofts, so while you don't have to be "on the list," you do still have to be in the know. Hopefully, this chapter serves as a solid start.

Bohemian Grove
Dan Barrecchia, Joey Giambra, Ed Weisgerber (Shred Flintstone)

Joey Giambra: It's an old punk house we played at. Apparently it's a generational punk duplex, and they have shows in the basement. They've been having punk shows for years.

Ed Weisgerber: It's like five-and-a-half foot ceilings, classic basement, shit everywhere, bad sound. But you know what, that's rock 'n' roll.

Joey Giambra: We have a YouTube video of our performance there. It was really fun. We had a really insane pit in that one.

Ed Weisgerber: I had a 101-degree fever. I was just sweating the entire time.

Joey Giambra: While Dan was doing a solo, someone suplexed him through a table.

Dan Barrecchia: I went out into the crowd and was like, doing some shit with my guitar while everyone was moshing, and then someone picked me up and suplexed me through a table.

Joey Giambra: That's in the video.

Dan Barrecchia: The table didn't break fully, it just kinda collapsed in. I don't want to oversell the story. Honestly, I think we should incorporate that into our set.

Ed Weisgerber: Big contact mics on everything.

Dan Barrecchia: Just body-slam each other.

Dodge 112
Johan, Jonathan, Jordan, Peter, Sahil, Sean (Glom); Quinn Devlin

Quinn Devlin: Dodge 112, the name is a room at Columbia, is the recording studio and venue space my good friends have built in Gowanus.

It's people I've made music with, people I went to school with. Up until then, we were still rehearsing at Columbia.

Sahil: I work full-time as a freelance producer and mix engineer, so it started with me looking for a space where I could basically just record bands. It's as simple as that, because at that point I was like, there's a lot of great music that my friends are making, and I wanted a space and the resources to be able to record them the way I wanted to for cheap, and not have to deal with the restraints of a commercial studio.

So I kind of teamed up with my friend Eli, who was also interested in making a space where he could record and make music, you know, in the kind of environment that was less stifling. But he kind of brought to the experience this idea of also having a performance space where bands could play lower-key shows, and kind of have a more intimate setting to try different things, or different arrangements, or just play for their friends. Again, without the restraints of a venue that was just trying to make money.

I mean, that is what the DIY aesthetic is, but it's a little bit more than DIY, because we're providing, you know, the resources and the gear and environment and the community for people to just try new things and be empowered to be making music, which sounds kind of hokey and precious.

And it wasn't like, that specific of an idea. It just turned into that, sort of ballooned into kind of a bigger thing, where all sorts of different types of music, all different bands around Brooklyn, some that we know and some that we don't know, have come to play at the space and appreciate it for what it is, which is kind of like a rare, small, intimate venue to try different things.

Peter: It's kind of a crazy thing to be a part of. Because you just realize that the DIY scene really is just a group of people who just decided that it's going to happen. Like, it's not going to happen any other way, so we are going to make it happen.

Sean: Make it happen for yourself, by yourself. You know, it's very inspiring to be a part of this community. I mean, I firmly believe that there's a movement going on, with all these respective DIY scenes.

The Dodge community means a lot to me, personally. There's a support system that we're a part of and you know, it's a commercial studio, and then it's also an art space, an event space. It's gonna be something very special, you know, like people are gonna look back on it and say that it was something big.

Sahil: Besides all the shows that we've been putting on, it is my office, and I've been very lucky to make a lot of amazing records there and have my own space where I can record a full band. Like I can pull in a band off the street and make a record in two days now for whatever I want to charge, which is like a really special, lucky thing to be able to do in New York, where real estate is expensive to rent and studio space is even more expensive. And just having enough square footage and the resources to be able to record at high-fidelity and do like creative, experimental music-making decisions. It's a really special thing.

In a year and a half, we've probably done like eight full-length records, ten EPs and maybe like fifty shows? That seems about right.

Johan: It's the only studio I've been in in New York, and I feel like I don't need to ever go to another one. It's got a great vibe. It all feels really good. It's a great space.

Jonathan: It's a definite family vibe. More often than not, you'll run into multiple bands while you're there, people coming in and out. It's really the epicenter of this Brooklyn musical community between all our friends.

Jordan: I moved November 2018, so Dodge 112 and the whole community were my ticket and introduction to the city. It's really special. The communal aspect, the family aspect, it's just genuinely good people who connect there.

I've heard a lot of stories of just the DIY scene and the ways it's been affected, [how] DIY scenes have been closing off, and it's still, like, a very live, living thing.

East Williamsburg Econo Lodge (EWEL)
Carlo Minchillo (Brooklyn Drum Collective); Zach Ellis (Dead Tooth); Jon F Daily (The Black Black)

Carlo Minchillo: East Williamsburg Econo Lodge (EWEL) in Brooklyn holds a very special place in my heart. A highly sought-after rehearsal space and haven for music lovers who prefer the modest, intimate settings for shows.

Zach Ellis: I've been in New York for a while, like going on fourteen years now. So I've seen a lot of the DIY spots come and go, you know?

We used to play this place called Big Snow Buffalo Lodge, which was like my favorite venue ever. All these kids like moved into this space, gutted it, built a bar, and they just ran an amazing venue. Like the sound was always perfect, the beers were really cheap. It was just the best place, and I guess Econo Lodge is like the only place I know that's still like that.

Carlo Minchillo: For the uninitiated, EWEL is tucked away in what was once the Third District of Williamsburg and borders on present-day Williamsburg, Greenpoint, Maspeth and Bushwick.

Surrounded by countless other practice studios and underground venues, EWEL is nestled in an industrial zone. The marriage of exotic smells from dumpling factories, coffee roasters, and exotic spice traders waft through this curious corner of East Williamsburg.

And like with any good love story, there's the pickle factory next door.

After a long night out in Manhattan at the Wetlands, Webster Hall or Roseland Ballroom, the scent of cigarette smoke and stale beer greets you from the fibers of your bedroom pillow, carried there on your hair and clothes. But to those who know, nothing quite stimulates like arising to pickle brine.

There are no fancy cocktails, coat-check, or mirrors in the bathroom. The beer is in the mini-cooler, put your jacket on the speakers, BYOKD (Bring Your Own Kosher Dills). There's a stage and equipment, but the thrift-shop decor, upright piano, and Persian rugs really tie the room together.

Zach Ellis: There's like this tiny door you go through to get in. It's almost like you're going through that door in *Being John Malkovich*. It kind of feels like you're going through that portal, and then you go in, and a really good show is going on.

Carlo Minchillo: Manager Jon Daily (The Black Black, Kissed by an Animal) keeps the torch burning. Before he began hosting EWEL livestream events through his website, bandNada, he was curating great shows with local and out-of-town bands at the spot.

Jon F Daily: It's an interesting space in that it kind of was just born out of necessity, I think to a certain point. We didn't really go looking for a space to do a semi-DIY venue kind of thing. It just kind of just happened randomly. We just started practicing there, and we're like, okay, this is a big room, we should have shows here.

I think summer of 2016 we had our first show. It was a Sunday afternoon thing. We really were just like, let's see if anybody shows up and if they're appalled at what this space is.

The first show was an earlier incarnation of The Black Black, and The Planes played it, and I was actually playing drums in The Planes at the time. It was just a super low-key kind of thing. And it was cool. And we're like, alright, I guess we'll kind of keep trying to do this.

Zach Ellis: They don't do shows often. There's no Instagram for it; there's only a hashtag. I don't even know if it's cool I'm talking about it. But it's just a really fun spot. They always do really good shows, the bills are always amazing.

Jon F Daily: The primary thing of importance to me are first, that we're providing this space that is comfortable and unpretentious, and just about seeing good local music in an affordable way that's just fun and cool and casual, and not trying to be anything that it's not. We just try to make it a cheap night out for people, where they can enjoy music and see their friends and meet new people.

The second thing is providing a space for my friends and friends of friends and people that play in bands and need shows or touring bands, whoever. And every time that a new band comes in, most of the time those bands come back again. They come to watch shows, they come to play shows, and the community just keeps on growing. And very slowly and organically.

Zach Ellis: They're just like, we're just here to have a good time, to have a good show. It's not like, some venue where they need to sell a certain number of tickets to make it. Clearly the space is used for something else, and then every now and then they're like, let's throw a bangin' show, so there's just always this good vibe there.

Jon F Daily: That really kind of can't be understated, how nice it is that we get to run it the way that we want to run it.

Some of the venues are wonderful, but they're businesses at the end of the day. I don't say this in a negative way, it's just the reality of the situation is that they're all businesses and they need to make money, so if you don't bring anybody, then they're going to be kind of upset they had you for the night, whereas we don't really care.

We're totally happy to do like, the weird, whatever solo project that you have, just noise pedals and whatever. Like, cool, let's hear it, you know. So, it's definitely lower pressure in that way.

And you know, I say this from a really fortunate position of having that space available where we aren't trying to make any money from it.

Zach Ellis: Some of these venues you play, I mean, I can only imagine they deal with so many bands and stuff and it's a pain, but they're not, like, *friendly*. It's a job for them. They might not be paid enough to do it.

Usually when you play a DIY venue like Econo Lodge, they're just more willing to roll with the unconventional way of doing it, willing to work with the situation and improvise and have fun with it. Usually you get a better sound, and usually it's just more fun of an experience for everybody.

Jon F Daily: It's a community. So everyone kind of pitches in the ways they can. That's what we're all doing, because we want to have something that we feel good about and are excited to do, and doing that with friends and people that we like and respect makes it great.

Carlo Minchillo: The majority of the shows I attended at EWEL were packed with people like pickles in a jar. At a Lumps show, I was certain that by the end of the set we'd all fall through the floor into a vat of sweet vegetable nectar.

Zach Ellis: I played guitar in Lost Boy ? for a tour, and our return show was there. The whole place was just packed [and] felt like it was like going up and down. It was one of the most fun shows. That's just kind of the vibe there.

Carlo Minchillo: One particularly fresh night featured the Non-Mutant Band Lottery. We put our names in a hat and formed random bands, returning later to play five to six hours' worth of music we wrote in one afternoon.

While our band was playing "I Wanna Be Sedated," I witnessed drummer Jeremy Duval (Haybaby, DAD) fly over the crowd, latch onto the rafters for a moment of frenzy, then surf his way to the end of the song.

Zach Ellis: There's just something about those home-built DIY spots that are pretty few and far between these days. When I first moved to Brooklyn, that was like all the places. That whole scene, those were always the most fun shows. And I feel like EWEL is kind of the dying, the last glimpse of that.

Jon F Daily: You know, everything changes. It's just kind of always about creating something new for this phase of New York, or this phase of music in New York.

You know, and the scene, they just kind of pop up and then go away and come back. It's constantly fluctuating. I think it's on us to just create our own reality, and to create the scene or the system that we want to see, that we think works for us and for our community.

Carlo Minchillo: If you haven't experienced how truly special it is to rock out in a cloud of dill and vinegar, I've got the spot for you.

Hartstop

Gillian Visco (Shadow Monster); Charmaine Querol (Nevva); Lily Reszi Rothman (Sloppy Jane); Jessica Louise Dye (High Waisted)

Gillian Visco: So, hartstop's amazing.

Charmaine Querol: It's an apartment in Bushwick run by really cool, kind, and just wonderful people. It's my favorite because house shows are the best! I grew up throwing a lot of house shows [and] art shows at my house back in Oakland, and they were always a positive turnout of support and fun.

Lily Reszi Rothman: I was booking shows and working events and with musicians for years before I moved in here, and then my friend and I found this apartment, and the shape of it was just so unique, and we were like, oh wow, that's the music corner! Like, the shape just like lends itself perfectly to having a stage.

Jessica Louise Dye: It's like one of those classic weird L-shaped apartments where you're like, you know, leaning on the kitchen sink and somebody's standing on a couch, but it just feels great. I came up in music in D.C., and it was all house shows, and so this is like, the only thing in Brooklyn that feels like that.

Gillian Visco: They'll have two stages when it's nice weather. They have the main room, which is in their living room essentially.

Lily Reszi Rothman: We had it down to a T, the switching between living space and venue space. It was almost like a dance. I'd throw all the furniture around. My roommate Paris and I run it together, so we each have our little things we would do, and we had our staff. Most of our staff are artists who also would play our shows. My bedroom was the green room.

Gillian Visco: And then they have the roof. I was there seeing a bunch of loud bands and went up to the roof and Joanna Sternberg was just placed right in the middle. And everyone's out there like smoking, getting their air and whatever. And I heard them playing, and I was just so stunned by their songwriting and voice, and it honestly made me cry. It was one of the most beautiful sets I've probably seen in years. It was absolutely incredible.

Charmaine Querol: Art is a way of communication, so it's nice to give an opportunity to share in a safe environment, especially if it is your first time.

Lily Reszi Rothman: I think making it feel like a house party, like you're in our living room, takes down some barriers between people.

I don't know, thinking about going just to normal shows, random people don't really just talk to each other that much at a venue. Like Alphaville or Baby's All Right, people just stand apart or stand in separate places. Here, I think a lot of random people just start talking to each other and people let their guard down. And I think that's also reflected in the way that people play.

Charmaine Querol: I also enjoy the intimacy and feeling serenaded or headbanging 'til my neck breaks a foot away from the performers. It's exhilarating.

Lily Reszi Rothman: We figured out the ways to keep the cops from coming. We started writing notes to all of our neighbors before, just to give them a heads up so there would be no noise complaints. We'd invite them also. We figured involving our neighbors in the community would make them less pissed off about it, and if they know what to expect, it's fine.

Jessica Louise Dye: People that live there are all musicians or photographers, and they put a lot of love into curating nights that are sometimes like, nineteen-year-old kids in a band from New Jersey that wouldn't be able to play venues, so they play this house party early on. I've gone there on nights where it's like, a band and then a Vogue competition, you know, and then another band and then drag queens. It's just always different.

Gillian Visco: hartstop does a great job of curating really eclectic bills.

Lily Reszi Rothman: I'm very sick of seeing the same bands on every lineup, and also I get sick of the vast majority of those bands being all straight white guys. So we make a huge effort to make sure our lineups reflect how diverse the community and neighborhood are. We try to have an eclectic lineup and representative in terms of genre also.

Jessica Louise Dye: They do a really good job of not putting the same bills together over and over, which is typically a complaint of mine. Like you go to a show, you end up seeing like the same ten bands, you know. I've never seen anybody play there twice at this point.

Lily Reszi Rothman: I noticed just from going to shows and playing shows and booking shows for so long that there were a lot of different groups and scenes of people that were kind of splintered. And the lineups that I booked a lot of the time are kind of all over the place, but I like doing that, because I like mixing everyone together. And there have been a lot of collaborations that have come from people who met at our shows and played together, so I think just sort of bringing people who are doing similar things, who otherwise wouldn't have been in the same space.

Jessica Louise Dye: They do painting nights too, drink and draw. They're really organized. They send out the newsletter, and they don't do any advertising on Facebook or Instagram just because it's still someone's house. So it's like, you're in the know, you're in the know. They take Venmo at the front door, they charge for drinks at their, you know, little bar. And it's just great.

Lily Reszi Rothman: Making it BYOB and having a bar made it also feel more house-party vibe. But also, buy stuff from our bar so we make money and pay people.

Jessica Louise Dye: I've just never had a bad time there, and it feels safe on top of it. Like, you know, you can dump your coat and your purse in a corner, and I've never been like hit on or assaulted there. Everyone's really kind, even when the room gets crazy with bouncing, you know. One time on Halloween, everybody did cover bands, and people were crowd-surfing but very gently helping people down.

Lily Reszi Rothman: People do associate hartstop with the physical space, but it is more of an entity and more of a community. A lot of what we do ties into the community and supporting and helping people, providing any form of support for artists beyond offering a platform and space.

I always loved having parties and shows because I was like, oh, at the end of the night I don't even have to leave. Everyone just comes here. We also, besides shows, put up touring bands a lot that needed a place to crash. There were often bands sleeping in our living room, which is fun.

Market Hotel
Nico E.P., Sean Wouters (Deaf Poets); Lydia Gammill, Tarra Thiessen (Gustaf); Tall Juan

Tall Juan: I like playing Market Hotel. It's not the best place, it's got a column in the middle of the room, but I think it's one of my fave places to play here now.

Sean Wouters: That's like the most DIY but cool spot. They don't have a liquor license, so they're giving free beer in the back.

Nico E.P.: Why are you ratting people out, bro?

Sean Wouters: Nah, that's legal. But it was so sick every time. The freaking subway is in the background. You can't get more New York than that experience in terms of a venue. It's so cool.

Nico E.P.: I was fortunate I was able to play that venue a few times. That was one of the venues when I first moved up that I played it, I'm like, holy shit, this feels like I'm in New York City. It's a cool spot, you know.

Lydia Gammill: My first show in Brooklyn was when I was a freshman in college, and I went to see Titus Andronicus at Market Hotel. And that was like a big city moment for me just to be like, *wow, New York City, yes, rock 'n' roll.*

It's one of those things too, kind of that like, *Gone with the Wind* moment where you're sitting there and you're looking at it like, *I will be on that stage someday.* You know it's like, this will be mine someday. And we played there a couple times, so that was nice. It reminds me of the days when I was just a wee pup.

Tarra Thiessen: We're like ancient in New York City scene years.

Lydia Gammill: We're old, but it's okay. It makes me think sometimes, you know, people will be like, "Oh yeah, remember that band Gustaf?"

Tarra Thiessen: Maybe, maybe not.

Lydia Gammill: We've played enough that I'd like to think that people who went to shows in New York know about us.

Pet Rescue
Jon F Daily (The Black Black); Michael Tarnofsky (Edna)

Jon F Daily: Pet rescue is like my favorite DIY space, apart from Econo, that's still doing it.

Michael Tarnofsky: It's a loft that people live in. The driveway is literally like a cargo-truck loading center or area. So it's like, I live in a converted warehouse space, and they seem to actually live in a real warehouse.

Jon F Daily: They have regular shows. I think there's a handful of spaces like it throughout Brooklyn where people kind of do these one-off shows, like one or two or three a year. Like, Cat Farm will do a few shows here and there. But Pet Rescue is more consistent, there's probably a couple a month. And just like, super casual, cheap, fun, and low-key, and so those are all the things that are kind of important to me.

Michael Tarnofsky: Those are always kick-ass parties. They're small, they always feel packed, even if it's like, only forty people. I came to music many years ago because I wanted to perform it. And so having a specific live energy feels important, and as I'm getting older and like, mellowing out, I think it's not as big of a deal if it's not a sweaty, drunk, everybody's-on-ten moment. I can just happily play my songs acoustic and sing and feel like it's getting a job done, but the experience of ecstatic body-on-body, that just makes a fucking show.

Jon F Daily: I think it was a Money Fire Records showcase there. We played it, and Best Behavior played it. And they weren't around all that long, but I would say that this was probably, at least for me, this was them in their prime. And that place was just *moving*. It was packed. And they just got that crowd. Everybody was dancing crazy. And it was just a super, super fun set, and super, super sweaty. The hot, sweaty shows, they just stick in your memory more. That one was really great.

Michael Tarnofsky: Every touring musician, probably most notably Jack White, would say New York is the hardest audience. And that feels so true, even at a very small show with all people you fucking know. Like everybody, if they move their hands or shoulders the wrong way. It could be snobbery or like, this is such an anxious place and that doesn't allow people to just kind of dole out compliments or gratification for anybody else so easily. But there's something about New-York-cool that permeates in New-York-cool music venues. So when you kind of cut out the pretense, you're in a better, at least for me you're in a more welcoming [space]. Your chances at scoring are way higher. You're just, you're dunkin' all night.

Rubulad
Dirty Mae (Ben Curtis, Cassie Fireman, Robin Frost); Kallan Campbell, Tcoy Coughlin, Shane Preece, David Johnson (Max Pain and the Groovies); Lily Reszi Rothman (Sloppy Jane); JW Francis

Dirty Mae: We love this super underground speakeasy because of its wild design, secret location and especially that they host amazingly creative events, many of which are for a cause.

JW Francis: One of my many endeavors is throwing murder-mystery parties with friends under the name J33. My favorite place in Brooklyn is without a doubt the location we threw our biggest murder mystery party to date, Rubulad, an explosion of creative force that leaves no rock unturned or mind unblown.

Shane Preece: What a fucking psychedelic place, man.

Tcoy Coughlin: We played there.

Shane Preece: It was just like, homies, kind of a DIY scene.

Tcoy Coughlin: And they were doing, what, tattoos and sandwiches? Count me in on this shit.

Shane Preece: Their outdoor area's like a fucking adult playground. It's just insane.

Lily Reszi Rothman: It's a crazy place. We get there like a couple hours early for load in and soundcheck, and when we walk in, it's like you never know what to expect, or what the room is gonna look like or who's gonna be there. One time we walked in and there was like a circle of people in masks with big hats dancing in a circle with kids in the middle. You just never know what it's gonna look like, which is exciting.

Kallan Campbell: The stage is great. It's just filled with art, which is nice.

Tcoy Coughlin: And you can tell the people there, because of that, are just so hungry for the tunes.

Shane Preece: That show was like a whole experience, totally DIY, covered in art, everywhere is visually satisfying.

David Johnson: It kinda feels like you're playing a mini festival. It's all decked out.

JW Francis: It is my favorite Saturday night spot because it's easy to participate in the action, whether that be a show or a happening, but it is just as easy to take a quiet moment to yourself or with someone else outside. Those are my favorite spaces.

ThL2

Michael Tarnofsky (Edna); Nick Louis (Almost Sex)

Michael Tarnofsky: I'm always trying to see who has a basement, which at nearly thirty years old is not a great career move. But I can't really work up the nerve to ask people to pay ten or more dollars to come to a show. Not without some incredible draw or some fire-breathing exotic dancer.

One that has been most welcoming to me and my band, and to friends of mine, who are also equally a little disheartened by how like, Sisyphean [it feels to be] playing in Brooklyn or in New York, is my friend's venue by the Bedford Nostrand G area. Real fire hazard of a place.

Nick Louis: ThL2 is close to me, not just because it happens to be located directly below my personal living space. Originally part of an old bar, separated from the street by a set of rusty hatch doors, the basement had been collecting junk for years before my old roommates, Adrien Espy and Ryan Cole, moved in and decided to clear the space out. Musicians themselves, in a city where square footage is precious, they saw it as a potential place to hang out and share music with their friends. Despite the low ceilings and occasional cobweb, it started gaining popularity, and when I moved in, in 2017, I began booking and managing the venue. We started ramping up the number of shows to a fairly ambitious two shows per month, and that summer alone, I booked close to fifty bands to play in our basement over the coming months.

I was thrilled to be part of the city's DIY music scene, I was getting to know so many great people, and it was also an opportunity for my band, Night on the Sun, to play alongside some of the most talented unsigned musicians in the city.

Michael Tarnofsky: There's no qualifications for the kind of music that they welcome. And I think that that's hard to come by, because usually, you know, it's like there's a garage scene, there's a post-punk scene, there's a synth-pop scene, and there's a noise scene, and never the twain shall meet. So, yeah, Nick's venue, that was just like, literally the last three years the majority of the shows played were down there.

Nick Louis: By 2020, a few of my closest friends, Dan Goldstein, Austin Brush, and Trevor Brenden, had moved into the apartment.

We just finished renovating the space with all-new sound equipment, a small bar, updated lighting and furniture, low ceilings hovering over an eclectic collection of instruments, mic stands, and furniture, all ready for the DIY enthusiasts and the revolving door of excellent musicians we've hosted to get back down there and play.

Zoos Studio
Tom Corrado, Mitch Meyer, Frank Poma (Zoos)

Tom Corrado: I had the space in Manhattan before I met these lovely fellows. And you know, I was just running it like a regular studio sort of business, but I was totally not creatively fulfilled by that at all. I wanted to join a band and wanted to actually have a creative outlet and spend time in the studio on things that actually were fulfilling, so I found these lovely chaps.

Mitch Meyer: Tinder for musicians. I met Tom and Frank through BandMix.

Frank Poma: It's just a crapshoot.

Mitch Meyer: It is a crapshoot. If you want a good laugh, go on BandMix. It's a sight to be seen. So then Tommy joined, and we started rehearsing at his place.

Tom Corrado: The lease was ending there. Plus, Manhattan is just not the feeling we wanted. The whole area, it's like being inside the internet, but it's real life. There's no soul.

Frank Poma: It's a creative desert.

Mitch Meyer: No windows, you know, like everything smells like smoke, everything's like, a hundred square feet. And honestly, it's really, really difficult after bombing a show in Bushwick to drive to fucking Eighth Avenue and Thirty-eighth Street at like four in the morning to drop off your gear and go up like eight stories when you're already mentally defeated. So, you know, there's that.

Tom Corrado: We wanted to make our own spot that had windows and daylight, and you know, its own feeling, so we would always have that oasis and real Zen atmosphere, to just always have that creative place.

Mitch Meyer: For music, like anything else, the time you put into it is the output you get, and we want a place where the environment is good enough and I'm down to hang out there for eight hours.

Frank Poma: Ultimately, what's interesting about Zoos personality-wise is we all treat each other like family. It is more than just like, four people getting together to play music. There's an energy that comes with all of us combined, and I think people do recognize that, our friends recognize that, and they feel it too. So when we built this space, what we had in mind was that this really is the physical embodiment of who we are as a band, so that when you come into this studio, you can *feel* the energy that we hold, the energy of the band. It's right here. It's in the walls. I mean, we fucking built the place, we painted the place. The blood, sweat, and tears, it's all here. None of this was artificially fabricated. It just exudes Zoos and who we are.

Tom Corrado: Some of our first jams in here were like, I feel like I've never really had, like I can only really describe as a floating kind of a feeling, almost an out-of-body experience, where we were completely in each other's minds, knew exactly what the next notes were going to be, you know, and that's a flow state. Getting to something like that as a group is something that's only happened a couple times in my life, and so right from there, I knew I was in the right spot with the right people and that we were right for each other.

Frank Poma: It feels like coming home. I'll walk in, and Tom is working at the desk, and Mitch is doing vocals. This feels more at home than anywhere else in the world. Even my own house.

Mitch Meyer: Even in the early days we were like, well, we want a space for us to be able to record and practice. But we also wanted more of a community space. We do want to have bands in here, we do want to have shows. I don't just want to release music, I want to connect with the Brooklyn music scene.

Frank Poma: We all work normal day jobs, you know, jobs that basically pay us to survive to go pursue the passion. We definitely recognize it's really special that all four of us are in that position where we're working hard at a job and in careers to fund this. We recognize that we've got some privilege here, that we are in a good spot that we're able to do this. Each of us individually couldn't do it alone.

We definitely want to give back and be participating in the community and helping other people use this space and take some of the energy and benefit from it as well. It's definitely how I think we see ourselves being ingrained in sort of the fabric of this culture, this community, and it's nice to see bands coming in and people smiling and really enjoying themselves.

Mitch Meyer: We want everyone to feel welcome and feel comfortable and want to come back. Even if it's a more minor hub, we wanted to have a hub in the music scene. We just wanted to be able to create a place we didn't think existed yet, for people to connect and be creative together.

CHAPTER 13
POP-UPS AND PLATFORMS

"I got to meet so many beautiful people who love art through performing in the subway. Busking showed me that there are a lot of good people out there."
- Lily Mao (Lily Mao and The Resonaters)

It might seem like a paradox in a book built around places, but some of the most memorable music experiences I've had over the last five years have been defined by an impermanence that's entirely by design. These are concerts with minimal tech, but maximum impact. One-of-a-kind, one-time experiences put on by artists, organizations, and innovative individuals for audiences across the city. It's art in transit, taking place on stages that are frequently unconventional and often totally temporary, where after the show is over, nothing but the memories remain.

I was introduced to previously mentioned singer-songwriter, multi-instrumentalist, and Taco Bell enthusiast Lizzie No when she played a set at Hygge Haus, a cozy space covered in the requisite amount of soft, Scandi-inspired decor inside a giant teepee-like structure in Industry City.

I had a religious experience when I heard the voice of indie-folk flower child Elizabeth Wyld vibrating through a secret show at a church one afternoon, an event that felt like even more of a miracle when I learned she had recently recovered from vocal fold paralysis.

I was introduced to Quinn Devlin's bold and bluesy voice at a sneaker store. I soaked up the soulful sounds of EZRAH as he held court in a yoga studio. I bopped along to progressive hip-hop artist Julian Xtra while he jumped around a Greenpoint backyard. And I first encountered indie folk-pop-Americana outlaws Bandits on the Run as they were singing and stomping it up in the office of a startup.

And while venues were closed and live music was effectively on hiatus between 2020 and 2021, Wayne Tucker and the Bad Motha's gave Brooklyn the greatest of gifts, putting on hours-long jazz jam sessions in the evenings at Grand Army Plaza outside Prospect Park, playing for diverse but universally thankful crowds composed of runners and bikers, wobbling toddlers and head-bobbing teenagers, stroller-pushing parents and paused passersby.

On each of these occasions, I was exposed to incredible musicians I didn't know in settings I didn't automatically associate with music, often spaces I wouldn't necessarily have found myself in otherwise.

But then there are the other types of unexpected events put on in locations that not just a few lucky fans but *millions* of visitors and native New Yorkers occupy every day. These are places where music isn't a destination but instead a surprise addition. And when talking unofficial shows in unconventional spaces, you can't forget the countless bands taking the original anything-goes, occasionally urine-scented stage, the subway platform, by storm.

These scrappy subterranean artists are some of the most extraordinary features of city life, serving crowds a surprise concert on their commute. And even when I'm head-down and headphones-in, dodging slow walkers and ladies selling plastic bags stuffed with sliced mango, the sound of a bucket drummer, a three-man mariachi band, or a little kid singing karaoke always snaps me out of my tunnel-vision trance and stops me in my tracks, inspiring me to pause and enjoy the music for a moment, deadlines and destinations be damned.

In some ways, this chapter could be considered a continuation of DIY in terms of intention and execution. The organizers and artists are typically doing it in bare-bones fashion, and while busking in the right station at the right time can pay some bills, the musicians seem to be doing it for the love, not just for the money. However, the following entries are different in that they're less about the specifics of whatever is serving as the stage, and more about what's happening on it.

In this case, all an artist really needs is enough space to sing, strum, or drum, and a willingness to play for unpredictable audiences in often unusual places.

Depending on the location, sometimes a really strong bladder helps too.

61 Local
Lizzie No

There's this once-a-month music series upstairs, Sunday Sounds. It's two or three acts, all donation-based, super cozy, and they do super sweet, intimate intros. I feel like I've never gone and not seen a great lineup. I love to do it with just myself and a guitarist, stripped-back. Because it's such a small room and people sit super close, you get the chance to do something a little more intimate and try out new stuff.

Barclays Center
Lily Mao (Lily Mao and The Resonaters)

So, my favorite pick feels pretty atypical, but I'm goin' with it! The Atlantic Barclays Metro, specifically off the 2 line at the top of the steps. Why is my favorite place in Park Slope a subway platform and not Lucky 13? Because I am a busker! I moved to Brooklyn in 2018 from Scranton, PA. Busking was [barely] paying my bills when I first moved here, and I did it consistently for three months at the Atlantic Barclays metro. I carried my cart and guitar from Crown Heights and set up at the top of the steps near the 2 platform towards the Q.

My set up was a cube amp, Boss RC-30 Looper, and microphone

and microphone stand. I would jam out to originals like "Run," "Sour Grapes," "Wolves" and "Omaha." It really helped me develop the songs into how we recorded them on my debut album *Run To Madness*.

Through performing in the subway I got to meet so many beautiful people who love art. I would let little kids strum my guitar, people would sing into the mic with me, dance, applaud. Busking showed me that there are a lot of good people out there. I also got really proficient in soloing from playing there five hours a day, I'm really good at holding in my pee! It was an amazing experience, and I cherish the memories.

I began busking in Philadelphia with my friend Sofiya Mariya, a professional hooper, in 2015 while we were both attending Temple University. Ever since then, I was hooked. The energy and improvisations are like no other mode of music when you busk. Busking in Brooklyn made me the musician I am today. Gritty with a heart of gold. The band, Lily Mao and The Resonaters, usually ends our set with an improv song with a word suggested by the audience. It's a lot of fun!

Feng Sway
Matthew Gibbs (Evolfo)

Nothing gets my heart rate going like the promise of solid thrift. Feng Sway in Greenpoint has all the soul, eclecticism, and mystery necessary to a beautiful dig. My love for this place begins with a secret, barely amplified Evolfo show that took place on their showroom floor in 2018. We were walled in by cactus brambles and loud tapestries. All the lights were extinguished except one red and one blue, and we sang sad songs from our album *Last of the Acid Cowboys*. Folks sat cross-legged on the floor and gave us that thing we have hardly known but often greatly crave. Silence and their full attention. The vibe was on ten thousand percent, and of course I have to give much of that credit to set and setting.

My ego and I visit Feng Sway together often, hoping the staff might recognize me and we can talk once more of that magical show. To their credit, they hardly ever let me and my ego play our rock-star games, and instead they direct me towards the pure act of thrifting. I return at least once a month to check their thoughtfully curated collections of plants and vintage clothes, jewelry, and home decor. The staff is knowledgeable and fun. It is a place where I feel comfortable telling them just what kind of freak flag I feel like flying that day, and they thoughtfully connect me with the items that support my vision. I am fairly proud of my bolo tie collection, and my favorite bolo tie comes from Feng Sway.

The Greenpoint Loft
Lydia Gammill, Vram Kherlopian, Tarra Thiessen (Gustaf)

Lydia Gammill: Our whole life changed. You can get married there, or something. It's like a venue space.

Cage the Elephant wanted to have, I guess, a tour celebration party and have local artists come perform. So it was Matt, and then, you know, he and Beck were on tour together and they were doing like, a little secret performance at the end. And a friend of Matt's was asked to help find people, and she DM'd me on Instagram, and it was just one of those moments. We were at Tarra's house shooting a music video, and you kinda see the DM, and you're like, *what?* None of us really knew what it was. All we knew was we were just gonna do it. It was just magical.

Tarra Thiessen: And now we're sendin' Beck birthday cards.

Lydia Gammill: They had techs, so you didn't have to set anything up. You just told them what you wanted, and then these people would do it. They tune everything, and you just walk on. And I was like, *people perform like this?*

Tarra Thiessen: You thought that Yoko Ono was there.

Lydia Gammill: They were like, "Yokko's coming!" And it turned out it was just a woman named Yokko.

Vram Kherlopian: It was Yokko Ono but she spells it with two k's.

She's online and stuff.

Tarra Thiessen: I looked, and I was like, she's too young to be Yoko!

Vram Kherlopian: But I was fooled. I was fuckin' fooled. It was the magic of the whole thing. It's like, there's all these famous people there. What's happening? Is this seriously Yoko Ono doing some weird kinda art dance?

Tarra Thiessen: She was like, painted white.

Vram Kherlopian: But it was Yokko, with two K's, and it was just hilarious, and I'm so happy. She just goes around and just pretends to be Yoko Ono, but she's like her own thing. But she's clearly ripping off Yoko Ono, the original, so it's just so good.

Green-Wood Cemetery
Mia Berrin (Pom Pom Squad)

One of my favorite experiences I've had in Brooklyn is when we played a show in Green-Wood Cemetery.

It was very unique. It was with a group called Rooftop Films, and we were the opening act for a movie. They set up basically a movie theater, a bunch of chairs and they had this big inflatable screen.

First of all, we were paid real money, and it was the first time we made like four hundred dollars, which is hilarious, because that's kind of nothing, but to us it was a huge deal at the time. I was like, oh my god, like, that's one hundred for each of us! Seemed like such a novelty.

We all got there early, and we did the soundcheck and then we sort of got to walk around the grounds. I think I actually came out as gay to one of my bandmates that day. It was just this crazy thing. There was sort of this magical air.

I had this heart-shaped stone that my partner had given me that I carried around in my pocket, like every day obsessively, anywhere I went, as just kind of a connection. And we went into this empty church, the four of us. And it was so quiet. It was like the quietest place in Brooklyn. And I laid down in the middle of the floor, and we all just kind of had this moment. And at the end of the night, I realized I lost the stone somewhere. And I just love the idea that it is somewhere in the church in Green-Wood Cemetery, living its life. It's like, you know, I left a part of myself there. It was a really beautiful night.

The Metropolitan G Stop
Shane Conerty (Color Collage); Bandits on the Run (Adrian Blake Enscoe, Sydney Shepherd, Regina Strayhorn); Cancion Franklin

Shane Conerty: One of my favorite places in NYC is probably not everyone's favorite, but it's where I've spent a good chunk of my time while living in Brooklyn. I go busking at the Metropolitan G stop and have been for many years. I have three hospitality jobs now, so I don't get out there as much as I used to, but I used to go a few times a week.

Bandits on the Run: This is one of the most important places in Bandits lore. It's truly where it all began for us, years ago, when Roy Dodger dragged us all down into the subway to play our first Bandits songs. And we weren't alone down there. The Metropolitan stop is practically an underground venue, a mecca for all [sorts] of buskers. Bird Courage, Gabriel Royal, and Andrew Kalleen are just a few that we looked up to, looking to try out their songs unplugged in a beautiful acoustic environment in front of a regular audience of commuters who have come to expect their wait to be scored by some platform crooner.

Cancion Franklin: I was a subway performer before I got into the band game. Anywhere in NYC where a fast train meets a slow train is a good place to busk, as the fast L for example would feed the platform on the G (this was a while ago!), and a solid audience would be there. The acoustics down there are great, and you didn't have to compete with too many announcements.

Shane Conerty: Why do I like it? One, it's paid practice. Two, every once in a while, something really genuine and magical will happen.

Earlier this year, I met this little girl named Ruby who's probably about eight or nine. She came up to me holding her mom's hand and said something like, "Hey, you're a good singer! I sing too!" So I was like, "Ok, let's hear it then," and she proceeded to make up an original song on the spot while I played some simple chords. I threw a few changes at her, and she followed them without a cue. She did the whole song with her back to everyone and staring at the subway wall because she was shy. It was incredible. Then the train came, and we said goodbye. I saw her a few times after that, but she didn't remember my name and was too shy to ever sing with me again. It was a really cool moment, though.

Cancion Franklin: I always did pretty well there and made friends with a waitress from Kellogg's Diner who would give me coffee and let me use the bathroom when I needed to. Using the bathroom becomes an issue when you are broke and playing the tunnels, as it was $2.75 to get underground, and if you are having a bad day, it can actually cost money to busk. Still, some beautiful memories from those days, and I was able to get a start in this city. Always will be a precious spot for me.

Bandits on the Run: If you're ever passing through this stop, we encourage you to keep an ear out, you may just happen on a fresh new musical discovery!

Two Boots
Lydia Gammill, Vram Kherlopian, Melissa Lucciola (Gustaf)

Melissa Lucciola: Vram and Lydia did an amazing performance called "Bird Funeral" that's one of my favorite Gustaf performances I've seen with my own two eyes. Lydia dressed up like a bird, and Vram played classical guitar and read a script about Lydia's life growing up as a bird and dying as a bird, and it was beautiful and tragic and amazing.

Vram Kherlopian: That was so fun.

Lydia Gammill: Tarra books Two Boots, where there's some free beer and pizza, and it's been a really wonderful way to spend an afternoon. It's kind of like it's the secret Alphaville in a way, our secret Alphaville, where you stop by and you're like, oh, who's in here? I know these people. And you usually get to see a friend playing some music, and she does a great job of curating stuff.

So you can try things out. I think it started with Vram being told by one of his friends that he'd make an ideal person to play a bird funeral, a funeral for a bird. And then he wrote a wonderful piece. I feel like I did the least in all that. I just showed up with some outfits. It was great.

Vram Kherlopian: You had like four costume changes.

Melissa Lucciola: It almost brought me to tears. It was that good.

Lydia Gammill: Vram's music was great. I forgot what a wonderful hidden gem Two Boots Pizza is. It's truly such a wonderful secret, safe, art space. You know Tarra, like, you can do whatever you want there.

SECTION 4
BEHIND THE SCENE

Generally speaking, there are two ways you can experience a band's music, on the stage and on the record. And in both formats, the artists responsible put in an extraordinary amount of work to perfect their performance through efforts that we, as fans and friends, generally know nothing about.

We see curated behind-the-scenes photos and video footage featuring fancy mics, dozens of dials, and miles of cords snaking across rugs above can't-wait-to-show-you-what-we're-working-on captions, but we don't witness everything going on behind the closed doors in the windowless rooms. None of us know which tools and tricks and tweaks were used to make the album that sound-tracked the wildest summer of our lives, or the amount of time and work, plus money, whiskey, and weed, that went into the record we had on repeat after our worst breakups.

And honestly, most of us are probably cool with that. We don't need intimate knowledge of every step of the assembly line or want to be privy to every part of the painstaking production process. Most fans are more into the outward-facing aspects of the art, the madness rather than the method. We'd much rather observe our favorite larger-than-life singer howl live and unrestrained on stage than witness dozens of takes as they try to hit that high note or nail a line with the right combination of sex and rage.

But despite the "pay no attention to the man behind the curtain" concept, that doesn't mean we don't still want a little peek behind the scenes, and for this book some artists were more than happy to provide it. After all, there is some definite punk-rock intrigue to band practice, and an undeniable sexiness to *in the studio*. And while we definitely don't need all the technical, often unglamorous details accompanying the rehearsing and recording process, let's be real. We're one hundred percent here for any and all tales involving blood, sweat, and tears.

Or, you know, bass, drums, and beers.

CHAPTER 14
OFF THE RECORD

"Band practice is a very special space. We all are very,
very vulnerable with each other, and the practice space is
kind of a physicalized version of that."
- Mia Berrin (Pom Pom Squad)

The moments in which you completely let go aren't always spontaneous. They're often thoroughly mapped out and planned for.

Before hosting a house party, you probably pick up booze and put away your most breakable belongings. If you're doing mushrooms, you might recruit the right mix of friends and select an upstate Airbnb with just-freaky-enough furniture. And while a concert can be a totally insane experience characterized by a big anything-can-happen atmosphere, it's also on some level a controlled chaos, an explosion of energy that's been bottled for this very moment, and an experience that's all possible because of the unseen hours of preparation that were put in beforehand.

That's all to say that while artists might be possessed by an unidentifiable spirit once they hit the stage, unless one only operates alone and in totally improvisational fashion, practice is still imperative. Which means, of course, that bands need a proper place to do it.

In NYC, apartments are stacked, shoved, and wedged above,

below, and beside each other like Jenga blocks, meaning that by virtue of noises and vibrations alone, your neighbors know things about your life—shower schedule, sex noises, Netflix queue—that in any other city only your roommates, pets, and personally assigned FBI agent would. Sure, this proximity does offer a small sense of security. If you're getting murdered, at least one person might call 911, or at least 311 a few days later once the smell gets too bad. But it also means you have the neighborly duty to, you know, not be a dick. And while there are plenty of ways to make enemies of the human beings existing on the opposite sides of your very thin walls, buying a drum set, accordion, or anything else that makes a lot of noise is right at the top of the list.

Of course, there are definitely living spaces that serve as exceptions to this rule, bohemian buildings and unconventional apartments where ordinary etiquette, and even occasionally safety, are thrown out the window in favor of creative expression.

When my friend, musician, producer, and engineer Jeff Citron (Moonglow) moved to Brooklyn in 2014, his goal was to find a place where he could have a full set of drums in his apartment, play as loud as he wanted, and record music at home. In many cities that might be a pipe dream, but Jeff managed to find a room that met those rent-paying rock-star requirements in what he described as a "crusty, kinda free-for-all" artist-occupied former factory in Bushwick.

"You just hear like metal bands practicing in their apartments, then you'd walk up a different floor and there's a jazz band practicing in their apartment," he told me of his first visit to the space. "There's just all kinds of, you know, loud music happening everywhere, and graffiti everywhere on the walls and dudes smoking cigs in the stairwell, and it just felt like what I wanted at that time of my life."

While Jeff succeeded in finding a place that checked his original boxes, the honeymoon period was admittedly short-lived, and he soon learned that this kind of freedom can come at a cost. Beyond the slumlord management and the roaches and mice that served as roommates, his literal breaking point came six months after moving in, when he awoke early one morning to water trickling into his bedroom, the first startling sign of a ceiling that would collapse just hours later. And in many ways, the building doesn't seem to have changed much since. It's still filled with musicians and their instruments, and when I visited a bassist friend who was living there in the summer of 2021, he casually pointed out the stack of buckets on top of the fridge that he and his roommates and bandmates kept on hand to capture living-room leaks.

So back to more, shall we say, *mainstream* living arrangements. For an artist in a more traditional apartment, proximity to one's neighbors and general societal expectations mean that, unless their style is coffee-shop acoustic, they're only interested in air drumming, or they're content perfecting their performance in their bedroom with headphones fused to their ears, they're going to need a separate practice space. A designated area where they can fuck around at high volume, let loose while they get tight, and run through their full set at top speed with their friends.

That's where Brooklyn's rehearsal hubs come in. Imagine small, typically shared spaces where artists can rock out while plugged in, and for a few hours at a time have all the freedom in the world to get loud and go wild. Places that are often still stacked, shoved, and wedged above, below, and beside each other, with noise bleeding out under doors and through walls, but without the risk of angry neighbors and noise complaints. Primarily because the people under that specific roof are also musicians, and no one's trying to do something insane like sleep at 3 a.m.

While my friend Alex and I spent every afternoon in high school praying for a thunderstorm to cancel soccer practice, and while we later took the outrageously extreme step of joining math club just to get out of it, for artists practice seems to be both a safe space and a happy place. And while it is definitely *work*, with progress being made and real goals and milestones in mind, it's also in some ways play. It's a cross between fun and therapy, a jam session meets adult pizza party, a time and place where bonding and breakthroughs happen, songs are written and refined, and band traditions are established while inside jokes are solidified.

Along with a "really convenient excuse to be social," Joe Dahlstrom of Brooklyn psych-soaked rock trio Hot Knives described for me the fun and fulfilling nature of band practice.

"The idea of like, working on a work project or a project in school, but with your best friends and people who agree with you creatively, challenge you creatively, and don't agree with you creatively in the right ways, is just so pleasant. That we get to do it three to four times a week is just incredible, and the more times we do it the more fun it is, and it's just a blast. It's the reason I live in New York."

I caught this creative process in action in May 2021, when Hot Knives invited me to sit in on a Saturday-afternoon practice session six days before the release of their record, *Making Love To Make Music To Make Love To*, a sexier spin on a Spacemen 3 title. The band was rehearsing at their longtime practice space at Savaria Studios, which is housed, along with outposts of various other businesses, in the massive former Pfizer plant on the border of Bed-Stuy and South Williamsburg. Decked out with string lights for artistic ambiance and a box fan for summer survival, Hot Knives' unit could fit maybe one-and-a-third Smart cars, but having played together for a decade and rented the room for years, the bandmates had long mastered the art of rocking out without knocking anyone out. Deftly maneuvering around each other like head-banging ballet dancers, but with far more flowing hair, Joe, Tom and Alex demonstrated an unspoken awareness as they played with and off each other, showcasing the band ESP they'd honed over hundreds of hours spent within those same walls, all while delivering me an eardrum-blasting, mind-blowing concert for one.

While the best bands appear to truly offer something of themselves on stage, this personal show was unparalleled on the intimacy front, and from my vantage point squatting in the corner I witnessed what appeared to be a totally unselfconscious experience, a group completely in the zone performing in the comfort of their music home.

Along with what I gleaned from my super-charged live experience with Hot Knives, the beloved, even revered, nature of practice spaces was really brought home by Mia Berrin, the fierce queer cheer captain of "Quiet Grrrl Punk" project, Pom Pom Squad.

During our interview and over email, Mia got a little sentimental as she explained how much she cherished band practice. She described the moments of self-discovery and catharsis that had occurred within the group's musical equivalent of a cubicle, where she says she first came into her own as a musician. And in 2020, when COVID made it impossible to convene indoors to sing and sweat it out, the artist was quite literally dreaming of the moment when she and her collaborators would be able to reunite and rehearse:

> We have a practice space at Our Wicked Lady, which is also a very loved bar and venue off the Morgan L. We've spent a lot of nights there working on music and talking and crying and doing drunk karaoke. I'm getting to the phase of quarantine where I'm having dreams about doing things like hugging or going to people's apartments. Last night, the dream was just me struggling to find an XLR for twenty minutes while my bandmates drank Gatorade or warmed up or talked about their day. It felt like heaven.

When I was seeking contributions for this book, LG Galleon (Clone, Dead Leaf Echo) shared his love for not just one spot, but an entire area, the border zone between Williamsburg and Bushwick to the east, located off the Montrose L train stop and along a polluted body of water.

When describing a decade's worth of experiences in this neighborhood he called Newtown, named for the toxic creek nearby, LG painted a picture of a gritty-glam paradise characterized by droves of artists and beloved small businesses, illicit parties and underground venues, local radio stations and indie record labels. Plus, and perhaps most notably, he spoke of Danbro Studios and The Sweatshop, two of North Brooklyn's most prominent rehearsal hubs where bands have been playing, partying, and perfecting their craft for years.

"You can feel the creative spirit that is constantly flowing through it," he told me of this bit of bohemian Brooklyn, a sacred section of the borough where art is on the walls and music is always in the air.

They say that practice makes perfect. Here are a few of the places where Brooklyn artists work towards it.

Brooklyn SolarWorks
Kallan Campbell, Tcoy Coughlin, David Johnson, Shane Preece (Max Pain and the Groovies)

David Johnson: These guys, Shane, Tcoy and Dallin, work for Brooklyn SolarWorks. They have a giant fridge with free beer, so we raid the fridge and then we go jam. They take care of us.

Shane Preece: It's the coolest company ever, and they have a jam space where we practice. We used to practice at our house, but our neighbor next door does not like it.

David Johnson: He threatened to shoot us. It was so cool for like six months, and all of the sudden we had this Halloween show at Knockdown Center, the Jonathan Toubin event, and Emily from Ashjesus was coming over to jam because we were doing Creedence Clearwater Revival as our little guest appearance, and every time she'd come over to jam, this dude next door would start freaking out. He called the cops.

Kallan Campbell: He was causing such a ruckus, and everyone on the block is sticking their heads out like, "What?"

Tcoy Coughlin: Dude lives at his mom's house. He's like forty-five.

David Johnson: He told us we can't sit on the stoop and smoke cigarettes in our boxers anymore, as well.

Kallan Campbell: So long story short, we don't jam in the house right now.

Complete Music Studios
Jon Sandler (Great Good Fine Ok)

For every tour and every big performance we've ever done, we've rehearsed at this place called Complete Music Studios.

We've spent countless hours in that place. And it's so funny being there, every band in Brooklyn rehearses there. So anytime we're there, like clockwork we're either friends with bands that are rehearsing next to us or freaking out because there's bands we're huge fans of performing next to us.

There was one time where literally every room in the studio had a band in it that we were huge fans of. We were like, we should just all get together right now and put on a festival! We'd pop our head out in the hallway to see if anybody would come out. And you could hear songs through the walls. [You're] hearing some of your favorite songs.

The time I'm thinking of right now is CHVRCHES. So we could hear that hit, "The Mother We Share," echoing throughout the halls of Complete. We were like, yes! We're doing something right that we're here right now.

One time we were there and one of the dudes from Earth, Wind & Fire was rehearsing, Philip Bailey, and GGFO actually did a cover of "Easy Lover," which is Philip Bailey and Phil Collins. And he was there, and we told him about it, and we played it for him, and he loved it. So that was incredible. You can understand why that's one of my places. Any given day, you could probably see your favorite band.

Danbro Studios
Ryan Foster (Warm Body)

To me, Danbro was a nexus point. It was absolutely one of those places that helped interconnect the community of musicians. Physically though, it seemed the opposite, a cold, imposing factory-like fortress that could literally withstand a nuclear blast. It stood conveniently on Meserole, mere blocks away from the legendary DIY venue Shea Stadium, where we, the scoundrels, would cut our teeth.

Ever the militant labyrinth of concrete and steel, the structure could make one truly feel like a rat in a maze. It was always vast and unknowable no matter how many times I'd been there, and every trip up and down the stairs with arms full of equipment seemed inviting of accidental death. It was a while before someone showed me the elevator! It was also strangely welcoming though, with a sort of tangible kinetic energy as well.

Our band Lost Boy ? never rehearsed all that much, partly because this spot's accessibility enabled us to just meet up right before shows sometimes to get the blood pumping a little beforehand. That was invaluable for us!

My man R.J. Gordon (Baked, Titus Andronicus) would hole up in a room overstuffed with equipment and hosting the permanent essence of cigarette smoke and alcohol, and produce records by Titus, Lost Boy ?, Baked, etc. in addition to having actual space to physically workshop that music. All of this was certainly common practice in the facilities here, but behind every door creativity was emanating and it was inspiring. You can't understate what that did for the artists and the arts in NYC.

Our Wicked Lady
Mia Berrin (Pom Pom Squad)

We've been practicing at Our Wicked Lady for about two years.

As sort of my induction into the Brooklyn music scene in a weird way, at least in the current lineup of my band, I met Maria and Shelby at [the Bushwick venue] Elsewhere. I was in the green room, and it was this crazy night where I had broken up with somebody the night before and was sort of just manic, and I fired my old band like, a week before, and it was the second or third time I was ever playing solo. When I went into the green room, they were sitting there, and they were in another band, and I kind of just spilled all my guts to them. At the end of the night, they both came up to me, and they were super drunk, and they were like, "So when are we gonna play together?" I kind of thought that they were fucking with me. But they actually ended up kind of taking me in. You know, I was like a little lost stray puppy.

They had been practicing at Our Wicked Lady for a couple years. So one day, they were like, "We have this space. Come bring your stuff." I didn't even have an amp. I barely had a pedal board, if I had a pedal board at all back then. And they were like, "Do you need this? Here you go. Do you need this? Here you go."

I have a lot of really special memories of Our Wicked Lady, just kind of coming into my own as a musician in this new lineup, where I actually got to be the boss of my own music project. I tended to sort of yield to everybody else, and when I fired my old band, I ended up going to music school, because I just had felt so pushed around that I wanted to know how to do everything. And so in this space, literally and sort of metaphorically, they kind of asked me, "Well, what do you want to do?" And instead of telling me what I should do or dictating to me what I was good at or what I was bad at, they let me sort of figure it out on my own.

We're still there to this day, and you know, it is not a glamorous space whatsoever. It's like, there's just trash cans and dead cockroaches, and you know, you can hear everybody else's music through the walls. But it's like when you're in your little cubicle, it's very homey, and band practice is a very special space. I mean, I'm sure it is for every band in their own way, but for us in particular, we're all extremely emotional. We all are very, very vulnerable with each other, and the practice space is kind of a physicalized version of that.

Pirate Studios
Connor Gladney, Laura Valk (Skout); Dang Anohen, Lip Molina (Sallies)

Laura Valk: It's this DIY rehearsal space, which is awesome. It's twenty-four hours a day, which is pretty unheard of. There are three rooms. And it's all about the musician code, which is leave the room as you found it. And we've been to so many shitty spaces.

Connor Gladney: They smell bad, and the floors are sticky.

Laura Valk: Yeah, why is everything sticky?

Connor Gladney: You have to wrap your shoes in plastic bags. [Pirate Studios] is just a nice rehearsal space. They've got a bunch of equipment. The rooms are comfy and warm. It's easily accessible.

Lip Molina: They have very nice rooms.

Dang Anohen: We met the owners. Really cool people.

Lip Molina: Every once in a while, they have surprise shows with bands that normally rehearse over there. Free beer, a bunch of bands, you meet a lot of people.

Laura Valk: It does feel like a built-in community. There's always chitter-chatter with the musicians coming in before or after you, too. We're all kind of in this for the same reason, while at other places, you're like, "Get out of my room."

Connor Gladney: A lot of places, they just feel like a rented room, and this one feels more like you're walking into a shared space. It's cool.

Lip Molina: Definitely a great place for a band in Brooklyn, Greenpoint, to rehearse.

Dang Anohen: Don't talk it up too much, man. We want to get our hours.

Lip Molina: So don't rehearse on Tuesdays, six to nine!

Savaria Studios
Minaxi (Steve Carlin, Liam Christian, Shrenik Ganatra); Joe Dahlstrom (Hot Knives)

Minaxi: The spot that has been a creative outlet for Minaxi since its inception is our rehearsal space at Savaria Studios. Located on the third floor in the Pfizer building, a multi-purpose space with a corporate-looking facade, the spaces within are hidden gems.

Joe Dahlstrom: The guy who runs it is named Tamas Vajda and he's in a band called The Unbroken. He runs it and he has a recording studio as well upstairs.

Tamas is really attentive to what we want in a practice space. He's really responsive. Think of the best landlord you've had in Brooklyn, and he's better than that, you know. Which isn't saying a lot for a Brooklyn landlord, but for a guy running a practice space, that's incredible. He's really accommodating. He answers text messages, emails. Just behind the scenes he's been one of those guys that's facilitated really strong creativity.

He puts together showcases of Savaria-only bands. He really tries to foster community in the space, and that's really cool.

Minaxi: We have also made quite a few band friends on account of us sharing the spot with other Brooklyn bands.

Joe Dahlstrom: I was trying to record these vocals, and we couldn't find a quiet enough area to record the vocals, because there were so many bands practicing. And as we walked around those hallways at Pfizer, like, okay where's the noise coming from, it's like, *holy shit!* There are eight bands playing right now and all of them are good. Like we stopped to listen to every single band.

To know that if some band is ripping, I can stand outside the door, knock on their door and be like, "We want to play a show with you," which we've totally done before and we've hooked up shows that way, is invaluable.

Minaxi: Minaxi's music comes to life collaboratively in our space at Savaria. The room being on the "cozy" side can barely fit three to four people. The vocal mics can only be turned up to a certain point without encountering feedback from the instruments. The room itself is very dry. Despite these limitations, we have managed to craft sonic parts for the songs in that space. We have also evolved from just rehearsing to tracking guitars in that room for our sophomore album.

Joe Dahlstrom: In a place where people are getting priced out and pushed around, Savaria, he's really holding it down. And you can tell he's battling against the building because we get moved around a lot, but he's making it a place for musicians, making it a place for people that don't have, you know, the kind of money that I assume some people do have in the city. And he's come through huge for us time and time again.

He could be charging out the ass for rent and be doing fine. Like people can afford rent in that building, but he chooses to keep it available for musicians that are going to use the spaces.

One day we walked by the room that's ours now, and this guy came out only wearing sweatpants hanging off his ass. He looked like he hadn't slept for a week, and he just like, came out and the smell just hit us like, death. There was a mattress on the floor, a computer, and a guitar amp. I think he had a drum set, but basically, we were like, oh, this dude's living here. We pay well under half of what a normal person would pay for an apartment in New York City, so yeah, if you can swing it.

The next week, we came for practice and there was trash everywhere, and the smell was less strong but it was everywhere. So this guy had gotten caught and evicted. It took about two weeks to air out the room. It's in the lease now that we can't live there.

A Shipping Container in Bushwick
Lydia Gammill, Vram Kherlopian, Tarra Thiessen (Gustaf)

Lydia Gammill: I just stopped renting a shipping container outside of the Jefferson stop. I shared that as a practice space with The Wants, my old band. Their album was called *Container*. It was recorded in a container. We recorded some demos in there. It's a blue shipping container, and that's where we practiced.

Madison and I from The Wants, we wanted to have a space that we could also use as a studio. And so we were looking at spots in Danbro, and they ended up just being too small and too loud. So we started looking at art spaces, and we found this one real-estate agent. And finally, one day Madison's like, "Okay, I'm going to meet this guy. Come meet me at this address." And he's just like, smiling in front of our shipping container. *What?*

It was a fun experience to have. Not always practical when you had to go to the bathroom.

Tarra Thiessen: I peed in front of a lot of box trucks. Remember when cops knocked on the door when we were practicing randomly?

Vram Kherlopian: They were like, "What's going on in here?!"

We're like, "We're playing music."

They're like, "What address is this?!"

We're like, "Uhh…"

Tarra Thiessen: They were looking for something else, I guess.

Vram Kherlopian: They were *not* looking for us.

The Sweatshop
Todd Martin, Michael Nitting (The Misters); Chayse Schutter (A Very Special Episode); Zach (Strange Neighbors); Michael Tarnofsky (Edna); Peter Wise

Peter Wise: So you don't think of a rehearsal space as your favorite place in Brooklyn, but when you're a musician, you spend a lot of time [there].

Todd Martin: I think it's a very personal spot for The Misters. It's honestly a great spot. There's like a bajillion rooms.

Michael Nitting: Hourly rentals.

Chayse Schutter: Sweatshop is special because it is literally where every band in BK sheds themselves for hours on end. It's a true mecca of music in that area. It's dank.

Zach: There's always interesting people hanging around outside and the sound of a hundred bands practicing at once bleeding through the walls.

Todd Martin: There's so many eclectic groups that go through, and you get to hear people through the walls and stuff. It's actually pretty fun.

Chayse Schutter: Never know who you're gonna run into.

Michael Tarnofsky: I love going to The Sweatshop only because I've run into Jeff Rosenstock three times there. I'm always like, *Ahh!* And it's a cheap, well-run place.

Todd Martin: It's truly a sweaty little shop.

Michael Nitting: It's gross, but it's amazing.

Peter Wise: The Sweatshop is just like the perfect Brooklyn rehearsal experience. You know, maybe not the cleanest in the world. Just all the good rock-n-roll smells that you need. A lot of sweat, cheap beer, cigarettes, all the good stuff.

Michael Nitting: Sometimes you walk into the room and you're like, I don't know who was in this room before we are, but it smells weird. We're getting in and playing two-five-one progressions and jazz chords, like *ya-dah-dah-bah-bah*, and meanwhile, beforehand it was like, uh, weird sex parties probably.

Todd Martin: We don't kink shame, dude. Sexual freedom for all.

Zach: The whole area also smells like dough because of the dumpling factory nearby.

Chayse Schutter: It neighbors an Asian food distribution plant, so outside always smells like uncooked ramen. It's hard not to love.

Todd Martin: We weren't going there for a while, we were in a different spot. And then we stopped going there and went back to Sweatshop. I remember the first time we went back. We were kind of like, we really like the vibe here.

Michael Nitting: It's like the equivalent, oh my god, I'm so glad I got to bring this up. *Cheer* on Netflix. It's just like going to the gym. It's like, we're comfortable with the space, we're showing up.

Todd Martin: Like I don't know what it is, but we really like how we feel in here.

Peter Wise: I don't know, it's everything you want in a rehearsal studio.

CHAPTER 15
STUDIO CITY

"It's a community of people who are all doing the same thing. We learn from each other, and teach each other, and we're all in music projects."
- Harper James (Eighty Ninety)

While music exists in rowdy, unrestrained form on stage and in practice spaces, recording studios are where a different side of band life goes down, and it's one I was recently lucky enough to witness and participate in firsthand.

In what is approximately a once-in-six-months occurrence, I was actually going to be on time to meet Gino Gianoli of Duke of Vandals at his band's recording session before my Uber driver Gerard "got caught up in the vibes" of the trance tunes on the radio and managed to miss our turn, instead landing us on a mystery street a mile or so away from the actual address before realizing his error.

That said, it was still a five-star transportation situation. After all, if there's one form of distraction I understand, it's getting lost in a music moment. I've overshot destinations due to dance-walking down the sidewalk. I've air-drummed my way through a fair share of subway stops. And I once snapped to attention in the adult-diaper aisle of Duane Reade after wandering through the store with my phone above my head, trying to Shazam whatever probably-

Taylor-Swift song was playing through the speakers.

And to my driver's credit, even if you're demonstrating a surgeon-like level of focus while observing perfect silence in your 2012 Toyota Camry, it's definitely not difficult to get turned around on the warehouse-lined streets with barbed wire-topped fences that make up Brooklyn's most industrial areas. Whether you're navigating by street sign or street art, it's easy to overshoot your destination when the address is a sign-less door that opens up into an unmarked building.

However, after some rerouting, U-turning, and backtracking, we eventually arrived. With more confidence than I felt, I assured Gerard that this was indeed my intended endpoint, and while obviously skeptical, he turned the radio up and sped off, probably to pick up a new nearby Brooklynite ready to start their Saturday night.

Shivering on the sidewalk and hunched against the brutal wind of the thirty-degree March evening, I used my suddenly frozen fingers to text Gino, "I'm HerEEe?" while trying not to think about what exactly I would do if I wasn't. Fortunately, the moment of uncertainty only lasted a moment before the curl-crowned head of one of Brooklyn's most charismatic musicians popped out of a door I hadn't even spotted and greeted me with an "Ah!"

While Gino isn't a particularly tall guy, I always forget that, because his personality is larger than life. And one of the things I love most about him is his insatiability, his desire to do everything and be everywhere and meet everyone while moving a million miles a minute, often in multiple directions. And while sometimes that means I emerge after a two-minute bathroom break to find he's completely vanished from the venue, the persistent pursuit of a good time is one search in particular that I'll always respect and understand.

Along with playing hard, Gino works hard, and he enjoys it. After beckoning me inside and wrapping me in a hug that instantly defrosted my frigid torso by at least twenty-five percent, he led me up the stairs, waving his hands while excitedly describing the progress of the new EP in whatever accent one develops from being half-Italian and half-Peruvian, living life on three continents, and spending a decade running and ripping around New York City.

Now, no matter how much time I spend in Bushwick and East Williamsburg, and the border between the two and even the validity of the latter label are somewhat debatable, I always forget how misleading the uninviting outsides of these ominous buildings often are. However, like a spiky, juicy pineapple or a crusty geode with a crystal center, the most *Saw*-like of exteriors often contain the most surprisingly delightful interiors. This studio epitomized this contradiction, a warmly lit and well-furnished enclave twice as big and twice as nice as my not-even-that-small-or-shitty apartment.

That evening, I was under the impression that I was meeting thrashy-trashy punk trio Duke of Vandals to have a drink, catch up, and perhaps capture some behind-the-scenes footage while the band wrapped the recording of their debut EP, *Vandalism*. However, after offering me a seat on the couch and an IPA from the brewery around the corner, Gino casually mentioned that I would not just be documenting that evening but participating, informing me for the very first time that, along with Brooklyn photographer Michelle LoBianco, I would be contributing backing vocals to the band's record.

Now, while I'm highly skilled in the audience art of the "Woo!" and can easily switch on a smooth radio voice, when it comes to singing, my vocal cords are yet another instrument I haven't mastered. In fact, one of the most mortifying moments I've experienced in my thirty-three years on this planet was being forced to attempt "Over the Rainbow" during a mandatory musical audition in highschool theater, a performance that landed me, I kid you not, the role of "Tree 2." However, unlike the Klein Forest High casting director, Gino had no illusions about my singing skills, and he wasn't exactly setting me up for a solo. Instead, the band just needed a few friends who could show up at 7:00 p.m. to shout some lyrics while clapping somewhat on beat. And it turns out that, as an individual whose trademark characteristics include enthusiasm and volume, this was a job for which I was perfectly suited.

Under the instruction of the engineer, Gino, Michelle, myself, and Duke of Vandals bassist Missy Scarbrough and drummer Danny Irizarry arranged ourselves in a loose semi-circle around a single mic. And after clearing throats and cracking both necks and beers to get appropriately loud and loose, the group recording session, led by DoV's percussion professional, officially commenced.

"Whoooa-ohhhh-ohhh"

"24! 24! 24!"

"Car crash TV! Can't stop watchin' eeeee-it!"

Maybe check out the Duke of Vandals EP for the full effect. But that was my musical debut, my first foray into experiencing a very small fraction of the mad science that makes up the recording process. While these few lines were short and simple to recite, they were still an important part of a much bigger picture. They needed to be done exactly right, and there was a major sense of satisfaction when, after stumbling our way through the first several takes together, we finally got the thumbs-up signaling that we'd nailed it. And then half of us went to a nearby bar to celebrate.

What I now understand about the studio, not just through this brief bit of personal experience but through the excitement and awe of artists themselves, is that *this* is where the magic happens. Where musicians, like kids in a candy store, often with a Willy Wonka-like genius behind the board, have access to the equipment, effects, and expertise to make anything happen. Where the music that bounces around brains, the lyrics that bleed out of pens, and the songs that have been demoed in bedrooms and basements across the borough are fully realized. Polished, perfected, and captured forever to be pressed onto vinyl, distributed in digital form, and sold as cassettes for cash at corner merch tables across the country.

While sometimes the process might be simply transactional, a matter of X dollars per hour for parts and labor, with bands carefully budgeting to bang out their next EP without breaking the bank, in the best of scenarios the set-up is not just professional but personal. It's a joint creative effort and a matter of true collaboration, musicians partnering with trusted producers and engineers who, over the course of a song or album's realization, become real friends who are just as obsessed with and invested in the vision as the artists themselves. And that's often because they *are* artists themselves, dividing their time between the booth and the board, helping others achieve their dreams in between bringing their own art to life.

When I'm working with an artist to promote or premiere a new release, it's not uncommon in conversation or the Bandcamp credits to come across names I recognize from my inbox, often because I've also worked with that individual to help push their personal music project. And there's no doubt that this firsthand understanding of the musician experience directly informs the way these detail-oriented creatives operate on the other side of the glass.

Of course, it must be mentioned that just like DIY venues allow artists to bypass barriers and do things their own way, free of rules and without reliance on industry gatekeepers, increasingly affordable technology has facilitated the boom of the bedroom producer, offering knowledgeable-enough artists the access and ability to produce their own music. It also offers them unlimited hours to experiment while saving incalculable amounts of money.

One November night in 2018, I was interviewing musician and producer Ryan Egan, who has since relocated both his project and his person to Paris, at Baby's All Right. In a front booth, under the magenta glow of the neon sign and over the sound of the Bee Gees song boogying through the speakers, the artist touted the benefits of this method and the freedom that comes with it:

> You just have all the time in the world. You have as much time to tweak and tweak and tweak until it's right. We're at this amazing time, which I think is why contemporary music is so unique and interesting and exciting, because you do have so many people creating in this format. It's just bringing out a really interesting phase in music history.

One artist known for this is Billie Eilish, whose brother Finneas recorded her Grammy-winning debut album at home. On the less famous, more local front, I saw this DIY process in progress in the Brooklyn bedroom of my friend Nick LaFalce (Atlas Engine) on a

Saturday afternoon, as I lay sprawled on his bed contributing moral support while he and his bandmates tracked vox in a makeshift closet-turned-vocal-booth.

I knew Nick and I would be best friends the moment he showed up as my guest on the first-ever episode of the Bands do BK radio show wearing a yellow t-shirt with a bear piloting an airplane that said "Flying is just plane fun!" And in adrenaline- and tequila-fueled fashion at Our Wicked Lady right after the broadcast, I'm sure I informed him of our destiny. A multi-instrumentalist who got his first guitar at six and has been playing music for almost as many years as he's been alive, Nick is not just an experienced artist but a true perfectionist. A year after our first meeting, as I was writing this book and he was working on his album, we had adopted a mutual mantra that we texted back and forth regarding our respective projects. *Do it right.* And the biggest benefit of the DIY approach was that Nick had the time to do just that, inching closer to the ideal as he poured his heart, soul, and countless hours into a complex, ambitious, and stunning set of songs exploring his decade-long battle with Lyme disease. All without lighting thousands of dollars on fire trying to perfect every single harmony.

But back to Brooklyn studios that aren't where someone also sleeps, mostly because Nick probably wouldn't be stoked if I gave out his actual address. Whether you're an artist or just a fan, you have to respect the role of these tune factories and of the facilitators who serve as music midwives, helping groups and individuals bring their art into the world. And in some cases, you've also got to appreciate the histories, which might pale in comparison to certain established Manhattan studios, but are nonetheless impressive. Beyond being stocked with high-tech tools and staffed with killer talent, many of these spaces double as modern music museums and meccas, where over the years both local legends and visiting visionaries have come to create. And in some studios, today's musicians might be sharing spaces with the spirits of their heroes, ghosts of NYC scenes and sessions past, as they record in the very rooms responsible for the records that have impressed, inspired, and influenced them, while making songs that in the future just might move and motivate others.

My artist and engineer friend Jeff, he of the collapsed ceiling, worked in seven New York studios in seven years before relocating to Vermont in 2021 to take a dream gig with record producer Rich Costey, who produced and worked on many of the records Jeff had listened to growing up. When I asked him what the most important attributes are in a studio, Jeff listed three, a good-sounding room, quality equipment, and something a little less concrete. *Vibe*:

> You don't want a space to be too clean or feel too slick and streamlined like some of these modern studios. It just feels vapid. There's no ghosts in the walls, you know, or stories. I think it's really important [for] artists to come into a place to make music where you feel comfortable and inspired in the space, and you feel like you're a part of something bigger, and you're tapping into something. And an artist in a studio, when they know somebody that they love has made a record or a song that they love in that space, their face just lights up, you know.

Whether it's price point, toy chest, talent, or a recording résumé that makes a studio stand out, it's these places and the people running them that we have to thank for the music on our playlists and on our turntables, in our headphones and inside our homes.

Even if, on occasion, the songs might cause us to skip our subway stop. Or our Uber driver to miss a turn or two.

Black Lodge Recording
Devin McKnight (Maneka); Jared Yee (Evolfo)

Devin McKnight: I'd like to highlight one place in particular, Black Lodge Recording. It *was* located on Broadway a block or two from the Myrtle Ave intersection. It's since moved due to pandemic-related complications I believe. My long-time producer and bandmate companion Michael Thomas III became a resident engineer and co-owner there maybe five-ish years ago? We were in Grass is Green together and attended Berklee together and he's recorded many, many albums that I've been a part of in his parents' basement in Boston. So in a sense, Black Lodge became the new Mike's basement for me and bands like Ovlov, Mister Goblin, and other Two Inch Astronaut-adjacent bands, Grass is Green, Maneka, Fern Mayo, and the list goes on.

Many times, we'd just jam and experiment with the gear he and his co-owner Vishal had been compiling along the way. So in that way it's even acted as a learning experience for me as a producer and songwriter. Having the opportunity to experiment really gave me ideas of how to bring my ideas in Maneka from my bedroom directly to the studio to accurately communicate and produce what I was envisioning.

This is a totally shortened description of hours of spliff-filled sessions where I'd get there in the morning and leave in the middle of the night having no sense of where time had gone because there are no windows.

Jared Yee: Black Lodge is definitely one of my favorite studios in which to record. The engineers, the gear, and the overall vibe are all top-notch. Also recording in those surrounding velvet walls puts you in a real good zone.

Devin McKnight: Additionally, I've been able to meet people in other bands who also used the space like Nick Hakim, Empress Of, and record in the same place as a slew of other super cool artists I'd never even dream of considering my peers in any way. There's also this great coffee shop, restaurant and party space next door called Cafe Erzulie, which was also a weird hub of sorts for creatives in the neighborhood. So like, we could oftentimes leave the studio for a coffee or drink and run into some pretty hip people. I also occasionally ran into people who'd been at Maneka shows, obviously the hippest people around.

Whether this vibe or purpose was intentional or unintentional, it became a place I was proud to show others and associate myself with. I feel like I could record at any number of places and achieve similar audio fidelity, but none with the added perks I've spoken of.

I've been on the edge of my seat, chomping at the bit, eagerly awaiting the studio to reopen in its new location so I can fill my life with a constructive creative outlet. It seems like now more than ever I'm somewhat starved for an outlet and some semblance of community and belonging. I doubt it'll be the same, but at least I know what to shoot for.

The Bunker Studio
Todd Martin, Michael Nitting (The Misters); Jeff Citron (Moonglow); Vanessa Silberman

Vanessa Silberman: I typically produce and engineer my own projects and I'll bring artists to different studios, so when I first got to New York, I was getting to know different rooms. You know, so you can take your time and find the right fit for the right artist. Having worked there, you understand the flow of how things are set up and whatnot.

I work at home and I record also at home, but there's a recording studio that I've worked at that I really like called The Bunker Studio.

Michael Nitting: Ugh, writing a song is like you hate it and you love it. Maybe you hate it again, and then you hopefully go back and love it again. And [our song] "Other People" was the silent creeper. Like, it came up and I was like, damn, like I actually am in love with this.

Todd Martin: It really wasn't until we finished it that we were like, wait, this song's kinda good!

Michael Nitting: We were so thankful we got to record everything. Thankful? We paid, but we're thankful, nonetheless. We recorded at The Bunker Studio, which is over in Williamsburg, with this guy Nolan Thies. And I think he was literally just the engineer on duty but like, lo and behold, we have formed this amazing relationship with him. Nolan, we love you! Shout-out!

Todd Martin: He knows what's up.

Vanessa Silberman: It's so purely New York music culture. Coming from LA and working around the country, I never worked on jazz records really. New York is such a big place for jazz, and the first time I helped out on a session, just kind of learned the room there, I think it was like a forty-piece choir, or maybe thirty people, and it was just insane. It was the most people I think I'd experienced or close to it. I thought it was really cool, and the quality is really amazing.

I also am super into hip-hop and the culture of that, and the first time that I worked there, at the same time I was watching this show on Hulu about the Wu-Tang Clan. I saw a scene and I was like, wow, that really looks like Bunker. They filmed it there!

Jeff Citron: I [part-timed] at this Brooklyn studio, Bunker, which is pretty cool. It's very Sear Sound-y in terms of equipment and ideology. The whole ethos of fifties and sixties tube microphones, in pristine condition. You know, [just] like the type of clientele that comes through. Big jazz groups and artists and world music and indie-rock bands, people that appreciate a really fine recording and working like it's [still] the seventies or eighties.

Vanessa Silberman: There's a lot of that culture from New York. I think it's a really great place, and I really like the guys who work there. There's a fellow named Andy [Plovnick], who's the manager there, and he's really cool, and he's got a band, and the guys who are there just running the place are really, really good.

Jeff Citron: The owners at Bunker, the engineers, are also a part of this band, I think it's called Nerve. It's all these performers that are really virtuosic, really talented players. So they're all approaching having a studio from a musician's perspective very much, but also honoring the art of having like a really fine recording studio.

There's a lot of great instruments, fine microphones, synthesizers and some fine pianos over there and a nice collection of amps.

Michael Nitting: We went in and tracked all the songs, like all the drums, all the pianos, all the guitars, all of the guitar tones and the synths, in one day.

Todd Martin: It's like you're shilling out this cash to really do what you want to do, so I think this was the first time we really went into the studio being super prepared. And I'm so happy that we did that, because we ended up getting so much more done in the studio. Now this is kind of the standard for how we should work. And I think that was a huge step for us.

Brooklyn Recording
Jeff Citron (Moonglow)

A lot of these other places I worked, like Sear Sound, when we made recordings, it was like, don't hit the compressor too hard, don't even use compression, record everything in a really proper way, give the client a really un-fucked-up recording that sounds great, but doesn't tie up anybody's hands in terms of making decisions down the line.

Whereas with Andy [Taub] at Brooklyn Recording, it felt like every session was like, seat-of-the-pants, just like, I'm along for the ride. His style was to do what he thought was right and what was cool in the moment. So things got pretty chaotic at some points, patching up a lot of different stuff at once and setting things up in a complicated way. But, you know, the recordings are pretty sweet and interesting and colored, and in that way I do think Andy was kinda really smart and a really interesting engineer.

And he had everything at the studio. Had all the sweet old organs that were used on different records, like a really nice Hammond B3, a Vox Continental, everything in really great shape and well maintained. You know, the kind of place you want to be if you were like, I want to be Brian Wilson making a Beach Boys record or something, and you have all these tools and orchestral instruments and things right there.

The Creamery Studio
Caitlin Mahoney

The Creamery is where I recorded my last album [*Story Still Left to Be Told*]. It's an amazing place, a very inspiring place to make music. The guys that run it are just wonderful humans, wonderful guys. They do such a beautiful job making it an inviting, relaxed space where you just want to create things. And it's kind of unassuming. It's what you need it to be, whereas I feel like some studios are kind of flashy because they feel like they need to be fancy to draw you to make music there. Here the equipment is incredible, but it feels like home. It's a nice place. It's where I've written and created so much music that at this point it's special to me.

Degraw Sound
Harper James (Eighty Ninety); Connor Jones, William Thompson (Yella Belly)

Harper James: That's where I live, basically. I mean, I live in my apartment theoretically, but I spend fifteen hours a day there. Degraw is one of my favorite places in the world.

William Thompson: I went to Degraw when it was getting built, when I first moved to New York. [Ben, the owner] was like a friend of a friend. A year later, I went in there, and me and Ben just automatically got together. And we have all these shared interests. He was more or less doing the rock 'n' roll resurgence thing in New York when I was trying to do it in Austin, when we were both kids. We've played with all the same people, we have all the same interests in music. So immediately I just felt some kinship, as opposed to those pay-by-the-hour studios that you go to when you first move here and you don't really know anyone.

[Ben's] passion is recording and producing and obviously running a studio. So to have someone in your age range that's just as passionate but doing that, to get together and collaborate is so cool. It's always been a good relationship. It's always great to have people like that.

We've been going there for a while. We've recorded all over the place and we always kept going back to Degraw. I think that kind of became like our primary spot to record and it definitely felt like a family of people.

Connor Jones: We've developed a great relationship with the other bands that record and work there as well.

William Thompson: Yeah. And then there's always new people coming in and out.

Harper James: It's a community of people who are all doing the same thing. We learn from each other, and teach each other, and we're all in music projects.

Figure 8 Recording
Jeff Citron (Moonglow); Gabriel Birnbaum (Wilder Maker)

Jeff Citron: Flatbush was, I think, the ultimate part of town that I've lived in in terms of just being around music and artists, and people recording stuff and writing songs. My roommate Lily Wen was really fucking cool and worked at this great studio called Figure 8. It's definitely not the biggest, it's a little smaller, but it's really fuckin' great. A lot of people like working there.

Gabriel Birnbaum: I love that place. It's in Prospect Heights. That's where we recorded *Zion*.

It's a beautiful place, a great space. It's really thoughtfully designed, great gear, really reasonably priced for how nice it is. Compared to other studios that cost about the same in New York, I'd say they have much better stuff. Then it's also the community around it. It's owned by Shahzad Ismaily, who's a musician who plays with tons of great people.

Jeff Citron: All the things I was mentioning make a great studio, they really nail it and try and approach it from an artist perspective. And Lily is very cool and has her own record label called Figure & Ground records, and she works with a lot of local folks and really cares about making interesting, eclectic music.

Gabriel Birnbaum: It's funny to me because it's like a storefront recording studio. I remember someone telling me it was going to be a recording studio, and I was like, no, no, no, there's no fucking way. But it's true. They just have frosted glass in the front, you can't tell what it is. There's an upstairs room and a downstairs room, there's a backyard, really nicely sound treated.

I actually do not smoke weed because I can't do it, but a lot of people who are musicians do, and it's good to be able to have a backyard to smoke in. My friend who works there was telling me about doing rap sessions, and every five minutes they're just going outside to smoke a fuckin' blunt.

It's also personally significant for me in making this record, which is the first record we put out on a label, a big forward step for the band, and also the last thing we did before our lineup kinda shifted. It sort of feels representative of that period.

Mousetown
Mia Berrin (Pom Pom Squad)

I had finished my show at Trans-Pecos, and this person came up to me and really liked the band, and they'd never seen us before and were super inspired, and it was basically like, "Oh, I have this studio called Mousetown."

I was looking for a place to record our EP [*Ow*]. I was trying to figure out where to go, what to do. I was really new to the whole thing, I'd only ever recorded in my bedroom or other people's apartments. So I was like, oh my god, yes, a studio. Yeah, absolutely. And we recorded for four hundred dollars, and we did it in like, two days.

The first day we showed up to the studio, it was like the tiniest, dustiest practice space, so dusty that I couldn't do the vocals, because every day that we would leave the studio I would have like, an asthma attack, and I don't have asthma. I like, would not be able to breathe.

So, it was hilarious, and I think the second all of us walked in, we all shared this glance of like, oh, fuck, what are we doing? So our friend, who is the person who produced *Ow* with me, his name is Tommy Ordway, left the room for a sec, and all of us kind of did the whisper of like, "I didn't expect this. What's going on?" And then, you know, we ended up recording the whole EP in this practice space.

Tommy is a fantastic engineer and was able to figure out how to set the mics so that even in this tiny space, there was very little bleed between the drum kit and the guitars, and it was very impressive, actually. We were just all so close, like physically close, that there was this lovely, frenetic, sweaty energy that I feel like made its way into the EP. And it was special. That was a magical process.

I think the last song we recorded, the second to last song on the EP, it's very quiet, and it starts with this section of just me playing a guitar solo and doing this kind of finger-picking thing. It's a song called "Cut My Hair." So for this first verse that's just me and guitar, there was this person playing somewhere in the practice space down the hall. And the only way I can describe the sound of this was it sounded like Transformers coming down from space and just moving their giant limbs. It was just this huge, crazy, synth sound. And it was so loud that we would have to stop recording because we would be getting bleed from this crazy Transformers band.

I remember at the very end of it, Tommy was just sitting on the floor with his knees to his chest, with his head down, and there was one take when we finally got it, and they had stopped playing, and I was like, "Oh, my god. Thank god we did this," and Tommy looked at me and goes, "I was praying." So that's what he was doing. He was making a silent wish for it to be quiet enough for us to record the song.

Spaceman Sound
Adam Holtzberg, Zack Kantor, Eric Nizgretsky, Manny Silverstein (Loose Buttons)

Manny Silverstein: We recorded the album [*Something Better*] in Brooklyn.

Eric Nizgretsky: In Greenpoint.

Manny Silverstein: It's this tiny studio. It's like half the size of this room we're in right now.

Adam Holtzberg: It's a great space.

Manny Silverstein: It's an all-one-room studio vibe.

Adam Holtzberg: We spent seven days basically tracking this.

Manny Silverstein: It's nice because you can rent it out for days at a time, as opposed to a lot of studios, where it's like, you have it for the full day, that means like eight to six.

Eric Nizgretsky: The guys there just give us the keys, and they're like, "Go have fun." The full twenty-four hours. Give them the shout-out, because we love them. Great guys.

Zack Kantor: We were definitely in there until like 5 a.m., especially the last day.

Eric Nizgretsky: They're just the coolest dudes. It's a beautiful studio that they built out there. I think our producer Gus slept on the couch there.

Manny Silverstein: No one's quite sure what he was doing.

Eric Nizgretsky: We were not sure what would happen when we would wrap for the day.

Studio G Brooklyn
Kate Black (THICK); Zach Ellis (Dead Tooth); Jake Derting, Matt Derting (Venus Twins)

Kate Black: This studio is a dream. There are so many talented people and smiling faces under one roof! I did my first ever studio recording session with Jeff Berner with my first band before he relocated to Studio G. He's the nicest man in the world! And he's worked on a ton of records for local bands, including two of my personal faves, Haybaby and Big Bliss.

Zach Ellis: Before Dead Tooth, my band was called The Adventures of the Silver Spaceman, and we recorded a record at Studio G and that was like a really awesome, fun experience. And they're super pro, but super cool. We made a record in like four hours.

Kate Black: THICK's first time at Studio G was when our friend Jack Counce mixed *It's Always Something*... When we were trying to decide where to record our first EP after we got signed to Epitaph, our first choice was to go back to Studio G and record with Joel

Hamilton. After a bit of pestering and some scheduling luck, we recorded our self-titled EP with Joel, then a few months later, our first ever full-length! On the first day of recording the LP, someone on the staff came down to let me in and we both did a double take, it was my childhood neighbor! As if the place needed to feel more like home.

Jake Derting: We recorded the drums and bass [for *The Whole Thing Is Sick*] at Studio G in Brooklyn, and that was a really cool experience being there. We'd never really played out of an actual studio. I guess once, but that was eye opening. Me getting to choose what drums I wanted, how many different snares I could use that weren't mine.

Zach Ellis: They also had the coolest toys to play with as a musician, like all the best guitar pedals and shit.

Matt Derting: Same with the basses there, like the pedals. I'm sure every studio has cabinets of pedals, but it was our first time to do it, so it was really cool.

Kate Black: It was such a great experience recording the LP that I almost cried leaving the last session and realizing I would be sitting at a desk the next day instead of waking up, making coffee in the studio kitchen, and playing music all day with Nikki, Shari, Joel and Francisco. I didn't grow up playing music, so I used to be really intimidated by being in a studio, but spending time at Studio G really solidified that's how I'd like to spend the rest of my life.

Trout Recording
Zach Ellis (Dead Tooth)

Lately, where I've been recording is this spot down in the Park Slope area called Trout Recording. The drummer of my other band that I play in, WIVES, he engineers there, and it's just a really cool spot.

They have all the sickest vintage gear from like the seventies and shit. All these tape machines, all the best microphones you could want. And it's pretty spacious. It's just really cool. I've recorded a bit of stuff there now, and anybody that I bring there to play, they're just like, "This place is amazing, holy shit."

They recorded some pretty huge records there in the nineties. Spacehog recorded there. Pavement recorded there. Antony and the Johnsons. Some pretty big names have been through there.

That place is a dream. All the toys that you always thought you could save up for but are clearly out of your price range. The equipment that you're using is like the same equipment that they made these great records with, so you're like, there's no reason my record can't sound good.

Wonderpark Studios
Kira Metcalf

As a wee preteen, I met Wonderpark Studios founders and co-conspirators in musical ingenuity, Eva Lawitts and Chris Krasnow, while opening for a former band of theirs at a now-defunct basement venue somewhere in Manhattan. We didn't so much meet as they played a wild set and I fangirled from afar before my brother drove me back to suburban Long Island.

Almost fifteen years later, I ran into Eva at a concert at the Brooklyn Bandshell. I'd been keeping up with her various projects and was stoked to learn she'd moved her studio into a space I'd been to in Gowanus. I was eager to work with a new producer, especially a woman, especially someone whose music I so admired. Isn't that always the dream? Eva and Chris proved to be a killer team. They've struck that elusive balance between calm and enthusiastic, professional and personal. Chris's impeccable ear for mixing and mastering and Eva's tactful candor and inspired production suggestions make working with them such a great experience.

Unfortunately, COVID [left] them in search of a new permanent home for their studio.

They have a great live studio session series up on their YouTube. They fully supported our daring move to cover the Mars Volta and made it sound incredible, and I feel very fortunate to know and work with them. Eleven out of ten.

SECTION 5
OFF THE CLOCK

Consider this the equivalent of *Us Weekly*'s "Stars—They're Just Like Us!" segment, but we're not talking about Julian Casablancas sucking down Frappuccinos or the phenomenon that is Lady Gaga pumping her own gas.

Instead, this section is dedicated to the outside-the-scene adventures and extracurriculars that our favorite Brooklyn musicians are embarking on and enjoying off-stage during their off-hours, when instead of playing instruments, they're often just playing around.

But first, a word on the work.

As I mentioned earlier, the hustle of many of the musicians I know is unparalleled, and their drive is one that never fails to impress. And when artists aren't working on their own music or doing whatever it is they do to make rent, you won't find them popping bon bons and binge-watching *Love Island*. Instead, the brains behind your favorite Brooklyn bands are often focused on other music-related projects and passions.

Favorite Friend Records and Totally Real Records. Plastic Miracles and Ghostie Recordings. Paper Moon Records and A Diamond Heart Production. All are indie labels with local artists at the helm. Meanwhile, musicians and photographers Justin Buschardt (Sharkswimmer), Jeanette D. Moses (Frida Kill), Keira Zhou (Climates), and Dalton Patton (a drummer in more projects than I have room to list here) are just as likely to be in the crowd and behind the camera as on the stage being shot. And as mentioned before, it's the musicians themselves who are literally setting the stage in the DIY space, simultaneously providing bands with a welcoming place to play and the rest of us with our Friday-night plans.

This unstoppable urge to produce seems to permeate most areas of artists' social, personal, and professional lives, with creation doubling as recreation and every conversation providing an opportunity for collaboration. There is truly a shared sense of purpose, a real rising-tide approach, and camaraderie and collaboration that extend beyond a slap on the back and a "Nice set, bro," resulting instead in real action. When I'm out with my musician friends, who are typically sporting t-shirts featuring their buds' bands, casual banter inevitably evolves into brainstorming, an ongoing discussion of plans and possibilities, different ways to work together, and how to combine strengths, assets, and ideas to lift each other up.

Gillian Visco of Shadow Monster, one of my favorite musicians and humans, has been making music in New York City for more than a decade. Before we went live for our radio interview in January 2020, we were casually chatting about her past and present playing music in Brooklyn. As she spoke, Gillian sprouted actual goosebumps describing the current state of the scene, expressing a sincere sense of awe and appreciation that she later reiterated on air:

> It's astounding. I've been in New York since 2007, 2008, playing in bands since 2008, 2009. The scene right now is absolutely incredible, and it's really kind of inspiring and humbling to be a part of honestly.

The hype is real, and the momentum is tangible. You can feel it. There are *so many good bands* in Brooklyn right now. And in my own years here, there have been moments when I've recognized in real time that what was happening around me was truly special, that this was an experience I would remember, not just as a one-off event but as part of a beautiful big picture.

Witnessing the first-ever live performance from alt-folk duo

Almost Sex, who connected on a dating app and sent lyrics and demos back and forth in 2020, courting each other as creatives before meeting to start a band, and a romance, in real life.

Jumping around with a gang of women in Brooklyn's best-smelling, most courteous mosh pit to the stirring sounds of "feelings-first" dream-rockers Ok Cowgirl, whose sweet songwriter Leah Lavigne simultaneously exudes confidence and vulnerability, warmth and effortless cool.

Screaming TVOD lyrics back in the face of Tyler Wright as the mic-wielding madman threw himself around performance spaces like a pinball with the ferocity of a pit bull during a series of summer shows, prioritizing showmanship over his personal safety in proper frontman form.

Watching the dynamic dudes of punk outfit Mary Shelley tear through their set with equal parts fun and finesse, genre-hopping, instrument-swapping, and demonstrating a rock-star energy so undeniable that I found myself spontaneously offering to manage the band after their show. Then forty-five minutes later, buying a how-to book on band management off Amazon while waiting on the subway platform for the train to go home.

I could go on. I *want* to go on. The unseen hustle that makes this magic happen should be acknowledged. This talent deserves to be recognized. And given the chance, I'd wax on about the work forever. But I'll stop here. Because rather than the effort being put in by these artists to perfect their craft, advance their art, and contribute to the community, which a good chunk of this book is already dedicated to, the following chapters are designed to encompass everything else, the well-deserved rest and the much-earned fun happening in between all the music.

After all, free time and relaxation are not only imperative to wellbeing but also integral to the creative process, and even the most energetic of players still require a small break to stay healthy, happy, and at least a little bit sane. So with that, consider these final three chapters a glimpse into the less-sceney segments of artists' lives. The portion lived off the stage and off the clock, out and about in Brooklyn with the rest of us.

CHAPTER 16
PARKS AND REC

"You feel like it sets a reset button on you. It slows everything down and gives you a lot more space to think again." - Gordon Taylor (Plastic Picnic)

If in Brooklyn the bar is your living room and the coffee shop serves as your office, well, that would make the park your backyard.

While it feels counterintuitive, no one appreciates the outdoors more than residents of the concrete jungle. In a notoriously expensive city, parks are places to congregate without the cover charge, one hundred percent free spaces that anyone is free to exist in and enjoy. Spots that collectively serve as the everyman's oasis where New Yorkers can escape the commotion and forget, at least momentarily, the extent of their steel-and-cement-encased existence.

With 526 acres of room to roam, Prospect Park is Brooklyn's answer to Manhattan's Central Park, but without the tourists and the uptown train ride. This glorious glob of green was referenced by many artists as a sanity-saving location and a breath of literal fresh air, and was lauded primarily for its distinctly un-urban elements. Trees, trails, a horizon unobstructed by skyscrapers, and plenty of space in which to slow one's pace. Scenic spots to walk, run, bike, or skate. Or on the less active front, take your bar experience al fresco to binge the live reality show that is park people-watching, with bodega beers tossed between blanket islands and nutcrackers purchased from the coolers of visor-wearing, Venmo-accepting, entrepreneurs.

Prospect is just one example, of course. Like dive bars and delis, every neighborhood has their own park, every individual has their favorite, and they all have a distinctly different feeling, with each person present utilizing the space in their own unique way.

Rock 'n' soul singer and mother Brandi Thompson takes her twins to the J.J. Byrne Playground. The Muckers smoke and throw frisbee in Highland Park. Gustaf's Lydia Gammill has conducted Full Moon Rituals at Maria Hernandez. And on the first warm day of the year, McCarren basically turns into Coachella, but with probably even more bands on site. Plus, while we're technically talking off-hours activities, plenty of musicians just can't put down their projects and utilize Brooklyn's outdoor settings as alternate practice spaces, open-air venues, and even the occasional music video set.

And it's not just parks. There are beaches, of course, where the above characteristics apply, but with far more sand and skin. There are also spookier spots like Brooklyn cemeteries, which many locals frequent for solitude, some history, and the unique kind of (rest in) peace and quiet that one can only find in the company of corpses.

One of the first artists I interviewed for this project was Tom Freeman. A British Brooklynite and creative force who makes music under the moniker Covey, Tom not only writes songs but builds worlds, taming the fox that haunts his sleep hallucinations into song, and Frankensteining toys in a Sid-of-*Toy Story*-style to create endearing mutant monsters for the cover art of his 2021 album *Class Of Cardinal Sin*. Given the artist's power to reclaim and reframe his trauma and transform the traditionally dark into something beautiful, it's no surprise that when I asked him about his favorite spots in Brooklyn, he named the Most Holy Trinity Cemetery off the Halsey stop, where he would go to get away from the sounds of traffic and have meaningful conversations with friends.

Theadora Curtis of glitter-grunge group Climates expressed a similar fondness for these types of (final) resting places, and when asked about her standout spots, the frontwoman told me that the first thing that comes to mind is a graveyard at Starr and Woodward in Bushwick.

"I used to get pretty anxious between my commitments and NYC energy, so I would go jogging and inevitably walk around this graveyard. The energy was always really light and peaceful not sad or dark, and there were tons of fireflies, more than I've seen anywhere. It would give me this jolt of mental space and comfort."

For some, the value of these areas was driven home even further, or maybe finally fully realized, when the performance leg of the music rat race was rained out by COVID in 2020.

Vanessa Silberman is a singer, songwriter, record producer, and the owner of A Diamond Heart Production, dubbed by Alternative Press as one of eleven LGBTQIA+ and women-owned labels that are changing the music industry. However, while the music maven had been playing hundreds of shows per year and working non-stop on "a gazillion projects," when she, like many of us, was finally forced to slow down for a bit, she traded the stage and the studio for the great urban outdoors, and it was Maria Hernandez Park in Bushwick where the artist spent her time.

Elise Okusami of Oceanator, another double-plus threat, also seems to have more than twenty-four hours in her day. Along with releasing her debut full-length *Things I Never Said* and signing to Polyvinyl in 2020, she launched her own "teensy" but mighty local label Plastic Miracles and dropped a string of songs, covers, and compilations to raise funds for non-profits. The artist still made time to step away though, and that year Elise claimed Prospect Park as her destination of choice when she wanted to get out of her apartment and out of her head, to work on music or to wander, wonder, or simply space out.

In a city, the importance of these open places can't be understated, which is probably why Mike Borchardt of BK trash-pop band Nihiloceros wrote me a few full-on odes, poetic and fact-packed descriptions of his favorites. Meanwhile, Gavin Snider of Sad American Night is not only a musician but an incredible visual artist, and is always out and about capturing architecture, landscapes, and street scenes paired with poetic musings under the Instagram moniker @gavindedraw. While he didn't sketch anything for Bands do BK, he did paint a picture with his words, sharing a full itinerary for intra-borough exploration and pairing each destination with a song to serve as the soundtrack.

Whether it's for elective rest or a forced break from a hard-working reality, a bike ride to clear the brain or a waterfront stroll to soothe the soul, the concept driving artists' recommendations here was generally the same. Outdoor spaces as mental and emotional relief. Scenic spots to stop, smell both the real and the metaphorical roses, and simply *take a time out*. Where one can flee the noise, hassles, and pressures of everyday urban life, ignore obligations, silence notifications, and instead let recreation and relaxation reign, all while waiting patiently for inspiration to arrive.

Brooklyn Botanic Garden
Evan Crommett

Big fan of the Japanese garden in the BK Botanic. It's good for turtle-watching, dog-watching, and finding a nice, fizzy type of serenity. There's a bright red archway in the middle of the pond that the fantasy-fiction-loving kid in me always imagines as a portal to another realm. It's magnetically significant seeming. When I look at that arch, I'm able to let go of my New York go-getter anxiousness, and just chill for a sec, an effect that's deepened when I see the cherry blossoms, and listen to the ducks laughing, and wryly watch the sweaty tourists forget to glance up from their phones.

Brooklyn Bridge Park
Eddie Kuspiel, Ray McGale, Kevin Urvalek (Color Tongue); Brandi Thompson (Brandi and the Alexanders)

Kevin Urvalek: I like to play basketball a lot in my free time, and they have the best basketball courts in the city there. It's just my favorite place to go on weekends, out of any place in Brooklyn. It's beautiful, it's right on the water, you can see all of Battery Park and the whole southern skyline and the Brooklyn Bridge.

Brandi Thompson: I know it's pretty pedestrian and touristy, but this area of Brooklyn has so much to offer for everyone. Places to sit and hang, boozy sand bars, playgrounds, even one specifically for toddlers, the carousel, food and drinks, views, space, and a little peace and quiet.

Kevin Urvalek: People are really good at basketball there and it's really good competition. Most parks have double rims. There they have breakaway rims. And this has nothing to do with music.

Eddie Kuspiel: It does a little bit, because every time Kevin gets hurt playing basketball—

Ray McGale: While we're on the record talking about basketball, Color Tongue will challenge any band out there in basketball. And we'll definitely win because we have Kevin, and he's gonna do most of the work.

Coney Island
Mike Borchardt (Nihiloceros)

For a Brooklyn musician, living south of Prospect Park provides its own set of challenges. Rock venues, rehearsal spaces, DIY rooftops, and basements littered the streets of Williamsburg when we moved here from Chicago, and over the years have picked up and pushed further into the ultra-hip corners of Bushwick. Meanwhile, financial constraints and the blessing of a rent-stabilized apartment pushed us further and further south, deep into the borough. And while the cool kids might consider the last stop on the G train the end of the universe, having spent eight years living in Brooklyn's upside-down has been one of the greater experiences of my life.

At the very bottom of Brooklyn, as far south as you can go before you fall into the ocean, is a little spot time forgot called Coney Island. About a century ago, a wizard cast a spell and froze time at this eerie carnival wonderland. During daylight, beaches littered in shadow beneath behemoth housing complexes that harken to another time kiss the expanse of sea where NYC ends, and the Atlantic Ocean begins. Back when we were a Chicago band touring NYC, we always flocked to this place to soak up that edge-of-world feeling that lurks on its shores. Its bones come alive at night, as the warped wooden planks of the Cyclone and the twisted metal beams of The Wonder Wheel rise above the skyline, as thousands of tiny incandescent light bulbs luminesce against the darkness of old Brooklyn and the Sea.

At dusk, Coney Island is a labyrinth of amusements twirling amidst the warm glow of the circus. Overstuffed teddy bear prizes, the clamor of buzzers and bells, rollercoasters, and bungee swings fill the sky. We can stuff our faces with pink and blue cotton candy after inhaling a Nathan's chili hotdog, then stumble into the shadows of the creaky weatherworn boardwalk. A mishmash of seventies disco in the distance and old-timey squeezebox music plays as we rush past the log flumes and bumper cars past the paint-peeled freak show museum. We stop only a moment to catch our breath and look up at the towering and fallen old king of rides, the mighty parachute drop. And there, apart from the rumble of the subway in the background, we can forget for just a moment maybe whether or not we are even in New York City and to what century we belong, as though the mighty elephants of Dreamland will carry us home for the night.

DUMBO
Raycee Jones

Somewhere I like to go when I want to feel romantic is DUMBO. I like to go stroll by myself along the water, and watch people on Jane's Carousel. But mostly I just watch the water hit the rocks under the bridge, and think about how lucky and lonely I am. NYC is wonderful at providing you with that super contradictory feeling!

The Edges of Brooklyn
Gavin Snider (Sad American Night)

To properly see Brooklyn, you need to find the edges. Go to the water. Ride a bike across the Williamsburg Bridge. The long, slow approach from the Brooklyn side gives you time to think. You get to the top and you're suspended above the East River, and all of New York stretches out before you. I'm always thinking about the Soul Coughing song, "True Dreams of Wichita." "You can stand on the arms of the Williamsburg Bridge crying, 'Hey man, well this is Babylon.'" I don't know what the Williamsburg Bridge has to do with Wichita, but that's where I grew up so that makes the song even better. Listen to the Jeffrey Lewis song "Back to Manhattan" as you're flying down the back span. It's about crossing the bridge after a breakup. The song just rolls over and over. Pick up speed and coast down to the Lower East Side.

Run up to Newtown Creek at the northern tip of Greenpoint, where Manhattan Avenue terminates at a sign that says "END." Across the creek and past the docked sailboats, Queens recedes into the distance, steeples and smokestacks and bridges. If I have my headphones, I'm usually listening to a Paul Simon song, something off *Graceland* or *The Rhythm of the Saints*.

Take the R train out to Bay Ridge and walk down to Owl's Head Park. I think I first heard about it from Eleanor Friedberger on her perfect record *Last Summer*. "I don't know the way to Owl's Head Park. I don't know why it always rains in Owl's Head Park." Walk down to the water and out on the pier. The Verrazano is to the south, large and grey. The Manhattan skyline is to the north, distant and blue. Hang out with the fishermen. They're sitting on egg crates and folding chairs, their bicycles are loaded with bait and tackle.

Go to Coney Island in the summer. Walk along the boardwalk, through crowds dancing to an unseen stereo. Drunk people are singing karaoke. Guys are playing hand drums in front of a Puerto Rican flag. Smell the sea, sand, sweat and carnival food. There are a hundred songs about Coney Island, but Tom Waits sings about it the best. It always seems like a place he returns to in dreams, a place where you could fall in love and hide away from the rest of the world. Dreamland was actually one of three amusement parks on Coney Island. Even though it closed in 1911, I imagine Tom Waits still found a way to go there. Listen to his song "Take It With Me." I think it's the best love song ever written.

The Gowanus Canal
Dana (Strange Neighbors)

It's a superfund site that is *super fun!* If you swing by Wednesday evenings or Saturday afternoons you can borrow canoes from the Gowanus Dredgers, an advocacy group raising awareness about the canal [and] the history of the Gowanus neighborhood [that] advocates for recreational boating in the city.

Maria Hernandez Park
Eddie Kuspiel (Color Tongue); Jeremy Neale; Vanessa Silberman

Jeremy Neale: This park has it all. Trees? Check. Music? Sometimes. People skateboarding? Forty percent of the time. Sunshine? That's entirely dependent on the weather.

Eddie Kuspiel: I like the park a lot. It reminds me of when I'm not working.

When I was an intern for a production company and first came to the city, I remember going to Tompkins Square Park and walking around, and I would always look at people running or at the dog park or playing the guitar. And I would be like, what the fuck do you do where you don't have to be at work wanting to kill yourself at eleven o'clock, and it's Tuesday, and you don't think any of this is worth it?

Vanessa Silberman: I spent just so many years just moving, hustling and in a positive way, just doing so many things, you know, constantly playing 150 to 250 shows a year and doing a gazillion projects. I never got a chance to sit and, you know, stop and smell the roses as they say.

So, during this time, with the kind of standstill of certain projects that I had going on, all of the sudden I had time to do some things that I never had time to do, like read a book. I discovered one of my favorite things to do is to read books and listen to music and write in the park.

Eddie Kuspiel: Now I'm freelance and I get a month or two off in between when I'm finding gigs. I get to walk [my dog] Thunder more, and I get to go for a run, and I get to go actually get sun on my skin, which people in New York don't often get to do.

Vanessa Silberman: Maria Hernandez sticks out to me because it's right in the thick of Brooklyn and Bushwick. It's just this cool local park, and it's definitely one of my favorite spots to just sit and be peaceful, just hang out. Be quiet.

Eddie Kuspiel: Every time I'm [at the park], it's when I'm not working, and that's when I'm happy.

McCarren Park
Paul Hammer (Savoir Adore)

McCarren Park is one of my favorite places. The last ten years of my life have been focused around this circle between Williamsburg, Greenpoint, and Bushwick, whether it's music venues, rehearsal spaces, where we hang out, where we get in trouble, where we don't get in trouble.

McCarren, as soon as it gets warm, I have these memories of Turkey's Nest. You get a Styrofoam cup with a margarita and you go to McCarren Park. There's something about it that for me is this landmark, you know, walking through the park, listening to our latest mixes, or walking home from rehearsal. It's definitely the most nostalgic place because I've walked through it so much in different seasons. I have all these memories. And it's interesting because every city has their McCarren Park, a smaller park in a hipper neighborhood, and I don't know what it is, but there's a certain energy to that. I love it.

McGolrick Park
Connor Gladney, Laura Valk (Skout); Jessica Leibowitz, Danny Ross (Babetown)

Laura Valk: When we get stuffed up, get tired of our surroundings, we'll go play outside. It's awesome. It's clean and beautiful.

Danny Ross: I hadn't heard of it, and when I first met Jess, she lived right near McGolrick Park. I would walk her home past the park. It's a hidden gem of New York, and Brooklyn in particular.

Jessica Leibowitz: There's a dog park there, too. And they do movie screenings in the summer.

Connor Gladney: There's a lot of adorable dogs. I love getting to play guitar and watch cute dogs walk by. That's my heaven.

Laura Valk: Remember that guy? He came up and asked to play our guitar, and was like, "Have you heard this song? Have you heard this song?" And he started playing and singing to us. And we're like, "Okay, first of all, give me my guitar back." But it's a cool spot in that it's kind of artsy and people are out there doing different things.

Danny Ross: It's our neighborhood park. When we did a music video for "Met a Boy on the Subway," that's the park we featured pretty prominently.

Connor Gladney: I'm gonna sound like a fifty-year-old man, but it's also cool because there's a grocery store off of it, so you can go play guitar and then pick up stuff to grill. I'm also just a sucker for nature, and living in New York, any park I can go to is very refreshing. It feels like you can escape for a little bit.

Laura Valk: [It's also] a good people-watching spot.

Connor Gladney: We've had times where we've gone to rehearse there and really adorable kids are at some daycare thing, and they'll run up and just be cute. One time one of them had a toy, and one of the others wanted to play with it. He was just like, "You want it? Here, you take it!" It was just a weirdly childish, adorable moment. And I was like, I feel like I just learned something from that. Sharing is caring.

Laura Valk: We learn lessons at McGolrick Park.

Connor Gladney: Life lessons, brought to you by McGolrick Park. Sponsored by the grocery store on the corner.

Most Holy Trinity Cemetery
Tom Freeman (Covey)

When I'm driving back from tour or from another state back to Bushwick, I know I'm nearly home when I see rows upon rows of graves. You would think it's a daunting feeling, but you know that feeling when you're pulling into your driveway at your home? I get that feeling whenever I see the graveyards. It's a strange feeling, but it's funny.

I don't necessarily believe in ghosts, but I like the concept of ghosts. I like dark things, and I like to go to the graveyard and hang around. I don't go like, every day of course. That'd be kind of weird. I usually go if someone wants to walk around and it's a nice night or we have something to talk about, maybe something depressing. You know when you're not ready to stop talking yet? It's a great place to aimlessly walk around.

It's quiet. That's what gets me. You walk in there, and you don't hear any of the roads. I never expected to like it so much.

Prospect Park
Lincoln Lute, Gordon Taylor (Plastic Picnic); Katie Martucci, Lucia Pontoniere (The Ladles); Ben Adams (Evolfo); Cody Fitzgerald (Stolen Jars); Elise Okusami (Oceanator); Lindsey Radice (PYNKIE); Brandi Thompson (Brandi and the Alexanders)

Gordon Taylor: It's a huge part of living in Brooklyn, or it should be. And we all use it in our own personal ways. I run a lot, so I go running through the park, and I know Lincoln goes biking through there a lot of times, but we also meet up in the evening and have a bottle of wine and hang out outside and watch the fireflies and stuff like that.

For us, being able to go hang out outside with friends, have something feel really simple like that, you feel like it sets a reset button on you. It slows everything down and gives you a lot more space to think again.

Lincoln Lute: Yeah, I think that a part of the birth of our band sound and the concept behind our band is that we are all from these areas with an abundance of nature, and that really supplies this therapeutic outlet, but we're taken away from that. So you're kind of looking at the world in a different way where you sort of don't have that comfortability. So those little places become really important.

Lucia Pontoniere: Parks are so important when you live in a city.

Katie Martucci: That park saved me. Living like half a mile from it, being able to walk there all the time and having a minute to be in nature and to go for runs and slow down. I feel like it just made all the parts that I was worried about New York not a problem. I just had that space to breathe.

Gordon Taylor: A thing that we would end up doing a lot [is] biking around at night with friends. It's like you're given the freedom to loop around, and it's quiet and just these empty roads that you suddenly have to yourself. You have so much space. It feels like the city's just kind of disappeared.

Lincoln Lute: Going on bike rides is so difficult in the city because it's always like start, stop, start, stop, traffic everywhere. Going to Prospect's nice because you can just go either run or bike or whatever it is, but the city doesn't have to control your pace. I just think it's always controlling your pace in one way or another, and usually it's too fast, but just being able to go and not have to worry about so much traffic and everything, you know.

Ben Adams: I couldn't imagine life in Brooklyn without our parks. I find that Prospect Park is a great place to breathe, look at trees, think about songwriting ideas, and generally quiet the mind a bit.

Lincoln Lute: It's just close enough and you can kind of feel like you have a little bit of your own space and just watch some really old trees blow in the wind and kind of slow down.

Cody Fitzgerald: As someone who works at home and lives fifteen minutes from the park and literally will write music for two or three hours, get annoyed at the third hour, and then leave my apartment, and walk around the entirety of Prospect Park for an hour and a half or two. I do that loop and I come back and I keep writing music. It's very much a part of my music-writing life and my general life.

Elise Okusami: I'll either put on a long podcast and head over there and just wander around for an hour or two, or I'll go sit for a bit and read, write, or listen to music, stare into space, whatever.

Lindsey Radice: It's so big, and you could probably never see every inch of it, even if you went every day for a year. I like walking around and listening to music for a long time, [just] losing myself. I could probably do that forever if I never got hungry.

Ben Adams: My favorite little spot is under the big tree planted by Boy Scouts in like, 1910 or something, by the Grand Army Plaza entrance.

Elise Okusami: I found a good spot that's uncrowded and also near a bathroom, but I'm not gonna tell y'all where it is, sorry.

Brandi Thompson: If you're on the south side of the park, you know the Parade Grounds. It's quiet, it's open. That whole area of Prospect Park is just cool. People always talk about Central Park, and I'm like, whatever, we've got this.

Cody Fitzgerald: Everyone loves Prospect Park. Even the guy who made it said it was better than Central Park. I think I'd go crazy without it.

Sunset Park & Green-Wood Cemetery
Mike Borchardt (Nihiloceros)

NYC. Central Park. Brooklyn. Prospect Park. Right? Wrong. Well I mean yes, those are your big iconic parks you may think of when you think of New York City. But let me tell you about a couple of Brooklyn's true green-space treasures a bit further south than you may be familiar with, Sunset Park and Green-Wood Cemetery.

These are two very different and unique green spaces, even though only a few residential blocks separate them from each other. The neighborhoods down here remind us more of the Chicago neighborhoods where we grew up. Down here, generations of very defined ethnic cultures exist independently side by side. For six years we lived on the edge of Borough Park and Sunset Park at the very intersection that split Brooklyn's Chinatown from the Orthodox Jewish community of Borough Park and the Latin communities of Sunset Park.

For that very reason, the namesake neighborhood oasis has always been a super unique blend of cultures. Sunset Park the park sits in the middle of Sunset Park the neighborhood. Flanked by Forty-fourth Street (our street) to the south and Forty-first Street to the north, and Fifth and Seventh Avenues to the east and west, the park has been neatly tucked between a series of neighborhood apartment complexes, single family houses, and rows of classic brownstones since the late 1800s. At the top end of the park stands an old brick rotunda that houses the old basketball courts and opens into the Olympic-sized outdoor pool that were all built in the 1930s, and since then very little has changed.

Senior citizens gather at sunrise to do morning exercises and then make their way back again in the afternoons to sit and play chess. Summer nights stir as the handball courts and soccer fields fill with a flurry of hands and feet, and the inflated pings ricochet off the cement, disappearing into the grass. The color flash of kites in the sky waft in and out between aromas of BBQed meats and burning charcoal among the chatter of children playing all around.

As the park slopes downward to the bustle of traffic lights and storefronts on 5th Ave, you can look over the remaining blocks of buildings that vanish into the bay. The green glow beacon of the Statue of Liberty calls your eyes out to her and beyond, to the shores of New Jersey and Staten Island. High atop the hill, you can completely ingest the deep grapefruit skies soaked in a blood orange sunset, so visceral that you could almost miss the entirety of Lower Manhattan rising in the distance. The mighty downtown skyline strikes the forefront as your eye-line vanishes to the Midtown skyscrapers shrinking in the distance.

The highest point in all of Brooklyn, however, is just a couple blocks away in Green-Wood Cemetery. Its altitude originally provided a key vantage point during the American Revolutionary War, and over the past couple hundred years since, more than a half million people have been buried there.

We originally wandered through its massive and ornate stone gothic gates on a quest to find Jean-Michel Basquiat's grave when we discovered that numerous other notables from Brooklyn's history pepper its massive expanse.

As Brooklyn's first public park, Green-Wood later inspired the creation of both Prospect Park and Central Park as additional urban oases became a necessary reprieve from the rapid urbanization of NYC.

Despite its size and historical significance, Green-Wood Cemetery to us was just our big park. The other iconic parks always felt like they belonged to Manhattan and to a whole different Brooklyn world of which we were not really a part. Green-Wood Cemetery was ours. Much like Coney Island and the Dyker Heights Xmas lights, it was weird and quirky enough and it was ours. Our park was beautiful and green and full of trees and dead people. We'd go there to watch the symphony perform sonic landscapes against purple sunsets. Or we'd go there for walks to watch history nerds play out war re-enactments from the 1700s and 1800s.

More recently were the unsolved clown sightings of 2014, mysteriously wandering the rolling hills of Green-Wood in broad daylight with a bunch of red balloons in hand before disappearing behind a stone mausoleum.

There are numerous swaths of green spaces both large and small throughout the borough. In a city of nine million, where you live, walk, and commute on top of each other, shoulder-to-shoulder every minute of every day, it's absolutely crucial to carve a little mother nature out of all the concrete and steel wherever you can. We'd suggest checking out a few of Brooklyn's southern parks as you make your rounds. They may not always be top of mind, but they are rife with cultural significance, and you might just create for yourself a strange new adventure that leaves its mark on your own personal history.

CHAPTER 17
SHOP TALK

"I crate-dig for obscure comics the way traditional hip-hop producers dig for rare groove records to sample. We're both trying to reach the same result."
- Darius VanSluytman (No Surrender)

Let's talk shop.

More than anything, the verb *shopping* conjures visions and stock images of fancy people strutting down city sidewalks or palm tree-lined boulevards, their arms laden with boxy bags and tiny dogs while swiping plastic most of us wouldn't be approved for at stores where many of us would be *Pretty Woman*-ed.

But with indie artists, shopping isn't an exercise in excess, and not solely because of the majority's distinctly un-Kanye credit-card limits. Instead, shopping is less of a spree and more of a search. A pursuit with intention, often in search of inspiration, and not just for music.

In what feels like an unfair distribution of talent, more musicians than not appear to have innate abilities that can't be confined to one mode of expression, talent that transcends their primary medium, and creativity and curiosity that bleed outside the lines of music to overflow into other artistic endeavors. And this phenomenon isn't akin to Michael Jordan's failed foray into baseball. The artists in question shine equally in these other arenas as well.

Goth-glam musician Alison Clancy doesn't just produce alt-pop but dances for The Metropolitan Opera, and "R&B princess" Ntu has choreographed and performed live for Black Movement Library. Artist-activist Debora Rivas created a program called Awareness Art to inspire change through murals and installations, while Gillian Visco is a Gill of all trades, crafting hipster-demon drawings, and writing, producing, and acting in a web series called *Stray Cats* about art, anxiety, and NYC. And then there's one of my favorite drummers, Charmaine Querol, who has nearly a half-dozen Instagram handles to her name encompassing her music, comedy, and entrepreneurial endeavors, including a satirical fitness-guru alter ego named Staycee Fitt, and a line of hats, as modeled on musicians like Mattie Safer, embroidered with a simple set of instructions: "Block His Number."

Keith Kelly (Jelly Kelly) creates massive mixed-media works featuring floral explosions. Gabriel Birnbaum (Wilder Maker) specializes in handmade linocut prints depicting abstract takes on parks, birds, and bars. And Alex Chappo (CHAPPO) twists wire into 3D female nudes and portrayals of pop icons past and present, from Prince to Lizzo, the Beatles to Bowie. Right next to their Spotify pages, these artists have websites and Etsy shops, and just like their songs fill my playlists, my apartment walls are adorned with their art.

So back to shopping. Whether creativity is more a product of nature or nurture, a fixed force, or, like a bicep or brain, something you strengthen, it needs nurturing. You have to feed the beast, and when artists need fuel for their creative pursuits, they head to the Brooklyn shops you'll find in this chapter, which aren't just home to unique inventory but interesting and truly inspiring individuals as well.

Once again, it all comes down to people and passion, so we're not talking about shiny boutiques staffed by snooty shop girls or corporate chains stocked with what everyone else is reading and wearing. Instead, the specialty shops in this chapter are run by careful curators who are as obsessed with their products as their patrons are, and who aren't simply participating in capitalism or fueling consumerism, but are focused on offering the best products and services available. And building real community while they're doing it.

In addition to playing keyboard in Wet Leather, Jason Katzenstein is a cartoonist for *The New Yorker* and the author of the comic book *Everything Is an Emergency: An OCD Story in Words & Pictures*. In our interview, he shared his love for Vinyl Fantasy, a combination record store and comic shop that serves as a meeting place for a clever contingent of NYC creatives, where the pen pals gather to share their work. Meanwhile, the artists who sang the praises of The Guitar Shop described it as a clubhouse of sorts, where fanatics loiter, friends linger, and musicians they know and admire are often cycling in and out.

Finally, along with stimuli and a social element, these shops also offer the thrill of discovery.

Perhaps it's an appreciation of art in all its forms, an insistence on originality, or a lifelong pursuit of beauty that impacts every area of life, but musicians often appear to possess an elevated aesthetic awareness, a superior sense of not only sound but self and style that's evident in one-of-a-kind wardrobes, carefully organized collections, and eclectically decorated apartments. In this context, shopping is not just a casual hobby or a form of retail therapy, but an adventure guided by an inherently cool internal compass that all artists seem to possess, one that might culminate in the purchase of an insane pair of thigh-high boots for an album-release show or a vintage fur-coat for a music video. It's the dream guitar, the perfect amp, a gorgeous mirror, or a funky lamp. A material muse in book, comic, or vinyl form. Or just some fluid to help the flow in a perfect-for-any-occasion bottle of wine, whether it be for a birthday, a breakup, or maybe just a Wednesday, selected by a shopkeeper turned trusted advisor and friend.

In this chapter, you'll find places where the selection is special, the beauty is in the bizarre, and the treasure hunt is half the fun. And while you can't buy cool with cash or with credit, if you're in search of some personal inspiration, a good conversation, or just some awesome stuff, here are a few artist-approved places to start your search.

The Cowrie Shell Center
Thaddeus Lowe

The Cowrie Shell Center is the hidden but not-so-secret gem of Bedford-Stuyvesant. When I moved to Bed-Stuy this year, I met Priestess closing her shop. I told her how much her store reminded me of my travels to New Orleans, the warm lights, world art, scent of oils. She invited me in and immediately I was greeted by her vast collection of plants, African spiritual products and garbs. Priestess (yes, that's her name) vented about how hard COVID had hit her business. She's been here since 1991 and has a loyal local foot-traffic base comprised of Zen-seeking made-with-love enthusiasts. As I left, Priestess offered for me to come by the next day and I've been soaking up the good vibes ever since. Please support The Cowrie Shell Center and go meet the light that is Priestess for some insightful conversation and flowering cacti, surrounded by enchanting African art in a brownstone building she lives in.

Earwax Records
Darren O'Brien (Wildly)

Was happy to recently see Earwax still kicking off Bedford. It's a small selection but well curated, and you'll want to know what they're playing on the stereo. That's how I first heard Gary Wilson, in fact. If you need to buy some Krautrock or French soundtrack jazz reissues, shop here first.

Green Village Used Furniture & Clothing
Raycee Jones

I've lived in a few neighborhoods in BK over the past eight years, but I've resided in Bushwick the longest. Green Village is this crazy second-hand store, with items piled high. Dressers stacked on dressers, old pots in a basket, #1 Grandpa coffee cups on shelves from somebody you'll never meet's grandpa. Sometimes I go just to look, but I definitely have decorated a lot of my home with their quirky items.

The Guitar Shop
Sarah Carbonetti (ESS SEE); Abner James, Harper James (Eighty Ninety); Matthew Iwanusa (Caveman)

Sarah Carbonetti: The Guitar Shop NYC is by far my favorite place to be in Brooklyn. It's a warm, inviting, and inspiring space. It's also where I met my husband, master guitar builder and Caveman guitarist, James Carbonetti.

Harper James: This guy, James Carbonetti, he's actually the guitar player in Caveman. They're awesome and they're one of my favorite Brooklyn bands. [He] runs a guitar repair shop and he builds his own guitars, Carbonetti Guitars.

Abner James: He's an artist.

Matthew Iwanusa: Our guitar player Jimmy's shop is awesome. We grew up together, we went to high school together. Just to see him have a place like that where, even though I didn't build any of it, it feels like our team of people. It feels very exciting. It just kind of feels like it's in the family.

Sarah Carbonetti: I walked into The Guitar Shop NYC in the late summer of 2019 on our first date. I was immediately impressed. Nestled just outside the gates of Green-Wood Cemetery (also a great date spot!), the Guitar Shop NYC is a legitimate candy store for musicians. The walls are saturated with new and vintage guitars, bass, pedals, amps, and other accessories from around the world. Photos of some of the greatest musicians of all time squeeze in every inch of free space where there is not an instrument. The shop has been open since 2015, but it oozes a sense of history beyond its years. There's a treasure trove of albums to sift through, play aloud and connect over. Everything in the shop has a story, and if you've got time to linger a bit, James or one of his partners, master builder Mas Hino or Eric Cocco (of La Bella Strings), will happily indulge you with every detail of an instrument's origins.

Harper James: Working in a studio, I'm a guitar player, but also I have stuff I need to maintain, and I've always been looking for someone who's the perfect guy. So I've tried a lot of the local shops, and there's some great shops, but he's one of these dudes who is a really well-kept secret and a complete master.

Sarah Carbonetti: Just beyond the retail showroom is a full workshop where James and Mas create custom-built instruments. Being able to witness a block of wood morph into a guitar is magical. And with each instrument being built entirely by hand, you can trust there's a ton of love going into the process.

Harper James: He just rebuilt my first college guitar, a 1950s Gibson. He basically rebuilt it from scratch, and it's better than it was originally. He understands how to do stuff that nobody really understands how to do. This guitar's been worked on by many people and has never been what it's supposed to be. But he did it.

He's sort of a secret weapon for anyone who's into guitar, and his shop is one of the coolest places in Brooklyn. And he's just a really nice guy.

Matthew Iwanusa: For me, it's comfortable, and I would say probably because Jimmy, he knows how I am, so he definitely has made spots where he knows I'll be like, okay, I'll sit over there. I think he's thought about that stuff for all of his friends. And I think it just works out for everybody.

Sarah Carbonetti: These days, I spend so much time in the shop it's an extension of my home. But that doesn't just apply to me. Many prominent musicians from around the world call this shop home. The vibe is communal.

Matthew Iwanusa: To be able to walk down, walk up the block, and know you can sit there and hang out and listen to music and look at records, and then some cool musician that you've known forever comes in.

Sarah Carbonetti: Often visitors will hang out for hours exploring and playing the inventory, or watching Mas or James carve and sand the contours of a new guitar while they wait for a repair to be finished. The shop hosts shows and events featuring phenomenal talent and the latest instruments and gear, where musicians, builders, brands and fans can all connect and get to know each other. I've met musicians here that have since recorded on my music. We even recorded in the shop on a bass that was built in the shop!

Matthew Iwanusa: When we were younger and his shop was in the actual city, like on Third Street, you know, we really just had nothing to lose. We would be out 'til four and then we'd go back there until who-knows-what time. So it's a little more tame you know, in Brooklyn these days, since we're a little older.

Sarah Carbonetti: The Guitar Shop NYC is a physical manifestation of what music can be for us all. Whether you're a musician or music lover, you can feel welcome and free to hang out, make some friends, soak in some music, and appreciate the beauty of craftsmanship and history in the space.

Human Head Records
Shawn Ghost (Ghostwood Country Club); Rafferty Swink (Evolfo)

Shawn Ghost: My favorite place in Brooklyn is Human Head Records. I've never found a retail space with a more friendly, welcoming, and authentic community vibe. It's an inspiring mecca of cool grooves where the tribes of music lovers and collectors assemble to search for new treasures and enjoy each other's company. They often host block parties with free food and crazy sales, so it's no exaggeration to say they're a vital and vibrant source of joy in the neighborhood.

Rafferty Swink: I started going to Human Head right when I moved to NY, which was also right around when they opened up. At that time, my friends Joe and Nick were working part-time for Travis when they weren't on tour. I'd loiter and spend what little money I had.

Shawn Ghost: Everyone who works there is super cool and many have become great friends. I think of the owners Travis and Steve as cool brothers or cousins I admire, and I've had the immense pleasure of playing a few shows with Steve's rad band Sweet Nothings, formerly known as Windbreaker. For the average price of a mixed drink plus tip, you can easily find two to three records you'll cherish and enjoy endlessly, from old favorites to new discoveries.

Rafferty Swink: Since the start, Human Head has been unpretentious, community-oriented, and deeply committed to the music. A tour of BK record stores would be woefully incomplete without a visit to this dusty vinyl haunt.

Shawn Ghost: If you're really lucky, the store dog and lovable official mascot Penny will be there hanging out. When you go, tell them Shawn says hello.

Koch Comics Warehouse
Darius VanSluytman (No Surrender)

I can name dozens of artists who are influential on my sound, but I've always been equally influenced by imagery. I was a big comics fan as a kid and still am. The older I got, the weirder my taste in comics became. I crate-dig for obscure comics the way traditional hip-hop producers dig for rare groove records to sample. We're both trying to reach the same result.

[Listening to] Slowdive on the headphones while reading issues of *El Topo* director Alejandro Jodorowsky's *Metabarons*, or blasting X-Clan while reading *Brother Voodoo*. Those kinds of days lead to late night sessions of hammering out synth and drum pattern ideas.

There is only one place left in Brooklyn you can go if you're looking for rare and obscure comics. Luckily that one place is literally a warehouse. Joe Koch is part owner of shiny, tourist-friendly Forbidden Planet in the city. Koch's warehouse is the polar opposite. It's filthy. There are cats running around. Middle-aged men baring plumber's crack shuffle through boxes of comic books, while their kids stare at them with pity. In the summer, the perfume of the slaughterhouse around the corner creeps into the halls, amplifying the joint's lack of AC.

But, where else can you find a stack of thirty-year-old *Heavy Metal* magazines looking for a new dad? It is a living monument to the days when New York was weird. I adore it.

Monday to Friday is appointment only. Saturday and Sunday, open to the public. 206 Forty-first Street. No Sign. Second floor. You'll find it.

Main Drag Music
Sam R. (Glassio); Darren O'Brien (Wildly)

Sam R.: I bought my first synth from Main Drag. I also met a dear friend and collaborator here, Ariel Loh, who would go on to mix a lot of my music. He worked there and sold me and my friends some of our first analog synthesizers back in 2013 when we first started making more synth-heavy music.

Darren O'Brien: Main Drag has saved my life so many times. Please keep them alive. Fuck Guitar Center, buy local, buy small.

Molasses Books
Jeremy Neale

You gotta have a second cafe on rotation cos sometimes you'll accidentally knock over a plant at Dweebs and have to lay low for a few days. My secret shame is that I don't read books, but nobody has to know that, and as the great Zoolander once said, "Words can only hurt you if you try to read them. Don't play their game!" But also, great selection of pre-loved books if you do read, friendly staff, and they're also a bar, which is very helpful for all those times when you go too far up caffeine mountain. Every. Single. Day.

Stranger Wines
Mattie Safer (Safer)

One of my favorite spots in BK is Stranger Wines in Williamsburg. I've been living in New York and a part of the music scene here since 1999, and as they got older, many of the big record nerd people I knew switched it up and became wine nerds. Basically, they moved from obsessing over obscure, short-run records released on small labels to obsessing over obscure, short-run natural wines released by small growers. While I don't buy into their mania myself, I appreciate having a small wine shop in my neighborhood run by a knowledgeable musician friend, Museum of Love's Dennis McNany, where I can walk in and say something vague about what I want, like "a dry white?" or "an orange that's funky but not *too* funky?" And walk out with something that I know is going to be superb. At the height of the COVID lockdown, it was nice to be able to walk in, get a bottle to help deal with the uncertainty, and chat with a familiar face. I love this spot and highly recommend you "do" it.

The Thing
Digo Best (Colatura)

The Thing in Greenpoint is a secondhand shop, with none of the romance that usually comes with vintage shopping. It's like shopping at your kooky aunt's place whose appetite for hoarding could land her on reality TV. Don't let its chaotic excess fool you, there are some serious gems hidden amongst the junk. I used to visit there a lot with a good friend of mine who was "serious" about collecting vinyl. Every time he'd get stoned, he'd tell me stories of all the priceless albums that had been salvaged from The Thing over the years. Every time I've been, I've spent hours digging through piles of scratched worthless Ace of Base B-sides, but the allure of scoring a priceless first-edition vinyl keeps me coming back.

Unnameable Books
Gabriel Birnbaum (Wilder Maker)

Unnameable is amazing. It's everything I want in a bookstore. They have really good shit, it's curated well, and it's also kinda messy. Almost always, if a bookstore is not messy, I don't like it. There's like piles of stuff in front of the shelves that you can pick through. It's my favorite feeling if I go into a bookstore and everything is piled to the ceiling and it's just a mess. I love a treasure hunt.

Vinyl Fantasy
Jason Katzenstein (Wet Leather)

Vinyl Fantasy is both a comic shop and a record shop. Ilana and Joe co-own the place, and Ilana also is a dog walker, so there are constantly cute dogs in there.

They have an event where cartoonists come in, and there's a big projector and they read work they're working on, which is really cool. I've done that reading. [It's] called Panels to the People. The cartoonist community in Brooklyn, we're all working from home all the time. It's nice to get everybody together, and a lot of people recognize each other based on their work but have never met, but we follow each other on Instagram. Suddenly everybody's doing readings and hanging out.

When Vinyl moved in, it was that place and Molasses Books. Those places made me fall in love with the neighborhood. A bookstore, a comic-book store and record shop, all within walking distance.

CHAPTER 18
JUST FOR FUN

"I love any place that is experiential, where you're encouraged to explore and try new things."
- David Van Witt (HNRY FLWR)

While this book is obviously heavy on places to play music and party with friends (*that's rock 'n' roll, baby!*), for our finale, we've got some think-outside-the-bar locations. A collection of musicians' miscellaneous favorites and a grab bag of go-to places. Spots outside the standard sort where artists go to enjoy their own company. And just as often, quality time with each other.

Throughout this process, what's been as delightful to witness as the music itself are the different dynamics that exist between individuals who aren't just co-creators and co-conspirators, but also siblings or spouses, lovers or best friends, who even when they're working hard, always make it seem more like play.

In other words, it's all about the bond between bandmates.

Now I'm not *totally* naive. I know all that glitters isn't Grammy or even Canal Street gold. That personality clashes and creative differences can cause even the strongest of connections to rupture, and that even the most passionate of intragroup romances can crash and burn in the forever-feared Fleetwood Mac effect.

Ego can't be separated from art, after all. There's emotional investment. And unless you're simply running a song factory cranking out jingles for snow tires and cereal, or it's more of a one-man show, less Tom Petty flanked by beloved Heartbreakers, more Bennie backed by anonymous Jets, people are going to have ideas and opinions and won't always be stoked when things don't go their way.

That said, while band drama definitely exists, I'm happy to report that I haven't encountered too much ego-tripping in my orbit. Instead, most of the Brooklyn bands I have interviewed and interacted with demonstrate a friendship that borders on infatuation, with music adding an additional dimension to the relationship that those of us uninvolved in this kind of creative partnership could never understand.

The joy is palpable, the excitement is contagious. And especially for those artists at a certain life stage, free of burdens and babies, willing to spend nine hours a day in a van, subsist on gas-station snacks, and sleep with limbs Tetris-ed under dining-room tables on new friends' floors in Topeka, all truly seem to be having the time of their lives together.

One example of a band whose members appear to be absolutely enamored with each other is snap-crackle-alt-pop trio Moon Kissed. Khaya, Leah, and Emily look like triplets, are synced-up like siblings, and make every show an event, sometimes even a gala, with on-site flash tattoos, designated themes like "Black Hole" or "Bikinis and Blazers," and a typically tops-optional ethos.

In our radio and video interviews, the three bandmates were giggly and almost giddy while recounting for me their festive and fortuitous meet-cute, which they commemorated in the most literal of fashions with the title of their first record, *I Met My Band At A New Years Party*.

Another such band is Gustaf. One of Beck's favorite live bands, the group of pals churns out playful punk that packs a punch, and since forming in 2018 they've taken the stage hundreds of times, combining music and mania into an art explosion fueled by both creative and personal chemistry.

While two of Gustaf's members have long been romantically attached, and one may have unwittingly walked across the room and into the frame naked while I was on a Zoom interview with the other, it feels more like a polyamorous love story involving all five bandmates, with enough best-friend bar stories, inside jokes, and mutual memories to constitute a collective consciousness.

And then there's indie-rock outfit Loose Buttons, whose intimacy was evident throughout our interview as they posed for photos prom-style with heads pressed together and arms wrapped around waists, and whose depth of friendship was demonstrated when they emphasized that it's not just what they're doing, but who they're doing it with. *Each other.*

And in a big departure from convention, the musicians were, unlike most bands, less about the bar scene and more about the bath scene.

When Loose Buttons aren't making music or throwing parties at guitarist Zack Kantor's apartment, also home to a pet chameleon with over ten thousand Instagram followers, you'll more likely than not find the band at the banya. In a nod to old New York and frontman Eric Nizgretsky's Eastern European background, the group even chose the Russian Bath on Neck Road as the literally steamy set where they shot the art for their debut full-length record, *Something Better*.

When we discussed this unconventional band clubhouse over beers (me) and borscht (them) during our interview at Tatiana Grill, a Russian restaurant on the Brighton Beach boardwalk, Eric put it simply when describing not just the return to his roots, but more importantly, the four friends' general philosophy:

We find any excuse to celebrate. At the end of the day, we find any excuse to just hang out with each other.

With that final, very necessary nod to friendship, we've come to our last chapter, where you'll find places like the banya. Picks that generally defied classification, or at least didn't fall cleanly into other traditional categories. Spots to break a sweat or cut a rug, catch a non-music show or just do a load of laundry while you play a game of pinball.

Which in true Brooklyn form, is both completely ridiculous and absolutely amazing.

Alamo Drafthouse
Kasey Heisler (A Very Special Episode)

So let's be fair, there are *much* cheaper places to see a movie, but nothing quite compares to the experience of seeing one at Alamo. I will travel to the ends of the earth for the herb parmesan popcorn they serve there, so it's extra lucky that you can find it right in Downtown Brooklyn! As a bonus, they also have one of the coolest, spookiest bars on the premises as well, the House of Wax. It's red and dark, windows covered in heavy blackout drapes and walls covered in cases filled with graphic medical wax figures, which honestly creates a perfect kind of vibe for discussing new music and other creative ideas. At least for us anyway. The selection of beers and ciders on tap are amazing *and* you can actually order the popcorn to the bar, so if you're not around to see a movie you can still get the world's best popcorn. It's one of the coolest bars, and you kinda have to know it's there. Is this whole experience a little kitschy? Yeah, but so are we.

Bossa Nova Civic Club
Felipe Giannella (Okay Okay); Ntu

Felipe Giannella: Bossa Nova is amazing. I didn't know much about the techno scene in Brooklyn, but one of my close friends is big into it and took me there and I loved it.

Ntu: Bossa Nova is a favorite spot of mine. I love to dance, and I grew to love techno there. I've worked at Half Moon BK, and the nights that friends and residents put on there were just incredible.

Felipe Giannella: It was totally different from what I was used to. Also, I'm Brazilian, so going to a club called Bossa Nova felt kinda familiar to me. The thing is, once I got there, it completely blew me away. Great place, cool crowd, good music. It's an awesome place to go to if you're into house or techno, or if you just want to have new experiences and meet new people.

The Brick Theater
Kegan Zema (Realworld)

The Brick Theater is one of those places where you can always expect the unexpected. Located in Williamsburg right off the Lorimer stop, it has been a home for experimental theater since 2002. But that designation really only scratches the surface. It's home to so many types of art and artists. I've seen and participated in plays, comedy shows, film screenings, dance parties and even a few rock shows.

Existing in a narrow space between two buildings, it has a slight "Platform 9-3/4" feel, expanding as you enter. Inside, the stark brick walls eschew the traditional black box theater feel. What it lacks in high-tech theater magic, it makes up for in heart and curatorial ethos that aims to provide a home for anyone and everyone to showcase their work.

What makes this place so special is the vast array of performances I've seen or been a part of. Reflecting back, most moments are a combination of beautiful and "wtf?" A queer wrestling parody, confoundingly hilarious plays about death, and people exposing themselves both metaphorically and literally.

At the stroke of midnight marking 2020, ownership was handed over to Theresa Buchheister who has been a longtime friend and collaborator. Even with the setbacks [that] year brought, especially for a theater space, Theresa and her team have found new ways to help curate performances online and provide a safe recharge spot for protesters.

Brooklyn Skates Club & Sugar Hill Supper Club
Tanner Peterson (Tanners)

If you're looking to show off your skating skills or just fall on your ass on a lacquered wood floor, Brooklyn Skates in Bed-Stuy is the way to go. The school gymnasium turned roller rink hosts skate nights every Wednesday and Friday. It's super inexpensive and you can either take some laps around the rink or watch the pros from the sidelines perform some of the most stunning OG roller disco moves. It's just good, clean fun.

If dancing sans skates is more your speed, I *urge* you to bop right down the street to Sugar Hill Supper Club. I went out dancing for a friend's birthday party there last winter and it was quite possibly one of the best nights I've had in years. Head downstairs and you walk into techno disco heaven. There's a huge space with tables and chairs, a massive dance floor with lights galore, a small yet extremely steamy bar in the back, and a little outside patio where you can go cool down. You might be hungover the next day, but I promise it's worth it.

Class One MMA
Viktor Longo

If I'm not writing, recording or playing out, I'm probably at this gym. The owner and head coach Ken Ng is a genius when it comes to striking and one of the most humble and generous people I know. His mind is like that of an artist when it comes to fighting. What drew me to this place was how creative and interesting the fighters and coaches were. And despite it being a place where we learn to kick, punch, elbow and knee each other, everyone has a pretty cool laid-back vibe. There's no egos. Not only is it great for the classes but after a while you find you can just come hang out while it's open and see your friends and train however you like. In that way it's almost like an old-school rec hall.

Some of my best friends and also biggest supporters of my music come from this gym. You'll usually see a few happy looking people in tank tops and joggers at my shows. I think making and performing music helps me in fighting and vice versa. There's an intense focus and joy that comes from this place. I don't really have any one particular story that comes to mind, I just spend most of my time here and it's made me a much better person all around. I think anyone that's serious about being the best version of themselves should come by. All are welcome.

Cobble Hill Cinemas
Caitlin Mahoney

Small theaters, and they have a very old-school concession stand. And it's a pretty affordable place to see a movie. I love seeing movies. I think with music, and touring in particular, I'll get, like, sensory overload from performing. There's so much adrenaline, and then talking to people. I'm a small artist still getting started, so I'll stay at people's houses. That's so wonderful, that's such a gift, but I'm learning I'm more of an introvert than I thought, and I run out of gas. So my favorite thing to do is see a movie by myself, put my phone away. Something about being in a dark room, I think, resets my vibes.

Friends and Lovers
Quinn Devlin

I discovered it from a show when I was in college. A friend ran a blog called *Rare Candy* out of Columbia, and they had their first print release party there. So when I moved back here, I went back there, like, this is the one place I know!

Every first Saturday they do a soul night, which has the feel of what I imagine Northern Soul nights in the seventies in Europe were like at places like The Wigan. I think it's a really cool thing that they do, and unfortunately, I have not been to enough of them.

The Lot Radio
Ryan Egan

Amazing in the summer. It's an open, fenced-in lot and they have a trailer with DJs booked throughout the entire day, every day. Inside they have a proper studio, and they project [the music] out. It's so cool on a June day or something.

You're just chilling there, you can buy bottles of wine, you can buy beers, whatever. [And] if you just pull up the website and listen at any given time, it's probably just really good shit that often is going to expose you to stuff you've never heard.

Russian Bath on Neck Road
Adam Holtzberg, Zack Kantor, Eric Nizgretsky (Loose Buttons)

Eric Nizgretsky: The banya's restaurant was ninth best in Brooklyn, I think.

Adam Holtzberg: They will remind you of that.

Zack Kantor: The guy told us that. I don't believe that at all.

Eric Nizgretsky: Or did he say ninth-best banya? But they're really great to us. They let us shoot our album there. They love us so much they said, "We'll open up the doors earlier." We got there at like four in the morning to shoot the album cover, and they were so nice about it. Then they've got the OG's, who show up at eight in the morning because they want to shvitz before anyone else. So they came in, and they saw all these lights and the cameras, and they were so chill about the whole thing. Some of them were posing, opening up the bellies a little bit more. Usually, people suck in their bellies. Russians do the opposite: They push out.

Zack Kantor: [The album cover is] a guy in the banya just sort of vibing out. He was a guy that we found online and just hired him basically to come and have a photo shoot with us, and he didn't really know what it was.

Adam Holtzberg: He had an Eastern European vibe about him.

Eric Nizgretsky: He very much embodied the look of the classic Russian guy who goes to the banya.

We go to the banya for fun. My family is from the Soviet Union, so I always grew up with that, and then we started going, and we had a great time, and we thought that was an embodiment of the record, the familial ties. It's a great spot. It's become a really important staple of our hanging out.

Adam Holtzberg: And celebrating usually.

Eric Nizgretsky: It's usually some kind of celebration. But we celebrate a lot of things.

Adam Holtzberg: And honestly, the things we're celebrating are not that big. We just like hanging out.

Sunshine Laundromat
Laney Lynx

Exactly one year ago I drove cross-country from New York to Los Angeles and back with no expectations, no real plans except to see the Grand Canyon, and in every single city along the way it just so happened I was drawn to the spots where pinball was present. It was inexplicable. I asked myself, "Is this my new thing?" I had realized a new love was taking form and there was nothing I could do about it.

Once back in Brooklyn believing I only had Barcade to turn to, it was recommended by an acquaintance that I check out Sunshine Laundromat in Greenpoint. Curious, I took the L Manhattan-bound to the G and wandered into a seemingly normal looking laundromat. It wasn't until I strolled all the way back past the row of washers and dryers that I heard the noises of a familiar friend. My companion on the long trek out west and back, the pinball arcade. The pinging sounds, the flashing lights, the drama, the flippers, the pocket full of quarters. My heart swooned. I had officially found my new favorite place. As it turns out, it seems I had traveled cross-country and back to find a new home away from home, and a much better place to do laundry, right under my nose!

Syndicated Bar Theater Kitchen
Bandits on the Run (Adrian Blake Enscoe, Sydney Shepherd, Regina Strayhorn); Beth Million; Jeremy Neale

Bandits on the Run: Syndicated is the best place in Brooklyn to catch an arthouse flick or a well-loved vintage cult movie on the big screen. Tickets are super cheap, because the theater in the back is also a restaurant, which means you can grab a brew, or two or five, while watching, say, *Booksmart*, or a David Lynch deep cut.

Beth Million: Syndicated has the best burger in New York City. Outdoors they project movies. Their cauliflower nuggets go stupid.

Bandits on the Run: The front bar area is decked out to the nines in an homage to the golden age of studio flicks, complete with wide viewing booths and a three-fourths marble bar. It's also a viewing room of a sort, complete with two gigantic screens that will be playing anything from random nineties flicks to *The Bachelor* to the Democratic debates.

Jeremy Neale: I was introduced to this place by a friend who took me here during the World Cup, but they also show classic movies. Like tonight they're playing *Jurassic Park* at midnight. By the time you read this I guess it'll be a different film. The entrance is very unassuming but once you're inside it's a whole new world of big screens and even bigger beers.

Whisperlodge
David Van Witt (HNRY FLWR)

I love any place that is experiential, where you're encouraged to explore and try new things. Whisperlodge [is] an immersive theatre experience for the senses, coaxing you to tune in to yourself with live ASMR.

ASMR is a divisive subject, but if nothing else I think it's interesting, and the body and mind are just as fun to explore as any place. If you're curious about experiencing it somewhere else than The Void of the internet, this is your chance. I was lucky enough to be part of Houseworld, an immersive theater experience, to try out my songs for the first time with a 1-on-1 concert in a bathroom. It was the most intense performance experience of my life, and it still informs me with bigger audiences. Some of the Houseworld people are behind starting Whisperlodge, and I'm so thrilled to see this coming back to Brooklyn.

A SNAPSHOT OF A SCENE: BROOKLYN TODAY, TOMORROW, AND BEYOND

"My favorite spots in Brooklyn always change because Brooklyn is forever changing." - Jon the Guilt

The bulk of the interviews, inquiries, and writing that went into this book were done both before COVID and right in the thick of pandemic panic, while the final months of work took place after the vaccine once again made live music a possibility. Venue doors were flung open, we snapped back to the scene, and reality semi-resumed as bands and fans were finally reunited, with joy and mostly without masks.

Of course, while normalcy has in many ways returned, much of the damage to the city and the scene is irreparable. I'm writing this conclusion in fall of 2021, and for the last year and a half, many small businesses have been fighting for their lives. Some have survived, countless others have already closed. And we still don't know the extent to which the city has been and will be re-shaped. We still have no idea what comes next.

Because we're working with the timeline and permanence of print, not the instant, ever-editable nature of digital, by the time this book is in your hands, there's no telling exactly which of these businesses will still be standing, how many artists will have abandoned the city or boomeranged back, and what exactly Brooklyn will look or feel or sound like. While one of my primary goals was to create a handy guide to Brooklyn and a useful book with which to bop and bar-hop around the borough, it now feels like it might exist equally, and down the line more so, as more of a snapshot of a very specific time. But to be honest, that was probably the case all along.

Long before COVID entered our collective vocabulary, well-documented pre-existing problems like gentrification, sky-high rents, culture-chasing corporations, and more had already established themselves as massive threats to creative communities and death blows to the borough's beloved and often longstanding small businesses. Residents are well accustomed to mourning the shuttering of their favorite spaces. It's the real reason Brooklynites wear black.

While the pandemic has presented an unprecedented challenge for businesses, obstacles are nothing new, and running a restaurant, maintaining a venue, or operating a store of any sort in Brooklyn has never, ever been easy. If there's one constant in this city, it's change. Temporary is typical, comfort is fleeting, turnover is a fact of NYC life. Fight for your right to party, but don't be surprised when the party ends because the building is being turned into condos or a Capital One.

This is an unfortunate reality, and no matter when you arrive, existing residents' retrospective rose-colored glasses will always make you feel like you *just* got here too late. And for those who have seen their friends struggle and their favorite places close, it can be all too easy to fall into a grass-was-greener mindset. However, without undermining the truly tragic nature of so much of this change, when it comes to the state of the music scene itself, I want to end on a positive note, with sincere hope and optimism.

While the venue names plastered on placards might change, band members might move, and scenes might shift, New Yorkers, particularly in the arts, are resilient by nature and by necessity. That's never been more evident than in 2020 and 2021, when the rug was instantly yanked out from under everyone, and musicians were not only robbed of their ability to practice, perform, and tour, but in many cases their jobs as well. Yet while they lost so much, artists were giving and doing so much more. The determined nature and DIY ethos of this community was on full display during the pandemic, as friends united not just in support of their own artistry but to give back to the community and contribute to causes bigger than themselves. I was endlessly awed and utterly moved by artists' generosity, creativity, and ingenuity as they worked together during this time, streaming to save threatened venues, collaborating on compilations to raise money for mutual aid, and donating proceeds from merch, albums, and singles to support social justice.

This is all to say that no matter what happens, the energy is here. Artists in this city are perpetually ready to innovate and always prepared to pivot, just like they always have been and just like they always will be. So, although the Brooklyn portrayed in these pages won't be the exact same one in existence whenever you're reading this book, and the borough won't be inhabited by an identical set of individuals, I have no doubt that whatever is happening *right now*, in this moment, still makes it the best place in the world to be.

This sentiment and an everlasting love for an ever-changing city was eloquently expressed in the form of some COVID-context but truly evergreen Instagram commentary from Digo Best of neo-surf garage-pop band Colatura, posted in February of 2021:

> When you first move to New York you'll always find someone willing to tell you New York is dead, that you should have been here a decade earlier. Rent was cheap, and real art was being made. I imagine a version of this has passed since Dylan left the village, since the Warholian days of Soho, up until the closure of the DIY scene. The one thing I know about New York is that it is resilient. It doesn't stand still. The version I know now will not be the one here tomorrow. I know that's its greatest strength. It's sad seeing places I love close, but I know what's on the other side will be worth its namesake.

Admittedly, during moments of weakness sparked by notorious city stimuli like rodents, a rent increase, or a particularly foul subway experience, we might find ourselves threatening a move to some easy-living town that calls itself a city and uses shopping as its primary selling point. However, the most dedicated and truly in-love of us will no doubt be sucked right back in again by the diversity, beauty, creativity, and utter insanity of the places, faces, music, and pure opportunity that Brooklyn has to offer.

As Brooklyn native Olivia K told me of her hometown during our interview at Cafe Erzulie a few years ago:

> It's like a trap. When you've had enough, that's when you meet someone like, oh, snap! This thing could work! Or you go to some crazy party that's so bananas that you can't even imagine going somewhere else. Because what could top this place?

So with that, go forth and go out. Check out these artists, hit these hot spots, buy some music, and go see some shows. I hope to run into you in the audience, on the street, or maybe, at some point, at home.

By which I mean your favorite Brooklyn bar or venue, obviously.

ACKNOWLEDGMENTS

It takes a village to raise the roof.

Like invitations to a wedding or birthday party, every time I thought of another name to include here, the list grew by ten, so instead of taking the 200 pages necessary to properly express my gratitude, I'm going to keep this short and sweet. That said, I truly appreciate each and every invitation, opportunity, piece of advice, and ounce of support that's been given to me by inspiring individuals, incredible organizations, and all the loved ones in my life since I started this journey. I am very lucky.

First and foremost, thank you to every artist who has offered their time, talent, energy, ideas, support, stories, and recommendations—those whose participation has made Bands do BK possible and whose music has served as my writing soundtrack throughout this process. This community truly means the world to me. To those featured in this book and to the countless others who have contributed over the years, I couldn't do what I do without you.

A similar thanks to Ben and the whole team at Lit Riot Press for believing in this project. For the big opportunity, the many calls, the thoughtful edits, and the note that six hundred EM dashes in one book might just be a *few* too many. I'm so, so grateful for everything.

Ter, Lar, Joe. Thank you for being the best family ever, for listening to me talk about Bands do BK twenty-four seven, and for not taking it personally that I've spent eighty-five percent of our time together over the last two years with my head buried in my laptop. I wouldn't be here, or anywhere, without you. Love you!

To the best friends who have supported me since the beginning, whether by lending industry expertise, hopping fences for photos, or providing words of wisdom at happy hour or endless encouragement via text. You know who you are. Thank you for showing up for me in every sense of the word. I love you all.

Of course, much love to my own favorite places, particularly The Crown Inn, where a good chunk of this book was written. Thank you to everyone there for being such a big, beautiful part of my personal Brooklyn experience, for accepting me in every state (and with every questionable date), and for bringing some truly wonderful people into my life.

And finally, Ms. Heitkamp, whose first name I don't feel comfortable using because the last time I saw you I was seven years old. Thank you for telling my mom I was a good writer after I crafted that truly captivating piece on how to make a peanut butter and jelly sandwich in your second-grade class. It was a little thing, but it meant everything.

SAM SUMPTER

Sam Sumpter is the founder and editorial director of *Bands do BK*. She is a journalist, emcee, and host of the popular radio show, *Bands do BK* on *Radio Free Brooklyn*, featuring live interviews with local artists. She is the manager of the punk band Mary Shelley, and produces, books, and promotes live shows on stages across Brooklyn and in Manhattan. Since founding *Bands do BK*, Sumpter has spent time in recording studios, music venues, performance spaces, restaurants, bars, and cafes in the borough of Brooklyn interviewing her favorite musicians about their favorite places while using *Bands do BK* as a platform to share and promote the amazing music of the artists she loves.

BANDS DO BK ONLINE

Bands do BK is a blog, radio program, weekly newsletter, and live shows and streams.

Keep up with the action at *@bandsdobk* and *bandsdobk.com*.

Subscribe to get THE SETLIST, a NYC weekend itinerary crafted by local musicians, in your inbox every Friday at *bandsdobk.substack.com*.

NAMES TO KNOW

The bands behind the names, the names behind the bands. For your cross-referencing convenience, here's a full list of the artists and groups who are quoted and referenced as contributors throughout this book:

Abner James (Eighty Ninety)
Adam Holtzberg (Loose Buttons)
Adeline
Aida Mekonnen (Forever Honey)
Aidan (Strange Neighbors)
Aleksi Glick (Snack Cat)
Alex M. (DD Walker)
Alison Clancy
Alex Chappo (CHAPPO)
Amelia Bushell (Extra Special, Grim Streaker, Belle Mare)
Andrew Possehl (Sooner)
Annie Nirschel
Anthony Azarmgin (The Muckers)
Bandits on the Run (Adrian Blake Enscoe, Sydney Shepherd, Regina Strayhorn)
Ben Adams (Evolfo, Ochre)
Ben Thornewill (Jukebox the Ghost)

Beth Million
Blu DeTiger
Brandi Thompson (Brandi and the Alexanders)
Brett Moses (Teen Commandments)
Brit Boras (New Myths, formerly of Future Punx)
Caitlin Mahoney
Cancion Franklin
Carlo Minchillo (Brooklyn Drum Collective, Murder Tag, The Planes, Glass Slipper)
Caroline Kuhn (The Ladles)
Chantal Mitvalsky (Snack Cat)
Charmaine Querol (Nevva)
Chayse Schutter (A Very Special Episode, Pocketsand, Amskray, Call My Husband, Wolves At Night)
Cody Fitzgerald (Stolen Jars)
Colin Lord (HYPEMOM, alex in the attic)
Connor Gladney (Skout)
Connor Jones (Yella Belly, Elliot & The Ghost)
Cory Peterson (Hollow Engine)
DAD (Jeremy Duvall, Jesse Fairbairn, Jon Murphy, James Watson)
Dallin Smith (Max Pain and the Groovies)
Dan Barrecchia (Shred Flintstone)
Dana (Strange Neighbors)
Dane Zarra (Oil Bay, Caged Animals)
Dang Anohen (Sallies)
Danny Ross (Babetown)
Darius VanSluytman (No Surrender, The Infesticons, Low Wave, Dead Tooth & No Surrender)
Darren O'Brien (Wildly, Activity Partners)
Dave Palazola (Evolfo, Holy Hand Grenade, Arthur Moon, Wsabi Fox)
Davey Jones (Lost Boy ?)
David Johnson (Max Pain and the Groovies)
David Van Witt (HNRY FLWR)

Deep Wimp (Trevor Courneen, Kyle Jutkiewicz, Wesley Rose, Charlie Waters)
Devin McKnight (Maneka)
Digo Best (Colatura)
Dirty Mae (Ben Curtis, Cassie Fireman, Robin Frost)
Dom Bodo (95 Bulls, Jelly Kelly)
Ed Weisgerber (Shred Flintstone)
Eddie Kuspiel (Color Tongue)
Elijah Sokolow (The Living Strange)
Elise Okusami (Oceanator, Plastic Miracles)
Elizabeth Wyld
Elliah Heifetz
Emanuel Ayvas (Emanuel and the Fear, Pale Ramon)
Emily Ashenden (95 Bulls, Ashjesus)
Emily Sgouros (Moon Kissed)
Emir Mohseni (The Muckers)
Eric Nizgretsky (Loose Buttons)
Ethan Alexander (So and So)
Ethan Bassford (Gemma, Ava Luna)
Evan Crommett
Felicia Douglass (Gemma, Ava Luna, Dirty Projectors)
Felipe Giannella (Okay Okay)
Frank Graniero (Caravela)
Frank Poma (Zoos)
Gabriel Birnbaum (Wilder Maker)
Gavin Snider (Sad American Night)
George Miata (Color Tongue)
Gillian Visco (Shadow Monster)
Gino Gianoli (Duke of Vandals)
Gordon Taylor (Plastic Picnic)
Hallie Spoor
Harper James (Eighty Ninety, Middle Youth)
Hayes Peebles
Hearth (Sara Horton, Melanie Rose Wiggins)
Impossible Colors (Adam Berrios, Chris Boecker, Scott

Greenberg, Ben Harwood)
Jack McLoughlin (Yella Belly, Forever Honey)
Jake Derting (Venus Twins, Mommy's Little Boy)
Jake Hiebert (Yella Belly, Elliot & The Ghost)
Jared Artaud (The Vacant Lots)
Jared Yee (Evolfo, Avant George, Aberdeen, Shubh Saran, Porterfield)
Jason Katzenstein (Wet Leather)
Jeff Citron (Moonglow)
Jenny Palumbo (Nevva)
Jeremy Neale
Jessica Leibowitz (Babetown)
Jessica Louise Dye (High Waisted)
Jim Hill (Slight Of, Trace Mountains)
Joe Dahlstrom (Hot Knives)
Joey Giambra (Shred Flintstone)
John Farris (Sooner)
John Zimmerman (The Muckers)
Johnny Dynamite (Johnny Dynamite and the Bloodsuckers)
Jon F Daily (The Black Black, Kissed by an Animal, EWEL)
Jon Sandler (Great Good Fine Ok)
Jon the Guilt
Johan (Glom)
Jonathan (Glom)
Jonathan Freeland
Jono Bernstein (High Waisted)
Jordan (Glom)
Josh Inman (Oil Bay, Rancho Cowabunga)
Justin Buschardt (Sharkswimmer)
JW Francis
Kai Sorensen (Evolfo, Karl's D Light)
Kalen Lister (Death By Piano, KALEN, Late Sea)
Kallan Campbell (Max Pain and the Groovies, GIFT,

Tilden)
Kasey Heisler (A Very Special Episode)
Kate Black (THICK)
Katie Martucci (The Ladles)
Kayla Asbell (95 Bulls, Bipolar)
Kegan Zema (Realworld)
Keith Kelly (Jelly Kelly)
Kevin Olken Henthorn (Cape Francis)
Kevin Urvalek (Color Tongue)
Khaya Cohen (Moon Kissed)
Kira Metcalf
Kristof Denis (Deep Sea Peach Tree)
Laney Lynx
Laura Jinn
Laura Valk (Skout)
Leah Lavigne (Ok Cowgirl)
Leah Scarpati (Moon Kissed)
Lexie Lowell
LG Galleon (Dead Leaf Echo, Clone)
Lily Mao (Lily Mao and The Resonaters)
Lily Reszi Rothman (hartstop, Sloppy Jane, fantasy)
Lincoln Lute (Plastic Picnic)
Lindsey Radice (PYNKIE)
Lip Molina (Sallies)
Lizzie No
Lucia Pontoniere (The Ladles)
Luke Santy (HYPEMOM, LUKEINTERNET)
Luna Rose (Hannah Rose Ammon, Sam Parrish, Jö Wagner)
Lydia Gammill (Gustaf)
Madam West (Sophie Chernin, Will Clark, Jory Dawidowicz, Todd Martino, Mike McDearmon)
Manny Silverstein (Loose Buttons)
Marble House (Gabe Friedman, Danny Irizarry, Nicole Pettigrew, Javier Vela)

Marina Ross (New Myths)
Mary-Louise Hildebrandt (Maladaptive Mistress)
Matt Bernstein (Wet Leather)
Matt Caldamone (HYPEMOM)
Matt Derting (Venus Twins)
Matthew Gibbs (Evolfo, Ben Pirani, Rodes Rollins)
Matthew Iwanusa (Caveman)
Mattie Safer (Safer)
Melissa Lucciola (Francie Moon, Pretty World, Kino Kimino, Gustaf)
Meredith Lampe (Work Wife, Colatura)
Mia Berrin (Pom Pom Squad)
Michael Hesslein (HESS, Mail the Horse)
Michael Nitting (The Misters)
Michael Tarnofsky (Edna)
Michelle Birsky (Birch)
Mike Borchardt (Nihiloceros, Treads, Murder Tag)
Minaxi (Steve Carlin, Liam Christian, Shrenik Ganatra)
Mitch Meyer (Zoos, Drive-In, Climates)
Mitchell Parrish (Fever Dolls)
Molly Schoen (Nevva)
My Son The Doctor (Brian Hemmert, Joel Kalow, John Mason, Matt Nitzberg)
NAHreally
Natalie Kirch (Sharkmuffin, Drew Citron)
Nicholas LaGrasta (Teen Commandments)
Nick Cortezi (Marinara)
Nick LaFalce (Atlas Engine, Edna, co-founder of Favorite Friend Records)
Nick Louis (Almost Sex)
Nico E.P. (Native Sun, Deaf Poets, Tall Juan, Ben Katzman's DeGreaser)
Nikki Sisti (THICK, TVOD)
No Swoon (Tasha Abbott, Zack Nestel-Patt)
Ntu

Obash (Bipolar, Yaasss)
Olivia K
Olivia Price (Forever Honey)
Papi Shiitake
Parrot Dream (Kiki Appel, Gonzalo Guerrero)
Patrick Phillips (Namesake, formerly known as Honduras)
Patrick Porter (A Very Special Episode)
Paul Hammer (Savoir Adore)
Peter (Glom)
Peter Wise
Phantom Wave (Ian Carpenter, Rachel Fischer)
Pouya (Bipolar, The Spits)
Proper. (Erik Garlington, Natasha Johnson, Elijah Watson)
Quinn Devlin
Quinn McGovern (Marinara)
Rafferty Swink (Evolfo, Low Noon, Oyinda, Ben Pirani)
Ray McGale (Color Tongue)
Raycee Jones
Razor Braids (Hollye Bynum, Jilly Karande, Hannah Nichols, Janie Peacock)
Richey Rose (Songs for Sabotage, ex-High Waisted, Tamaryn, Jennie Vee)
Ronnie Lanzilotta (Evolfo, Pronoun, Rodes Rollins, HNRY FLWR, Misst, Holy Hand Grenade, Charles Fauna, Cape Francis)
Rosie Slater (New Myths, Delicate Steve, Sharkmuffin, Catty)
Ryan Egan
Ryan Foster (Warm Body, Lost Boy ?)
Sahil (Glom)
Sal Garro (Mount Sharp)
Sam R. (Glassio)

Sarah Carbonetti (ESS SEE)
Sarik Kumar (Mars Motel)
Satin Nickel (Sam Aneson, Nikola Balać, Morgan Hollingsworth, Ariana Karp, Andrew Shewaga)
Scott Kodi
Scott Martin (Scott Martin and the Grand Disaster)
Sean (Glom)
Sean Carroll
Sean Wouters (Drunk Ex, Deaf Poets)
Shane Conerty (Color Collage)
Shane Preece (Max Pain and the Groovies)
Shari Page (THICK)
Shawn Ghost (Ghostwood Country Club)
Sonny Hell
Steele Kratt (Steele FC)
Stephen Berthomieux (The Big Easy)
Stephen Graniero (Caravela)
Steve Vannelli (Yella Belly, Forever Honey)
Superbloom (Tim Choate, Brian DiMeglio, Matteo Dix, David Newman)
Tallbird (Danny Sullivan, Erica Marchetta-Wood)
Tall Juan
Tanner Peterson (Tanners)
Tarra Thiessen (Sharkmuffin, Gustaf, Kino Kimino, MamajoeVramajoe)
Tcoy Coughlin (Max Pain and the Groovies, Dead Things)
Thaddeus Lowe
Theadora Curtis (Climates)
Tine Hill (Gustaf)
Todd Martin (The Misters)
Tom Corrado (Zoos)
Tom Freeman (Covey)
Tom Wolfson (Sooner)
Tracey (Strange Neighbors)

Vanessa Silberman
Viktor Longo
Viktor Vladimirovich (Prince Johnny)
Vram Kherlopian (Advanced Ant Party, The Big Drops, MamajoeVramajoe, Gustaf)
William Thompson (Yella Belly, Elliot & The Ghost, The Steps, Static Jacks, Grits., The Rassle)
Yuta Shimmi (Marinara)
Zach (Strange Neighbors)
Zach Butler (95 Bulls, The Mystery Lights)
Zach Ellis (Dead Tooth, Dead Tooth & No Surrender, WIVES)
Zach Inkley (95 Bulls, Smock)
Zack Kantor (Loose Buttons)
Zoochie

INDEX

Symbols
61 Local 86, 201
95 Bulls 119, 120, 132, 136, 159, 161, 171, 295, 297, 301

A
A&A Bake and Doubles 97
Aberdeen 296
Abner James 157, 267, 293
Adam Berrios 295
Adam Holtzberg 100, 166, 167, 168, 239, 240, 282, 283, 293
Adirondack 51
Adrian Blake Enscoe 93, 127, 164, 205, 283, 293
Advanced Ant Party 301
Aida Mekonnen 22, 30, 31, 293
Aidan 34, 35, 293
Alamo Drafthouse 278
Aleksi Glick 57, 58, 69, 71, 110, 111, 171, 174, 293
Alex Chappo 144, 157, 264, 293
alex in the attic 294
Alex M 55, 293
Alison Clancy 54, 171, 174, 264, 293
Ali's Trinidad Roti 97
Almost Sex 193, 245, 298
Alphaville 88, 140, 141, 142, 143, 188, 207
Amelia Bushell 23, 24, 25, 144, 146, 293
Amskray 294
Anchored Inn 4, 19, 20, 21, 22, 23, 24, 25, 90
Andrew Possehl 65, 110, 140, 141, 293
Andrew Shewaga 30, 300
Annie Nirschel 158, 293
Anthony Azarmgin 84, 169, 170, 171, 172, 173, 293
Ariana Karp 30, 300
Arthur Moon 294

303

A Shipping Container in Bushwick 222
Ashjesus 42, 136, 216, 295
Atlas Engine 159, 229, 298
Ava Luna 295
Avant George 296
A Very Special Episode 151, 223, 278, 294, 297, 299

B

Babetown 113, 255, 294, 296
Baby's All Right 12, 44, 50, 87, 88, 144, 145, 146, 172, 188, 229
Bamonte's 109
Bandits on the Run 93, 127, 164, 200, 205, 206, 283, 284, 293
Barcade 51, 283
Barclays Center 55, 201
Bar LunÀtico 26
Bay Ridge 253
Bedford-Stuyvesant 266
Bed-Stuy 31, 59, 75, 80, 83, 88, 96, 102, 151, 169, 178, 214, 266, 279
Beer Street 52
Belle Mare 293
Ben Adams 257, 258, 259, 293
Ben Curtis 192, 295
Ben Harwood 296
Ben Katzman's DeGreaser 298
Ben Pirani 298, 299
Bensonhurst 105
Ben Thornewill 109, 112, 164, 165, 166, 293
Best Deli 126, 127
Best Pizza 88
Beth Million 283, 284, 294
Bipolar 23, 120, 136, 297, 299
Black Lodge Recording 231
Blu DeTiger 169, 170, 171, 294
Bohemian Grove 180
Boobie Trap 61
Borough Park 260
Bossa Nova Civic Club 278
Branded Saloon 52
Brandi and the Alexanders 99, 154, 250, 257, 294
Brandi Thompson 99, 154, 248, 250, 257, 259, 294
Brett Moses 45, 46, 53, 116, 117, 294
Brian DiMeglio 158, 300
Brian Hemmert 61, 154, 298

Brick Theater 279
Brighton Beach 277
Brit Boras 169, 170, 171, 294
Broadway 42, 48, 88, 128, 132, 146, 147, 148, 231
Brooklyn Botanic Garden 250
Brooklyn Bridge Park 250
Brooklyn Crab 99
Brooklyn Drum Collective 152, 183, 294
Brooklyn Gourmet Deli 127
Brooklyn Ice House 61
Brooklyn Inn 26
Brooklyn Recording 235
Brooklyn Skates Club 279
Brooklyn's Natural 127
Brooklyn SolarWorks 216
Brooklyn Steel 32, 149, 150
Bunker Studio 233
Bushwick 13, 29, 40, 51, 59, 61, 62, 67, 70, 75, 78, 80, 86, 90, 92, 96, 104, 122, 126, 137, 140, 142, 154, 161, 173, 178, 179, 183, 187, 195, 212, 215, 218, 222, 227, 249, 251, 255, 257, 266
Bushwick Country Club 59, 62

C

Cafe Eloise 75, 76, 77
Cafe Erzulie 95, 96, 99, 232, 288
Cafe Madeline 79
Caged Animals 294
Caitlin Mahoney 235, 281, 294
Call Box Lounge 53
Call My Husband 294
Cancion Franklin 294
Cape Francis 90, 166, 297, 299
Capri Social Club 63
Captain Dan's Good Time Tavern 53
Caravela 42, 57, 295, 300
Carlo Minchillo 183, 184, 186, 294
Carmelo's 27, 28
Caroline Kuhn 69, 70, 294
Cassie Fireman 192, 295
Catty 299
Caveman 61, 89, 114, 267, 298
Champs Diner 86, 87
Chantal Mitvalsky 171, 174, 294

CHAPPO 144, 157, 264, 293
Charleston 63
Charlie Waters 36, 295
Charmaine Querol 42, 120, 187, 188, 264, 294
Chayse Schutter 223, 224, 294
Cheryl's Global Soul 100
Chinar 100
Chris Boecker 295
Class One MMA 280
Climates 243, 248, 298, 300
C'mon Everybody 150, 151
Cobble Hill 87
Cobble Hill Cinemas 281
Cody Fitzgerald 257, 258, 259, 294
Colatura 63, 88, 272, 287, 295, 298
Colin Lord 36, 37, 64, 65, 294
Color Collage 205, 300
Color Tongue 29, 132, 168, 250, 251, 254, 295, 297, 299
Commodore 28, 29
Complete Music Studios 216
Coney Island 111, 251, 252, 253, 261
Connor Gladney 54, 80, 86, 151, 219, 220, 255, 256, 294
Connor Jones 23, 24, 45, 46, 121, 147, 148, 166, 167, 236, 294
Cory Peterson 23, 24, 26, 294
Covey 248, 257, 300
Cowrie Shell Center 266
Crema BK 79
Crown Heights 11, 75, 80, 83, 96, 98, 137, 201
CUP 80
Cup of Brooklyn 80

D

DAD 128, 186
Dallin Smith 67, 68, 294
Dana 254, 294
Dan Barrecchia 147, 149, 180, 294
Danbro Studios 215, 217
Dane Zarra 23, 25, 159, 161, 163, 164, 294
Dang Anohen 31, 32, 65, 66, 219, 220, 294
Danny Irizarry 37, 228, 297
Danny Sullivan 300
Darius VanSluytman 136, 263, 270, 294
Darren O'Brien 33, 171, 172, 266, 271, 294

Dave Palazola 122, 294
Davey Jones 82, 294
David Johnson 44, 45, 57, 58, 119, 122, 192, 193, 216, 294
David Newman 158, 300
David Van Witt 275, 284, 294
Daytime 80
DD Walker 55, 293
Dead Leaf Echo 215, 297
Dead Things 300
Dead Tooth 136, 140, 147, 159, 183, 240, 241, 301
Dead Tooth & No Surrender 294, 301
Deaf Poets 33, 34, 53, 63, 64, 147, 171, 190, 298, 300
Death By Piano 90, 296
Deep Sea Peach Tree 144, 297
Deep Wimp 36, 295
Degraw Sound 236
Delicate Steve 143, 299
Der Pioneer 79, 81
Devin McKnight 231, 232, 295
Di Fara Pizza 110
Digo Best 63, 88, 272, 287, 295
Dirty Mae 192, 295
Dirty Projectors 295
Ditmas Park 79
Dodge 112 180, 182
Dom Bodo 136, 171, 172, 295
Do or Dive 59, 64, 65
Downtown Brooklyn 278
Drew Citron 298
Drive-In 298
Drunk Ex 131, 300
Duck Duck 29
Duke of Vandals 147, 151, 152, 153, 225, 227, 228, 295
DUMBO 252
Dweebs 78, 81, 271
Dyker Heights 261

E

Earwax Records 266
East New York 106
East Williamsburg 23, 37, 66, 175, 183, 227
East Williamsburg Econo Lodge 175, 183
Easy Lover 30, 217

Eddie Kuspiel 29, 250, 251, 254, 255, 295
Edges of Brooklyn 252
Edna 34, 67, 144, 191, 193, 223, 298
Ed Weisgerber 147, 149, 180, 295
Eighty Ninety 79, 81, 157, 225, 236, 267, 293, 295
Elijah Sokolow 92, 295
Elijah Watson 168, 299
Elise Okusami 249, 257, 259, 295
Elizabeth Wyld 69, 70, 199, 295
Elliah Heifetz 67, 68, 295
Elliot & The Ghost 294, 296, 301
Emanuel and the Fear 52, 171, 295
Emanuel Ayvas 52, 171, 173, 295
Emily Ashenden 42, 136, 159, 161, 295
Emily Sgouros 116, 155, 295
Emir Mohseni 33, 115, 144, 145, 169, 170, 171, 172, 174, 295
Empanada Lady 101
Erica Marchetta-Wood 300
Eric Nizgretsky 100, 166, 167, 168, 239, 240, 277, 282, 295
Erik Garlington 168, 299
ESS SEE 267, 300
Ethan Alexander 42, 56, 146, 147, 148, 149, 295
Ethan Bassford 28, 97, 98, 102, 295
Evan Crommett 250, 295
Evolfo 122, 128, 179, 202, 231, 257, 269, 293, 294, 296, 298, 299
EWEL 183, 184, 186, 296

F

Favorite Friend Records 243, 298
Felicia Douglass 28, 83, 97, 295
Felipe Giannella 278, 295
Feng Sway 202, 203
Fever Dolls 150, 298
Fiction 81, 82
Figure 8 Recording 237
Flatbush 80, 87, 158, 237
Forever Honey 22, 30, 293, 296, 299, 300
Fort Greene 22
FourFiveSix 54
Four Seasons Grill Deli 128
Fourth Avenue Pub 55
Francie Moon 298
Frank Graniero 57, 295

Frank Poma 195, 196, 295
Freddy's Bar and Backroom 22, 30
Fresh Kills 48, 49, 50, 55
Friends and Lovers 281
Future Punx 142, 294

G

Gabe Friedman 37, 297
Gabriel Birnbaum 69, 70, 71, 80, 101, 237, 264, 272, 295
Gavin Snider 249, 252, 295
Gemma 28, 83, 97, 102, 295
George & Jack's 65, 66
George Miata 29, 295
Ghostwood Country Club 269, 300
GIFT 296
Gillian Visco 135, 137, 144, 146, 147, 149, 159, 160, 162, 164, 187, 188, 244, 264, 295
Gino Gianoli 147, 148, 151, 152, 225, 295
Giuseppina's 89, 90
Glassio 51, 105, 271, 299
Glass Slipper 294
Glom 26, 180, 296, 299, 300
Golden Years 39, 40, 41, 42, 43
Gonzalo Guerrero 159, 299
Gordon Taylor 64, 69, 70, 127, 247, 257, 258, 295
Gowanus 180, 242, 254
Gowanus Canal 254
Gravesend 111
Great Good Fine Ok 157, 216, 296
Greenpoint 36, 79, 88, 93, 103, 131, 168, 183, 200, 202, 220, 239, 253, 255, 272, 283
Green Village Used Furniture & Clothing 266
Green-Wood Cemetery 204, 205, 259, 261, 267
Grim Streaker 23, 144, 293
Guitar Shop 265, 267, 269
Gustaf 23, 31, 34, 68, 140, 146, 155, 156, 169, 190, 191, 203, 206, 222, 248, 276, 297, 298, 300, 301
Gutter 86, 151, 152

H

Hallie Spoor 31, 295
Hannah Nichols 28, 299

Hannah Rose Ammon 121, 297
Harper James 79, 81, 157, 225, 236, 237, 267, 268, 295
Hart Bar 154
Hartley's 31
hartstop 178, 187, 188, 190, 297
Haybaby 42, 136, 186, 240
Hayes Peebles 43, 85, 93, 123, 164, 165, 295
Hearth 109, 116, 117, 295
He Cherokee 121
HESS 91, 164, 171, 298
Highland Park 101, 248
High Waisted 146, 169, 187, 296, 299
HNRY FLWR 275, 284, 294, 299
Hollow Engine 23, 294
Hollye Bynum 28, 299
Holy Hand Grenade 294, 299
Honduras 11, 140, 299
Honore Club 67
Hot Knives 159, 214, 220, 296
Human Head Records 269
HYPEMOM 36, 59, 64, 109, 294, 297, 298

I

Ian Carpenter 164, 299
Impossible Colors 120, 295

J

Jack McLoughlin 22, 30, 31, 166, 167, 296
Jake Derting 87, 88, 89, 240, 241, 296
Jake Hiebert 21, 23, 25, 45, 46, 166, 167, 296
James Watson 128, 294
Janie Peacock 28, 299
Jared Artaud 33, 34, 296
Jared Yee 231, 232, 296
Jason Katzenstein 41, 42, 43, 265, 273, 296
Javier Vela 37, 297
Jeff Citron 212, 233, 234, 235, 237, 296
Jelly Kelly 109, 136, 264, 295, 297
Jennie Vee 299
Jenny Palumbo 120, 296
Jeremy Duvall 128, 294
Jeremy Neale 75, 77, 81, 254, 271, 283, 284, 296

Jesse Fairbairn 128, 294
Jessica Leibowitz 113, 255, 256, 296
Jessica Louise Dye 146, 147, 169, 171, 187, 188, 189, 296
Jessi's Coffee Shop 82
Jilly Karande 28, 299
Jim Hill 120, 126, 296
Joe Dahlstrom 159, 160, 162, 214, 220, 221, 296
Joel Kalow 61, 154, 298
Joe's Pizza 88
Joey Giambra 147, 149, 180, 296
Johan 180, 182, 296
John Farris 65, 110, 111, 140, 141, 142, 296
John Mason 61, 154, 298
Johnny Dynamite 136, 159, 160, 161, 296
John Zimmerman 28, 33, 144, 145, 169, 170, 296
Jonathan Freeland 57, 59, 62, 84, 296
Jonathan H. 296
Jon F Daily 175, 183, 184, 185, 186, 191, 192, 296
Jon Murphy 128, 294
Jono Bernstein 146, 147, 148, 169, 170, 171, 296
Jon Sandler 157, 158, 216, 296
Jon the Guilt 285, 296
Jordan W. 296
Jory Dawidowicz 23, 297
Josh Inman 80, 296
Jö Wagner 121, 297
Jukebox the Ghost 109, 112, 164, 166, 293
Justin Buschardt 34, 243, 296
JW Francis 192, 193, 296

K

Kai Sorensen 179, 296
KALEN 296
Kalen Lister 90, 91, 296
Kallan Campbell 42, 44, 45, 57, 58, 192, 193, 216, 296
Karl's D Light 296
Kasey Heisler 278, 297
Kate Black 19, 23, 24, 25, 26, 102, 159, 160, 164, 240, 241, 297
Katie Martucci 26, 69, 70, 79, 257, 258, 297
Katzman's DeGreaser 298
Kayla Asbell 23, 24, 120, 171, 172, 297
Kegan Zema 90, 91, 125, 126, 279, 297
Keith Kelly 109, 110, 264, 297

Kensington 79, 81
Kevin Olken Henthorn 90, 166, 168, 297
Kevin Urvalek 29, 250, 251, 297
Khaya Cohen 61, 155, 171, 172, 297
Kiki Appel 159, 299
Kino Kimino 298, 300
Kira Metcalf 159, 162, 163, 242, 297
Kissed by an Animal 176, 184, 296
Koch Comics Warehouse 270
Kristof Denis 144, 145, 146, 297
Kyle Jutkiewicz 36, 295

L

La Isla Cuchifrito 88
La Loba Cantina 101
La Mesita 122
Laney Lynx 283, 297
Late Sea 296
Laura Jinn 102, 297
Laura Valk 47, 54, 86, 151, 152, 219, 220, 255, 256, 297
L&B Spumoni Gardens 111
Leah Lavigne 149, 245, 297
Leah Scarpati 155, 297
Left Hand Path 41, 56
Le Paris Dakar 102
Lexie Lowell 128, 129, 297
LG Galleon 215, 297
Liam Christian 220, 298
Lily Mao 199, 201, 202, 297
Lily Reszi Rothman 178, 187, 188, 189, 190, 192, 193, 297
Lincoln Lute 64, 69, 70, 127, 257, 258, 297
Lindsey Radice 257, 259, 297
Lip Molina 219, 220, 297
Littlefield 154
Little Purity 112
Lizzie No 86, 92, 100, 199, 201, 297
Loose Buttons 100, 166, 239, 277, 282, 293, 295, 297, 301
Lost Boy ? 82, 186, 218, 294, 299
Lot Radio 281
Loving Hut 86, 88
Low Noon 299
Low Wave 294
Lucia Pontoniere 166, 257, 258, 297

Lucky Dog 32, 92
Luigi's Pizza 89
LUKEINTERNET 297
Luke Santy 64, 65, 297
Luna Rose 121, 297
Lydia Gammill 23, 25, 31, 32, 34, 35, 36, 68, 69, 140, 142, 190, 191, 203, 206, 207, 222, 248, 297

M

Mable's Smokehouse & Banquet Hall 121
Madam West 23, 25, 297
Mail the Horse 91, 164, 173, 298
Main Drag Music 271
Maladaptive Mistress 154, 298
MamajoeVramajoe 300, 301
Maneka 231, 232, 295
Manny Silverstein 166, 167, 239, 240, 297
Maracuja 56
Marble House 37, 297
Marcy & Myrtle 83
Maria Hernandez Park 249, 254
Marinara 56, 298, 299, 301
Marina Ross 169, 170, 298
Market Hotel 123, 129, 190
Mars Motel 79, 300
Mary-Louise Hildebrandt 154, 298
Matt Bernstein 39, 42, 43, 159, 161, 298
Matt Caldamone 36, 109, 110, 298
Matt Derting 86, 87, 88, 89, 240, 241, 298
Matteo Dix 158, 300
Matthew Gibbs 202, 298
Matthew Iwanusa 61, 89, 114, 115, 267, 268, 269, 298
Mattie Safer 264, 271, 298
Matt Nitzberg 61, 154, 298
Max Pain and the Groovies 42, 44, 57, 61, 67, 69, 119, 122, 159, 192, 216, 294, 296, 300
McCarren Park 255
McGolrick Park 79, 255, 256
Melanie Rose Wiggins 116, 295
Melissa Lucciola 31, 169, 170, 206, 207, 298
Meredith Lampe 151, 298
Metropolitan G Stop 205
Mia Berrin 204, 211, 215, 218, 238, 298

Michael Hesslein 50, 91, 164, 166, 171, 172, 173, 174, 298
Michael Nitting 223, 224, 233, 234, 298
Michael Tarnofsky 34, 67, 68, 144, 145, 191, 192, 193, 194, 223, 298
Michelle Birsky 144, 145, 159, 161, 164, 298
Michelle LoBianco 227
Middle Youth 79, 295
Midwood 110
Mike Borchardt 4, 107, 111, 114, 115, 249, 251, 259, 298
Mike McDearmon 23, 297
Minaxi 220, 221, 298
Mitchell Parrish 150, 298
Mitch Meyer 195, 196, 197, 298
Molasses Books 271, 273
Molly Schoen 120, 298
Mommy's Little Boy 296
Momo Sushi Shack 102
Moonglow 212, 233, 235, 237, 296
Moon Kissed 61, 109, 116, 155, 156, 171, 276, 295, 297
Morgan Hollingsworth 30, 300
Most Holy Trinity Cemetery 248, 257
Mount Sharp 104, 299
Mousetown 238
Mr. Kiwi's 128, 129
Muchmore's 155, 156, 157
Murder Tag 294, 298
Music Hall of Williamsburg 12, 34, 157
My Son The Doctor 61, 120, 154, 298

N

NAHreally 155, 298
Namesake 11, 132, 140, 299
Nam Nam 90
Natalie Kirch 140, 141, 142, 298
Natasha Johnson 168, 299
Native Sun 298
Nevva 42, 120, 132, 187, 294, 296, 298
New Myths 142, 169, 294, 298, 299
Newtown 90, 91, 215, 253
New Utrecht 111
New York City 7, 10, 63, 77, 104, 109, 190, 191, 222, 227, 244, 252, 259, 284
Nicholas LaGrasta 45, 46, 53, 166, 298
Nick Cortezi 56, 57, 298
Nick LaFalce 159, 160, 162, 163, 229, 298

Nick Louis 193, 194, 298
Nico E.P. 33, 34, 35, 53, 63, 64, 147, 171, 174, 190, 298
Nicole Pettigrew 37, 297
Night of Joy 33
Nihiloceros 107, 111, 114, 249, 251, 259, 298
Nikki Sisti 23, 25, 104, 159, 161, 163, 298
Nikola Balać 30, 300
North Brooklyn 215
No Surrender 136, 263, 270, 294, 301
No Swoon 88, 298
Ntu 264, 278, 298

O

Obash 23, 24, 25, 299
Oceanator 249, 257, 295
Ochre 293
Oil Bay 23, 80, 159, 163, 294, 296
Okay Okay 278, 295
Ok Cowgirl 149, 245, 297
Olivia K 96, 99, 101, 105, 288, 299
Olivia Price 22, 30, 299
One Stop Beer Shop 43, 123
Our Wicked Lady 4, 132, 136, 137, 138, 159, 160, 161, 162, 164, 215, 218, 219, 230
Oyinda 299

P

Pale Ramon 295
Papi Shiitake 120, 128, 299
Park Slope 201, 241
Parlay 83
Parrot Dream 159, 160, 161, 162, 299
Partners Coffee 84
Patrick Phillips 11, 140, 141, 142, 143, 299
Patrick Porter 151, 152, 299
Paul Hammer 32, 48, 49, 50, 55, 61, 144, 166, 255, 299
Paulie Gee's 113
Paulie Gee's Slice Shop 88, 113, 114
Peaches Shrimp and Crab 91
Peter Wise 81, 223, 224, 299
Pete's Candy Store 164
Pet Rescue 191

Phantom Wave 164, 165, 299
Pies 'n' Thighs 91, 92
Pinkerton Wine Bar 68
Pirate Studios 219
Plastic Miracles 243, 249, 295
Plastic Picnic 64, 69, 127, 247, 257, 295, 297
Pocketsand 294
Pokito 42, 44, 45
Pom Pom Squad 162, 204, 211, 215, 218, 238, 298
Ponyboy 103
Porterfield 296
Pouya 23, 24, 25, 299
Pretty World 298
Prince Johnny 52, 75, 76, 83, 301
Prospect Heights 22, 75, 237
Prospect Park 120, 166, 200, 247, 249, 251, 257, 258, 259, 261
PYNKIE 257, 297

Q

Quinn Devlin 180, 200, 281, 299
Quinn McGovern 56, 57, 299

R

Rachel Fischer 164, 299
Rafferty Swink 269, 270, 299
Rancho Cowabunga 296
Raycee Jones 103, 111, 112, 252, 266, 299
Ray McGale 168, 250, 251, 299
Razor Braids 28, 299
Reclamation Bar 45
Red Hook 59, 61, 81, 99, 103
Red Hook Lobster Pound 103
Regina Strayhorn 93, 127, 164, 205, 283, 293
Richey Rose 33, 299
Risbo 103
Robin Frost 192, 295
Rocka Rolla 34, 35, 65
Rodes Rollins 298, 299
Roll N Roaster 114, 115
Rosie Slater 140, 142, 143, 144, 146, 169, 170, 299
Rough Trade 3, 166, 167, 168
Rubulad 178, 192, 193

Russian Bath on Neck Road 282
Ryan Egan 144, 145, 149, 150, 229, 281, 299
Ryan Foster 217, 299

S

Sad American Night 249, 252, 295
Sahil 26, 27, 180, 181, 182, 299
Saint Vitus 168, 169
Sal Garro 104, 299
Sallies 31, 59, 65, 219, 294, 297
Sam Aneson 30, 300
Sam Parrish 121, 297
Sam R. 51, 105, 271, 299
Sarah Carbonetti 267, 268, 269, 300
Sara Horton 116, 295
Sarik Kumar 79, 300
Satin Nickel 30, 300
Savaria Studios 214, 220
Savoir Adore 32, 48, 49, 55, 144, 166, 255, 299
Scott Greenberg 295
Scott Kodi 151, 152, 300
Scott Martin 66, 300
Sean Carroll 59, 65, 66, 104, 113, 117, 300
Sean Wouters 33, 34, 35, 53, 131, 171, 172, 190, 300
Shadow Monster 135, 137, 144, 146, 159, 176, 187, 244, 295
Shane Conerty 205, 300
Shane Preece 44, 45, 122, 159, 161, 192, 193, 216, 300
Shari Page 23, 24, 25, 91, 300
Sharkmuffin 140, 144, 298, 299, 300
Sharkswimmer 34, 243, 296
Shawn Ghost 269, 270, 300
Shred Flintstone 147, 180, 294, 295, 296
Shrenik Ganatra 220, 298
Shubh Saran 296
Skinny Dennis 57, 58, 65
Skout 47, 54, 80, 86, 87, 151, 219, 255, 294, 297
Slight Of 120, 126, 296
Sloppy Jane 146, 178, 187, 192, 297
Smock 136, 138, 301
Snack Cat 57, 69, 110, 171, 293, 294
So and So 42, 56, 146, 295
Songs for Sabotage 33, 299
Sonny Hell 51, 300

Sooner 59, 110, 140, 293, 296, 300
Sophie Chernin 23, 297
South Brooklyn 110
Spaceman Sound 239
Static Jacks 301
Steele Kratt 63, 109, 116, 117, 144, 146, 300
Stella Di Sicilia Bakery 82
Stephen Berthomieux 27, 300
Stephen Graniero 57, 300
Steve Carlin 220, 298
Steve Vannelli 22, 30, 31, 300
Stolen Jars 257, 294
Strange Neighbors 32, 34, 61, 69, 223, 254, 293, 294, 300, 301
Stranger Wines 271
Studio G 240, 241
Sugar Hill Supper Club 279, 280
Sultan Room 42, 169, 170
Sunny's 59, 62, 69, 70, 71
Sunrise/Sunset 84
Sunset Diner 115
Sunset Park 83, 259, 260
Sunshine Laundromat 283
Superbloom 158, 159, 300
Sushi Noodle 104
Sweatshop 20, 37, 215, 223, 224
Sweetwater 104
Sydney Shepherd 93, 127, 164, 205, 283, 293
Syndicated Bar Theater Kitchen 283

T

Taco Bell 87, 92, 199
Taco Rapido 92
Tacos, Twins and Trains Taco Cart 93
Tallbird 120, 300
Tall Juan 114, 115, 190, 298, 300
Tamaryn 299
Tanner Peterson 122, 279, 300
Tanners 122, 279, 300
Tarra Thiessen 31, 32, 34, 35, 68, 69, 140, 144, 146, 155, 156, 190, 191, 203, 204, 222, 223, 300
Tasha Abbott 88, 298
Tcoy Coughlin 44, 45, 57, 58, 69, 70, 192, 193, 216, 300
Teen Commandments 45, 53, 116, 166, 294, 298

Temkin's 36
Thaddeus Lowe 266, 300
Theadora Curtis 248, 300
The Big Drops 301
The Big Easy 27, 300
The Black Black 183, 184, 191, 296
The Brooklyn G 127
The Creamery Studio 235
The Graham 66, 67
The Greenpoint Loft 203
The Infesticons 294
The Ladles 26, 59, 69, 79, 166, 257, 294, 297
The Levee 31, 32
The Living Strange 92, 295
The Misters 223, 233, 298, 300
The Muckers 28, 33, 84, 109, 115, 143, 144, 147, 169, 171, 248, 293, 295, 296
The Mystery Lights 136, 162, 301
The Nest 158, 159
The Palace 34
The Planes 176, 184, 294
The Rassle 301
The Spits 299
The Steps 301
The Thing 272
The Vacant Lots 33, 296
THICK 19, 23, 25, 91, 102, 104, 159, 163, 240, 297, 298, 300
ThL2 193, 194
Tim Choate 158, 300
Tina's Place 116
Tine Hill 34, 35, 140, 142, 300
Todd Martin 223, 224, 233, 234, 300
Todd Martino 23, 297
Tom Corrado 195, 196, 300
Tom Freeman 248, 257, 300
Tom's Diner 117
Tom Wolfson 65, 300
Tortilleria Mexicana Los Hermanos 122
Trace Mountains 296
Tracey 32, 61, 69, 70, 300
Tradesman 37, 38
Treads 298
Trevor Courneen 36, 295
Troost 36, 37
Trout Recording 241

TVOD 245, 298
Two Boots 206, 207

U

Union Pool 34, 171, 172, 173, 174
Unnameable Books 272

V

Vamos Al Tequila 93
Vanessa Silberman 233, 234, 249, 254, 255, 301
Venus Twins 85, 86, 87, 88, 240, 296, 298
Viktor Longo 280, 301
Viktor Vladimirovich 52, 75, 83, 301
Vinegar Hill 121
Vinyl Fantasy 265, 273
Vram Kherlopian 68, 69, 140, 142, 155, 156, 203, 204, 206, 207, 222, 223, 301

W

Warm Body 217, 299
Wei's 105
Wesley Rose 36, 295
Wet Leather 39, 40, 41, 42, 49, 159, 265, 273, 296, 298
Whisperlodge 284
Wilder Maker 69, 80, 101, 237, 264, 272, 295
Wildly 33, 171, 266, 271, 294
Will Clark 23, 297
Williamsburg 12, 23, 29, 30, 34, 37, 39, 44, 46, 50, 51, 57, 59, 65, 66, 75, 81, 86, 88, 105, 109, 123, 127, 155, 157, 175, 183, 214, 215, 227, 233, 251, 252, 253, 255, 271, 279
Williamsburg Pizza 88, 123
William Thompson 20, 45, 121, 147, 148, 166, 167, 236, 237, 301
Windsor Terrace 51
WIVES 136, 241, 301
Wolves At Night 294
Wonderpark Studios 242
Work Wife 151, 298
Wsabi Fox 294

Y

Yaasss 299

Yella Belly 19, 20, 21, 22, 23, 45, 121, 147, 166, 236, 294, 296, 300, 301
Yolanda 105
Yuta Shimmi 56, 57, 301

Z

Zach Butler 119, 301
Zach Inkley 119, 301
Zack Kantor 100, 239, 240, 277, 282, 301
Zack Nestel-Patt 88, 298
Zoochie 103, 301
Zoos 178, 195, 196, 295, 298, 300
Zoos Studio 195